GOD ABOVEGROUND

GOD ABOVEGROUND

Catholic Church, Postsocialist State, and
Transnational Processes in a
Chinese Village

———————

ERIBERTO P. LOZADA, JR.

STANFORD UNIVERSITY PRESS

Stanford, California, 2001

Stanford University Press
Stanford, California

© 2001 by the Board of Trustees of the
Leland Stanford Junior University

Printed in the United States of America
On acid-free, archival-quality paper

Library of Congress Cataloging-in-Publication Data
Lozada, Eriberto P.
    God aboveground : Catholic Church, postsocialist
state, and transnational processes in a Chinese village /
Eriberto P. Lozada, Jr.
     p.   cm.
  Includes bibliographical references and index.
  ISBN 0-8047-4097-6 (alk. paper)
    1. Catholic Church—China.   I. Title: God
aboveground. II. Title.
  BX1665.L69 2001
  282'.51—dc21   200102910

Original Printing 2001

Last figure below indicates year of this printing:
10 09 08 07 06 05 04 03 02 01

Designed by Janet Wood
Typeset by BookMatters in 10/13 Aldus

To my parents

This study could not have been completed without the help and support of many wonderful teachers. My deepest gratitude goes to Professor James L. Watson, who patiently guided me through many challenges—academic, professional, and personal. No matter what the problem, Woody offered solid and honest advice on navigating the waters of anthropology. I am also greatly indebted to two other teachers, Professors Michael Herzfeld and Rubie Watson. Michael constantly raised theoretical challenges, helping to place my own thoughts in the wider context of the field. Rubie continually questioned my assumptions, prodding me to approach phenomena from different perspectives. I also want to thank my other professors in the Department of Anthropology at Harvard University who shared their experiences and approaches with me, especially Begona Aretxaga, Sally Falk Moore, and Stanley J. Tambiah. Teachers in other places have also shaped my thinking and offered valuable assistance, including Peter Barry, Daniel Bays, Nicole Constable, Paul Hanson, Susan M. Kenyon, Ellen Oxfeld, Jean-Paul Wiest, and John Lagerwey. John and his wife, Veronique, were particularly kind hosts to my family and me during our numerous visits to Hong Kong. Father Edward J. Malatesta, S.J., shared his knowledge and guidance when I first began my research on the Chinese Catholic Church, and I deeply regret that he passed away before seeing what he helped to start.

Many students, friends, and colleagues read drafts of this work and provided insightful comments that kept me going through the writing process. I was fortunate to receive help and encouragement from Sangmee Bak, Melissa Caldwell, Sidney Cheung, Maris Gillette, Tracey Heatherington, Jing Jun, Kathleen M. Murphy, Gregory Ruf, and Pam Summa. I also want to thank the undergraduates in my Religions of China course at Butler University who helped me refine my thinking on many details, especially Ashley Anderson, Elizabeth Cannon, Daniela Diamente, Lisa Greene, Ryan Overman, Jeff Payne, and Florian Stamm. I also owe a debt of gratitude to Muriel Bell, Matt Stevens, and Janet Mowery of Stanford University Press for their support and editorial guidance in the final stages of writing.

My graduate career and field research were funded by several institutions. Generous grants and support came from HEA Title VI Foreign Language and Area Studies Fellowships, the Committee on Scholarly Communication with China, the Frederick Sheldon Traveling Fellowship Fund, the Mellon Predissertation Fellowship Fund, the Harvard Department of Anthropology, and the Fairbank Center for East Asian Research. Ellen Pierce and others at the Maryknoll Mission Archives helped me explore their extensive collection. I would also like to thank Jiaying University in Meizhou, China, which graciously hosted my fieldwork. Special thanks go to Professor Fang Xuejia of the Hakka Research Centre for his collegiality during our many trips to communities in the Hakka homeland, as well as for his family's patience and generosity during our extended fieldwork. I would also like to thank the Pizzutelli family in Meixian for their companionship and inspiration.

My special thanks go to friends and neighbors in the village that I call Little Rome, who welcomed me over a period of many years. Omitting their surnames to protect their privacy, I would like to thank Father Joseph, Sisters Chunzhen and Xirong, Zanlin and his family, Zhifang and his family, Teacher Joseph and his family, Danian and his family, Changyuan and his family, Yonggang and his family, Qiaofen and her family, and Liping and her daughter, Jingya. Their faith and hospitality were truly inspiring.

Most of all, I would like to thank my family, who endured much to allow me to finish this research. My wife, Rebecca Ruhlen (also an anthropologist) and our son, Patrick, accompanied me to Little Rome and were with me on my research every step of the way. Patrick has been to more Hakka funerals than most Chinese boys, and he shared his love for baseball, Monopoly, and Gameboy with many "little friends" in Little Rome. Rebecca shared her skills as an anthropologist with me during the fieldwork in Little Rome and during the editing process in Massachusetts and Indiana. My brothers John, Phil, and James and their families took care of many details in the United States while we were abroad.

These brief acknowledgments cannot begin to thank everyone adequately, and I beg forgiveness from the many people I have failed to thank by name. Any mistakes in this work are of course my own. This work is dedicated to my parents, Eriberto Sr. and Divinia, who have unfailingly given me the love and strength to keep going.

CONTENTS

GOD ABOVEGROUND

CHAPTER 1

Being Local in a Global World

Madam Speaker, let me remind my colleagues [in the House of Representatives] that President Jiang Zemin is president of a country which systematically imprisons Catholic bishops and priests, imprisons Protestant pastors and lay people, tortures Buddhist monks and nuns. . . . But, Madam Speaker, Christianity will rise in China. Christianity will be there when President Jiang Zemin is gone. And the Catholic church will prosper and the evangelical church will prosper, and the church will rise up and be there long after President Jiang Zemin is gone from there.

—U.S. Representative Frank Wolf (R), April 28, 1998, speaking on the House floor in support of the Freedom from Religious Persecution Act, which was signed by President Clinton on October 27, 1998

Mr. Lozada, let me tell you something about the Chinese Catholic Church. American Catholics are too liberal in matters of morality such as divorce, and they don't listen to the Pope. The Chinese Catholic Church is a martyr [*lieshi*] church and has learned about God through our suffering. The American Catholic Church can learn something from us about faith.

—Mr. Wang, speaking to me in Little Rome, China, on March 11, 1997

From my living room in a northern Guangdong Hakka village, the Chinese Catholic Church looked very different from the picture painted by Representative Wolf. My Catholic neighbors in a village that I call Little Rome (a pseudonym) were beginning to prosper, religiously and financially, after almost two decades of China's "reform and opening" (*gaige kaifang*). They have been able to prosper and practice their faith because transnational Catholicism has become a local religious tradition, a social fact embedded in their everyday lives and in their identity as a rural community in post-socialist southern China.[1] Thus the localization of the Chinese practice of Catholicism has a wider political and social context, which speaks to the more abstract question of what it means to be local in a global world.

Living in a deterritorialized community, though perhaps a novel theoretical idea for anthropologists, has been a part of life in Little Rome since its formation as a Catholic village in the late nineteenth century.[2] As Hakka, members of a diaspora ethnic group, people in Little Rome have a history and tradition of sojourning and migration; as Catholics, believers in a transnational religious tradition, they have long maintained overseas connections through foreign missionary groups. The thirty years of the Maoist period (1949–77) interrupted these transnational links as the new government of the People's Republic of China implemented a socialist vision of society that severely constrained mobility and connections outside China.

With the institution of the reform-oriented economic policies of Deng Xiaoping in 1979, China's national boundaries gradually became more open and the people of Little Rome rapidly reestablished their transnational links. These connections were symbolically manifested in the resurfacing of the Catholic Church in 1983. With the maturation of reform policies and the rapid economic development of southern China in the 1990s, transnational processes—the global movement of people, goods, and ideas across national boundaries—became very much a part of everyday life in Little Rome. In the midst of all these traces of globalization, people in Little Rome have redefined what it means to be part of the Little Rome community. This is a study of transnationalism from the perspective of those who are supposedly the most local of people, not global jet-setters. In examining what it means to be local in a global world, this book also serves as a case study of the return to public life of transnational Catholicism in postsocialist China.

Situating Little Rome

Little Rome is about an hour's bus ride north of Meizhou City, the prefectural capital of what is known as the Hakka homeland (see Map 1). The Hakka (*kejia*, "guest people," in Mandarin) are a diaspora ethnic group, considered by most scholars and Chinese people to be a subcategory of the dominant Han ethnic group of China; there are over forty million Hakka scattered throughout China and many more in at least fifty other countries (CHCR 1987).[3] The village is called Little Rome by other Chinese Catholics and missionaries because nearly all the people who live there are Catholic.[4] And they are not just Catholic, but fervently Catholic: the many young men and women from this area who sought vocations in the Catholic Church, especially before "liberation" in 1949, have been the vanguard of the Church

Figure 1   Little Rome in 1996; the white spires of the new church are visible at the center of the photograph.

in Guangdong. Throughout the Church's turbulent history in China, the persistent faith of such villagers has enabled the Catholic Church to survive many movements of persecution, including the latest during the Cultural Revolution. In good times, the Chinese Catholic Church flourishes politically and intellectually in the cities; but in bad times, which have occurred regularly since the Nestorian Christians first showed up in the Tang courts, the Church survived through its rural strongholds.

Rice fields surround the village, spatially separating Little Rome from other villages in the Jiaoling valley. Of the one thousand people (from more than thirty different surname groups) whose household registration is recorded as part of Little Rome, nearly all have a family member who actively farms as well as at least one family member who is actively Catholic, meaning he or she attends mass weekly. Nearly all of the households also have major nonagricultural sources of income, whether through collective ventures (such as a distilling company) or private ventures (such as a roadside restaurant, retail store, or motorcycle repair shop). Most young adults leave the area to work in the more developed areas of Guangdong such as Shenzhen and Zhuhai, as factory workers, drivers, and hotel staff. On the eastern side of the village is the largest elementary school in the township, Fudan Elementary, which was established during the Republican period and named after the university in Shanghai founded by the Chinese Jesuit Ma

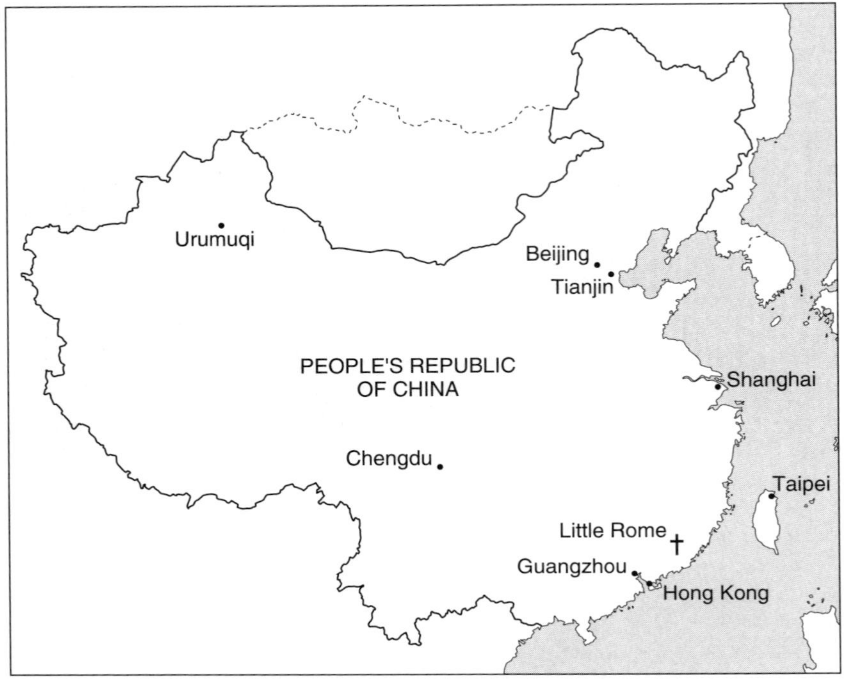

Map 1.   Location of Little Rome in the PRC

Xiangbo. Although Fudan Elementary has always been state-run, its name reflects the dominant Catholic character of its community, its students, and, in Republican times, its teachers.

Little Rome is less than five kilometers south of the county seat, Jiaoling City, one of the least affluent parts of Guangdong (Vogel 1989). During the 1990s this county seat was continuously under construction, although it grew more slowly than Shenzhen or the Pearl River delta. Before 1850, Little Rome was a dual-surname village more typical of the villages in Jiaoling County.[5] Little Rome was probably an offshoot of a village nearer the Shiku River, since the French missionaries referred to the village as Shiku in 1861 (Launay 1917). Descendants of the original two families (surnamed Tang and He) still live in the area. The families are reported to have moved into Jiaoling two to three hundred years ago, when the area was still a frontier. One man (surnamed Tang) sojourned in Malaysia and came back in the 1860s a converted Catholic. He built a chapel in part of his house and invited Father Bernon, a French missionary of the Mission Étrangères de Paris (MEP), who was then in Meixian doing missionary work. The MEP, based in Hong Kong and Shantou, did not initially assign a permanent priest to Jiaoling, but gradually built up a presence, buying land from the Xu lineage in the more established village of Dalubei (just north of Little Rome). As the MEP increased its landholdings (in the end buying about 100 *mu* [7.7 hectares] of land around Little Rome), poor Hakka families, who were either new converts or Catholics from other nearby MEP Hakka areas, gradually moved onto land given to them or rented at a very low price by the MEP priests.

A Catholic presence was already established by the time the Christianity-inspired Taiping armies swept through the area (they retreated from Jiaoling in 1866). The MEP's Father Bernon started with two churches operating out of houses, a men's church and a women's church. By 1872, a large church with a capacity of over a thousand was in operation. Because of bandits and tension between locals, sometime before 1887 a wall was built encircling the village, complete with cannons, gun ports, and four large gates, and the skyline was dominated by a multistory church and other church buildings (see Map 2). Other mission stations were set up throughout the county, with Little Rome serving as the focus of Catholic activities.

After World War I, the French reduced the scale of their mission activities in China and ceded the mission territory of Jiaying (the old name for Meizhou prefecture) to the newly formed Catholic Foreign Missionary Society of America, or Maryknoll.[6] Maryknoll first arrived in China in 1919, where their priests and sisters were very active in building schools and hospitals, and especially in expanding the Chinese clergy.[7] The minor seminary in neighboring Mei county (the diocesan center under Bishop Ford) was especially important as an educational resource for Little Rome villagers. St. Joseph's Minor Seminary (later, shortly before liberation, St. Joseph's Middle School) prepared many young men for vocations as priests and for further education outside the region and overseas.[8]

With "liberation," however, the expanding American missionary presence in the Jiaying area came to an abrupt halt, marked in 1950 by the arrest of Bishop Francis Ford and Sister Joan Marie Ryan, along with the deportation of American priests and nuns. As he was being arrested, Bishop Ford entrusted the diocese to Little Rome's Father Lan. (Bishop Ford died in a prison in Guangzhou one year after his arrest.) Father Lan, whom the local Catholics called Bishop Lan, though he was never consecrated as such, was confined to house arrest, with intermittent assignments to labor reform

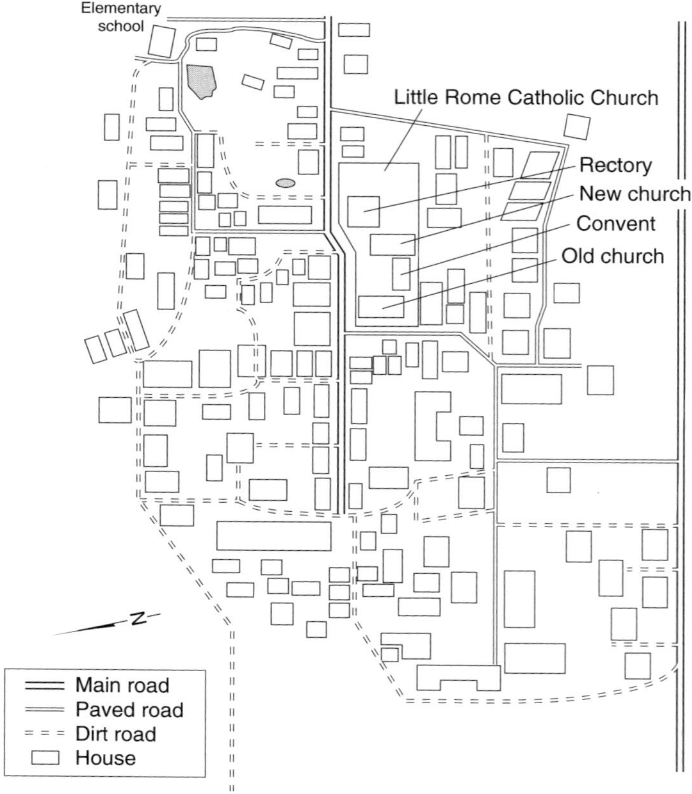

Map 2.   Little Rome in 1996

camps, until the Deng period. Other Chinese priests (including Bishop Zhong)[9] and Chinese sisters were sent back to their homes and put under house arrest or in labor camps. Many Catholics from Little Rome were also persecuted by the Chinese Communist Party (CCP), Church property was seized, and all public religious activities ceased. Officially, the churches remained open until 1964, but without their clergy the Catholics considered the churches closed from the time of the arrests of their priests shortly after liberation. Little Rome residents reported that in the countryside the Cultural Revolution was not as severe as it was in more urban areas like Meizhou City, but that it was still a very difficult period.

Throughout the Maoist period, Catholics were targeted because of their longtime association with foreigners and their kin ties overseas (especially in Taiwan). By the time of the Cultural Revolution in 1966, many Catholics in Little Rome had already been marked as unreliable during the earlier antirightist campaign, and many who had earlier been repatriated home after imprisonment or labor camp now were returned to labor camps. One villager told me that it was lucky for the Catholics that the priests, especially Bishop Lan, were kept away from the chaos of the Cultural Revolution by being imprisoned in a controlled labor reform camp. Though public Catholic activities had already been banned, with the renewed fervor of the Cultural Revolution after 1966, private activities such as prayer and possession of Catholic books and icons were also curtailed.

The ascension of Deng Xiaoping, however, marked a sea change in the life of Little Rome. In 1980, Bishop Lan participated in a national meeting of Catholics in Beijing, where the new line of "freedom of religious belief" was introduced. When Bishop Lan returned from his trip to Beijing, local authorities resisted the shift in policy but were divided, so Bishop Lan was able to begin reorganizing public Catholic activities. The first public activity was held in 1981, the funeral of a hundred-year-old woman. Masses were conducted in large houses, rather tentatively, since the villagers of Little Rome were still skeptical about the party's intentions. However, with the return of church property, and the reopening of the church on August 14, 1983 (Assumption Day), the ritual life of Little Rome gradually came back to life. Two Maryknoll-trained sisters from Little Rome and various lay leaders helped Bishop Lan reorganize the church in Little Rome. Bishop Lan, recognized as the successor to Bishop Ford, also was a key leader in the reorganization of the Meizhou diocese. Because of his age and previous political opposition to joining the Chinese Catholic Patriotic Association (the government structure created to administer the Chinese Catholic Church during the Maoist period), Bishop Lan confirmed the selection by the Catholic community of Bishop Anthony Zhong Quanzhang, who continued to head the diocese during my fieldwork there. When Bishop Lan died in 1991, the Little Rome church did not have a pastor (Bishop Zhong presided over the diocese in Mei County), and the four remaining priests rotated through the seven counties of the diocese. With the reopening of the seminaries, the first priest from Meizhou to graduate from the Wuhan regional seminary (ordained in 1991) was assigned to Little Rome. The diocesan convent was reestablished in the late 1980s, and in 1996 a daughter of Little Rome was in the first group to take final vows.

Little Rome in 1997 was a transnational village community. Its very existence was a result of China's penetration by a prototypical transnational organization, the Roman Catholic Church. Participation in this transnational religious organization has been an integral part of the community's history and identity. The villagers are part of a global diaspora, the Hakka. From the first person in the village to convert to Catholicism until the 1990s, many of Little Rome's offspring lived overseas and in other regions of China. The movement of community members in and out of Little Rome has been a central feature of the local social reality. Migration is an essential element of Hakka cultural identity (see Leong 1997). Because of the penetration of rural China by transnational capitalism, most young adults must leave their natal village to earn their livelihood and pursue careers. Despite these transnational influences, where spatial disjunctions are created through the scattering of community members far and wide, Little Rome still maintains its sense of community identity.

Transnational Anthropology

Transnational processes can be found throughout history and have existed as long as nations (Eric Wolf 1982; Mintz 1985). Local communities have always found ways to define themselves, to set up boundaries (however porous and shifting) that mark off insiders and outsiders. Similarly, transnational organizations like the Catholic Church that provide institutional support for this global movement have long influenced social and international relations (Vallier 1973; Hanson 1980; Nye and Keohane 1972; Huntington 1973). Transnational processes are not a new phenomenon, and anthropologists of the past—using staples of anthropological discourse such as migration, cultural diffusion, and acculturation—have tried to provide theoretical frameworks for understanding transnationalism.[10] What makes transnational processes today a dominant concern of anthropologists (and of villagers in Little Rome) is the rapidity and influence of transnational flows, which make boundaries even more porous than before. In international relations, transnational processes historically were not as influential as other factors, notably nationalism, in shaping the domestic practices of pre–World War I nation-states. But by the end of the twentieth century, local communities were more fully integrated by global communication networks, world trade and market networks, and labor migrations—creating a global system of interdependence (Featherstone 1990). Transnational processes increasingly challenge the boundaries of traditional social structures such as the family, the local community, and the nation-state (Wakeman 1988).Thus, understanding everyday social life now requires understanding the connections between a local community and the rest of the world (Moore 1994, 1987; Strathern 1995).

Analyses of transnational processes have emphasized one of two perspectives. One perspective is found in studies that have focused on what Strathern calls the "concrete models of globalisation" (1995: 159)—the structural implications for the "world capitalist system" of transnational organizations (Wallerstein 1974; Frank 1969). These studies privilege global capital and international relations in their examinations of multinational corporations (Sassen 1997, 1996), interest-based nongovernmental organizations (Haas 1992), and transnational religious communities (Rudolph and Piscatori 1997; Baker 1997; Eickelmann 1997) and lead to debates over issues such as sovereignty and security. From this viewpoint, transnational processes are seen as invasions of national space that result in major political challenges to governments in an interconnected global environment. Transnational organizations such as the Catholic Church and multinational corporations are portrayed as appropriating elements of state authority. For example, Duara (1997) portrays the struggle between Chinese nationalism (1900–45) and transnational ideologies as challenging the Chinese state's consolidation of sovereignty.

However, closer examination of the practice and regulation of transnational processes paints a different picture—transnational processes do not necessarily challenge state sovereignty, and in many cases buttress state legitimacy and authority. According to Saskia Sassen global capital, while appropriating some elements of economic control to agents outside of a particular state's sovereignty, can only function and flourish in localized spaces ("global cities," major financial and trade centers like New York and Hong Kong) that fall within the domain of state control. Transnational organizations and states are thus symbiotic, dependent upon each other for their own agendas: "The strategic spaces where many global processes take place are often national; the mechanisms through which the new legal forms necessary for globalization are implemented are often part of state institutions; the infrastructure that makes possible the hypermobility of financial capital at the global scale is situated in various national territories" (Sassen 1996: 27–28; see also Sassen 1997). State sovereignty is therefore reconfigured but not lost, with the increased penetration of transnational processes.

In her examination of the Chinese diaspora, Aihwa Ong concludes that state sovereignty in developing Southeast Asian states, while becoming more flexible, still structures spatial order in a "system of graduated sovereignty," wherein citizens with differential access to political and economic capital are subject to different state regimes (Ong 1999: 214). According to Ong, the result of this co-optation of transnational processes by Malaysia and Indonesia has resulted not in the loss of sovereignty but in the deepening of the domestic political realm into other areas such as ethnicity and religion. In China, similar processes have resulted in the strengthening of the Communist state. Transnational processes may have introduced new challenges to the state, but they have also supported its legitimacy. Studies have found that both the central and local state apparatuses were strengthened in the transition from a centralized to a market economy deeply linked to foreign investment and trade (Smart 1993; Oi 1992). State structures have developed to meet the challenges of transnational processes in China, containing political challenges in the form of a rising civil society and loosely harnessing the transnational material and cultural flow (see Madsen 1998; Pei 1998). Guangdong province has been in the forefront of state attempts to co-opt transnational processes, the result of which has been the growing prosperity of southern Chinese communities like Little Rome.

Transnational religions have been of particular concern for the Chinese government, but in the postsocialist period, new and reformed structures have struck a precarious balance between state sovereignty and transnational processes. During the postsocialist period, the local Catholic Church in Little Rome has maintained extensive ties to the universal Catholic Church while recognizing state authority under the umbrella of the government's Catholic administrative structure. Although Sino-Vatican relations have not yet been formalized, many other public Catholic communities had extensive exchanges with the universal Church by the mid 1990s.[11]

In Little Rome, the resurfacing of the church in the reform period demonstrates an optimism that the state will respect the documented constitutional right of the freedom of religious belief. Sociologist Richard Madsen describes a much more pessimistic attitude toward the state among Catholics near Tianjin in northern China. In the area where Madsen did his research, public and underground Catholics, especially their respective clergy, have been in intense conflict (see Madsen 1998). Such continuing conflict raises the key political questions about China's development: How will the Chinese state evolve to meet the challenges of transnational processes? Can the state successfully integrate Catholicism into the structure of Chinese society?

The other perspective found in studies of transnational processes has focused on their cultural implications, in such areas as development (Escobar

1995), public culture (Appadurai 1996; Morley and Robins 1995), and diaspora identity (Clifford 1994; Basch, Schiller, and Blanc 1994; Olwig and Hastrup 1997). In these works, a more detailed analysis of the impact on culture of transnational processes takes theorizing about transnational imaginings beyond simplified models of cultural imperialism. For example, Ulf Hannerz examines the medium for transnational cultural flows, embodied in his social category of cosmopolitans (mediators who straddle the global and the local), in the formation of creole cultures, and in unique nonterritorially defined cultural systems (Hannerz 1992: 264–65). "Locals" are rooted in the "more circumscribed territorial culture" (1992: 248), but cosmopolitans interact with global cultural centers and serve as the primary mediators in the creation of creole cultures. Hannerz's perspective, however, misses the active agency of the "locals" like the people in Little Rome. As I explain in later chapters, people in Little Rome interpreted and transformed transnational processes according to their own local needs.

In an examination of another quintessential transnational organization in East Asia, James Watson (1997) finds that locals are indeed active in shaping both the business practices and the cultural meaning of McDonald's. People in the local context exert much more agency than Hannerz's model would imply in transforming the meaning of eating a fast-food meal in a McDonald's restaurant. Localization of transnational processes, Watson concludes, is "[not] a unilinear process that ends the same everywhere" but instead varies with local contexts (James Watson 1997: 37). Similarly, in a study of Kentucky Fried Chicken in Beijing, I found that in the process of consuming KFC, locals generated their own specific interpretation of fast food and modernity (Lozada 2000). Gewertz and Errington further identify the agency of locals in the creation of a "sociality based in substantial measure on personal choice rather than on 'external' constraint or precedent" (1996: 477). In Little Rome, the process of localization is thus linked to the locals' exercise of choice in performing Catholic ritual in the way that they understand as appropriate, and not necessarily as prescribed by the state.

Rituals, Charisma, and the Localization Process

Ritual events are special times that punctuate the otherwise mundane affairs of daily life—they provide the stuff of memories. During holiday periods like Christmas and Spring Festival (*Chunjie*, the Chinese New Year) and special days like All Souls' Day, members of the deterritorialized community return to Little Rome to renew ties with their families, neighbors, and friends. Nonetheless, even nonritual events reveal structural tensions resulting from the localization process. Public construction projects in Little Rome and throughout the Hakka homeland are often funded by nonstate groups, from a small road built by neighbors to a Hakka museum. Alternative sources of capital are filling the gap left by the state's retraction from a centralized, socialist economic system. The state, however, is not yielding sovereignty to the foreign groups that supply the bulk of this capital. Ritualized events such as a church-opening ceremony confirm the Chinese state's strategy of co-opting transnational processes.

Ritual events themselves illustrate how transnational processes are localized. The events described in the chapters that follow, from baptisms, Sunday mass, weddings, and funerals to opening a church and building a road, reveal how something general is transformed into something specific. Rituals provide a special forum for the localization process—the meanings communicated in this privileged domain, such as a nuptial couple's claim to modernity, are enhanced and publicly performed through ritual. Rituals can be modified to alter their meanings, but Maurice Bloch is partially right in his assertion that rituals are "an area of human activity very low indeed in creativity" (Bloch 1986: 186). People alter their rituals to match changes in the wider social context, but making too many changes risks accentuating the invented nature of ritual and undermining its legitimacy (Myerhoff 1978). Rituals create liminality, using bodily practices informed by symbolic systems to compress time and space. They can thus connect participants to a wider community in both time and space. In Little Rome, participating in Catholic ritual connects people in present-day Little Rome to their Catholic ancestors, who in an earlier time participated in similar Catholic ritual. But it also connects them to a wider global community, the universal Roman Catholic Church. In fact, it is this very conservatism in ritual that creates the opportunity for legitimizing something new, for localizing something transnational. As a result, Catholic funerals in Little Rome can fit very well into Chinese orthopraxy.

But there is something more behind the privileging of ritual in the maintenance of community cohesion that can help explain the localization process. Rituals can define social groups and mobilize people for group action because they generate (or regenerate) charisma. Charisma was defined by Max Weber as "a certain quality of an individual personality by virtue of which [a person] is considered extraordinary and treated as endowed with supernatural, superhuman, or at least specifically exceptional powers or qualities" (Weber 1978: 241). In explaining the origin of social organizations that transcend the scale of kinship organizations, Weber says charisma is the source of legitimacy and authority that leads to the establishment of mobilized social groups. As they grow in scale and distance from the original charismatic leader, these communities routinize charisma by developing formal rules and administrative practices that are necessary for continuity and order. This routinization of charisma results in a bureaucracy where authority is associated with fixed positions in the system.

Edward Shils and Stanley J. Tambiah expand Weber's definition of charisma to make it more heuristically powerful as a social property. Shils extends charisma to become a social property not just of individuals, but also of institutions, actions, and objects, where charisma is a "potentiality of the moral, cognitive, and expressive orientations of human beings" (1975: 127). Shils further differentiates intense and concentrated charisma from attenuated and dispersed charisma. Intense and concentrated charisma creates a source of authority that conflicts with traditional practices. Corresponding to Weber's definition of charisma, such intense charismatic authority is incompatible with the legitimacy of the routine. Societies use and control intense charisma by segregating or disciplining potential sources in institutions such as monasteries and universities. Attenuated and dispersed charisma corresponds to Weber's routinized charisma, where charisma is attenuated or dispersed in the rules, norms, offices, institutions, and strata of society. However, in Shils's model, attenuated charisma is still a creative social force—active, effective, capable of renewal, and essential to the maintenance of routine order in society. Tambiah shows how charisma can flow over time and space through the distribution of "objectified charisma"—the sedimentation of the virtues and powers of the charismatic leader into objects such as talismans, amulets, and palladia. These objects have iconic and indexical properties that allow for greater participation by devotees in the original charisma of the leader and can be used to renew or redirect the original charisma. Charisma, then, is a function of the "social classification and cosmology of a society and . . . reflect[s] and stem[s] from the society's differentiated statuses and its hierarchy of persons and objects" (Tambiah 1984: 339; cf. Bourdieu 1984).[12]

In a study of the American Catholic Charismatic Renewal movement, Thomas Csordas demonstrates how the rhetorical performance of ritual generates charisma. Weber, Shils, and Tambiah say charisma is an imputed quality of a subject as interpreted by participants.[13] In contrast, Csordas says charisma derives from the *interpretation of actions* instead of people:

charisma is a "product of the rhetorical apparatus in use of which leader and follower alike convince themselves that the *world is constituted in a certain way*" (Csordas 1997: 139; my emphasis). Charisma is not inherent in an individual or attributed to a person by others—it comes from the interpretive action itself. Rituals are rhetorical performances that are only efficacious in producing charisma when people are convinced by the action. In other words, the practice of rituals itself generates a potential for charisma, a potential that is achieved when people interpret the messages of the ritual in a certain way.

Charisma thus configured can help explain the localization process. Before expanding on the relationship between charisma and localization, I need to unpack the connections between localization and the maintenance of community. Arjun Appadurai's model of transnationalism reveals these connections as the focus for anthropologists in the field, through his explication of *neighborhoods*—"situated communities characterized by their actuality, whether spatial or virtual, and their potential for social reproduction" (1996: 179). I use the term "communities" here, primarily because in Little Rome and elsewhere in the Hakka homeland this is the term with which people themselves problematize their deterritorialized sociality (*gongtongti;* see Fang 1994).[14] As a community, Little Rome is both context and context-generator. As context, Little Rome is the "frame or setting within which various kinds of human action . . . can be initiated and conducted meaningfully" (Appadurai 1996: 184). As a context-generator, people in Little Rome interpret the "contingencies of history, environment, and imagination" as they reproduce the social forms that reproduce the community (Appadurai 1996: 185).

I define the process of localization as the interpretation and incorporation of these contingencies into the social imagination of people in Little Rome. Little Rome struggles to maintain its sense of community in the context of (and sometimes against) three major processes: (1) the disciplinary practices of the nation-state, which seeks to solidify and expand its position of sovereignty within its borders; (2) the increased deterritorialization of its community members owing to the conditions of global capitalism; and (3) the erosion of community boundaries against the outside world owing to the heightened flow of local and transnational media and commodities (music, television, clothing, and other aspects of popular culture) (see Appadurai 1996: 189). Localization is Little Rome's answer to these challenges. For the people considered in this book, the challenge of the disciplinary practices of the nation-state centers on their practice of Catholicism. The challenge of global capitalism is embodied in labor migration and new sources of livelihood.

If the process of localization is the interpretation and incorporation of the contingencies of history, environment, and imagination into the context of a social group, then charisma can be seen as the authority that ensures this incorporation of meanings into the imagination of people in Little Rome. Such interpretive moments become incorporated into the local context only because of a charismatic force, concentrated or attenuated, in a multiplicity of structures and actions. The authority generated by such different sources of charisma provides the narratives that make up the "work of the imagination" (Appadurai 1996) for the people of Little Rome—some ideas and social organizations are more believable than others because they are more convincing. The process of localization, therefore, involves the negotiation of authoritative claims between different sources of charisma that themselves contain different cosmological orientations.

In Little Rome, two dominant and competing sources of charismatic authority are present—the PRC state and the Catholic Church. Since the revolutionary period, with its dependence on the intense charisma of Mao Zedong and other revolutionary heroes, the authority of the PRC was routinized with the rise of bureaucratic forms of authority that based their legitimacy on Maoist ideology. After the 1978 succession contest between Deng Xiaoping and Hua Guofeng, Mao's immediate successor, the PRC shifted its bureaucratic authority to incorporate "socialism with Chinese characteristics," basing its legitimacy on the success of the Chinese economy and rising living standards (Shirk 1993). By the late 1990s, the authority of the post-socialist government in Little Rome was characterized by the attenuated charisma of the bureaucratic state. In contrast, the local Catholic Church bases its authority on the attenuated charisma of the Roman Catholic Church—an "office charisma" that follows lines of episcopal ordination, lines that are legitimized through apostolic succession. Both everyday and calendrical Catholic rituals, centered on the office of Little Rome's young pastor, Father Liang, reinforce this attenuated charisma.

Another source of attenuated charisma is linked to the negotiation between these two dominant and competing sources of authority in Little Rome—the charisma of the ancestors. In Chapter 7, I describe how funerary ritual and ancestor veneration are essential to identity formation, arguing that they provide a connection between the living generations in Little Rome and their ancestors. James Watson has established one model that explains the importance of the link between the living and the dead. The obligation to participate in funerary rites and ancestor veneration results from an economic exchange between the living and the dead. Because land inheritances and shares of ancestral estates are owned by the ancestors, Cantonese villagers are in essence exchanging food offerings, death pollution absorption, and other ritual services for the economic benefits provided by ancestral estates and good fortune conferred through the geomantic power of ancestral tombs (James Watson 1982). The use of charisma as the lens through which to view the importance of ancestors does not negate Watson's model but adds a political dimension—one that is intrinsically connected with the economics of exchange with the ancestors.

There are also competing sources of intense charisma that challenge the attenuated charisma of church and state in Little Rome. One is the charisma of the sojourning young adult, the returned overseas relative or friend, who through performances of consumption embodies a perceived quality of modernity. The many individuals who return for events such as the building of the church make tangible the images of modernity depicted by the media, in advertisements and in television programming. Philanthropic demonstrations further support the rhetoric of charisma in diaspora community members. Similarly, objects of modernity, such as a motorcycle paraded as part of a dowry, contain an objectified charisma that is consumed by young newlyweds who then become endowed with the charisma of modernity themselves. These commodities of popular culture provide the stuff of dreams and become evidence of living the good life.

Charisma as an anthropological concept is thus a powerful abstraction in understanding localization and transnational processes. Analytically, the biggest challenge in understanding transnational processes is how to unravel their myriad global interconnections. Because charisma applies to people, institutions, material objects, and actions, different transnational processes can be juxtaposed and compared. Second, charisma implies a processual analysis; in its original sociological formulation by Weber, charisma is dynamic, catalyzing change as it achieves routinization. A more static model of transnationalism would fail to account for the spatial and temporal shifts in the current social environment, where time-space compression serves as the hallmark of life in a transnational world. Third, charisma by definition is interpretive and thus lends itself to subjective analysis. To understand how transnational processes differentially affect local social groups is to understand the subjective implications of displacing a person, commodity, or idea from one context to another. Localization accentuates a particularity that can only be explained through the specificity of cultural and historical exigencies. Ethnographic analyses must account for the "work of the imagination," but the imagination that must be examined belongs to those living in our fieldsite, not to ourselves (see Appadurai 1996: 2–11).

Understanding localization by using charisma is particularly applicable in this study of a Chinese Catholic village, because charisma was originally a theological concept. In its theological usage, charisma is the gift of the Holy Spirit that legitimizes the Catholic Church in both its spiritual and worldly hierarchy. In the Vatican II restructuring of the Catholic hierarchy, the hierarchical structure of the institutional church is dependent upon the authority of the Pope, and the Pope's authority (and infallibility) as successor of Peter is based upon charisma. In an examination of the role of charisma in the post–Vatican II Catholic institutional hierarchy, noted Jesuit theologian Avery Dulles concludes that the institutional church is dependent upon the charismatic to maintain the office of the priesthood and for the renewal and reform of the church: "The lordship of Christ in the Church as a social system is exercised, always provisionally, through the interplay of the institutional and the charismatic" (Dulles 1980: 180). In practice, however, because everyone is potentially a recipient of the "gifts of the Holy Spirit," there has been great tension between charismatic and institutional sources of authority, as depicted in many ethnographic case studies (e.g., Csordas 1997). Lawrence Taylor (1995) highlights the connection between this tension and the localization of Catholicism through the specificity of sacred sites in Ireland. Nagle's (1997) account of the impact of liberation theology in a Brazilian community also addresses this tension as competing social groups make claims to an icon of the Virgin Mary. The issue of competing authorities and negotiated legitimacy lies at the heart of my study of Little Rome and these other studies of local practices of Catholicism.

Since the formation of Little Rome in the late nineteenth century, the most disruptive charismatic force in its community life has been the persecution and harassment of people during the Maoist period, largely because of their Catholic belief. The state's suspicion of all elements of Chinese religious culture, let alone transnational religions like Catholicism, goes beyond the ideological content of communism and is firmly rooted in a long history of statecraft.

Writing About Little Rome

Because the localization process is contingent upon the particularities of historical and contemporary social contexts, this account is not representative of Hakka villages or of other Chinese Catholic communities in general. My research paints only a partial picture, like any other ethnographic study based largely on participant-observation fieldwork. It looks at the Chinese borderland, which includes such different places as the global cities of Shanghai and Canton as well as rural villages in the southern littoral areas, and documents how transnational processes have become localized, resulting in *specific yet deterritorialized* communities. Multiple transnational processes are transformed into local processes in many ways, involving consumption, production, and ritual celebration—the stuff of everyday life. What should become clear is a view of a developing Chinese modernity, a lifestyle that is somehow made specific to the needs and dreams of Chinese society. People in Little Rome, in their multiple identities as Hakka, Catholics, grandparents, and young adults, are pursuing every day their vision of a happy, modern life, implementing the work of the imagination in particularistic ways that define what it means to be local in a global world.

Each of the following seven ethnographic chapters focuses on a particular event that depicts how different aspects of transnational processes become localized in Little Rome. Chapter 2 describes Chinese religious culture, showing how charisma can be used to situate Catholicism and religion in Chinese society. Chapter 3 documents the opening celebration and centrality of the new church in Little Rome and describes how Little Rome is in effect a transnational village. Chapter 4 examines key historical events in Little Rome to demonstrate how transnational processes have always been significant there and how global history plays out in local history. Chapter 5 surveys the ritual life of the local church, describing everyday rituals in Little Rome by examining a baptism, Sunday mass, and the celebration of Christmas and Spring Festival to further clarify the role of the local Catholic church in Little Rome. Chapter 6 examines a wedding to demonstrate how transnational capital intersects with transnational religion in a highly personalized manner, embedding transnational processes into local social memory. Chapter 7 examines a funeral, including death ritual and ancestor remembrance, to show how transnational Catholicism becomes localized. Chapter 8 focuses on a nonritual event, the building of a road, to show how national processes—here, the retraction of the state from the local economic context—affect village life in Little Rome. As the postsocialist state transforms a command economy into a market economy, it co-opts transnational processes, making the state complicit in its own apparent abrogation of sovereignty. Chapter 9 examines the impact of diaspora Hakka ethnicity in the homeland. In this chapter, I describe how an ethnic movement that developed and matured in the diaspora rebounds in the Hakka homeland, and as a result links diaspora ethnicity with modernity. In the conclusion, Chapter 10,

I describe how charisma can clarify the process of localization. The interpretation of the contingencies of history, environment, and imagination, and the incorporation of that interpretation into the context of Little Rome, requires the negotiation of authoritative claims between different sources of charisma.

Doing Fieldwork in Little Rome

How does one do grounded, locally based fieldwork on transnational phenomena? What is "'real anthropology' defined by 'real fieldwork' " in a deterritorialized fieldsite (see Gupta and Ferguson 1997)? In my fieldwork in Little Rome, I tried to do precisely what Akhil Gupta and James Ferguson have suggested, to focus not merely on the local but on the social *location* of this rural community. This study is an attempt to determine what makes a local church local. It is based on summer field trips to Little Rome in 1993, 1994, 1995, and 1996, and an extended fieldwork period between September 1996 and February 1998.

I first became interested in the Chinese Catholic Church as a traveler, when as a U.S. Marine Corps officer on a Pacific deployment I attended Catholic mass in Hong Kong.[15] Even though mass was conducted in Cantonese, which I could not then understand, there was something very comforting about seeing familiar ritual practices there, and on every shore leave throughout the Pacific. In Hong Kong, I was definitely an outsider in the local church, yet as parishioners we were all linked as Catholics in something that we profess every week: "one holy, catholic, and apostolic Church."

I am Catholic, active in my own church in Cambridge, Massachusetts, and, more recently, Indianapolis. My identity as an American Catholic was the first thing that people in Little Rome knew about me. In 1993, Bishop Anthony Zhong Quanzhang from Meizhou City took me to Little Rome for my first visit. I knew of the churches in the area from previous archival research in Maryknoll, New York, and had letters of introduction from the Maryknoll research director, Dr. Jean-Paul Wiest, and the Hong Kong Maryknoll liaison to the mainland churches in former mission areas. I was one of many nonkin foreign Catholic visitors to the village, the majority of whom are priests and nuns touring China. The people of Little Rome warmly welcomed me as a full participant in their faith community. On my next visit in 1994 I was accompanied by Prof. Fang Xuejia of Jiaying University and Jiaoling county cadres. I knew of Prof. Fang from other Hakka researchers and was introduced to him by Prof. Hsieh Jiann, then in the Department of Anthropology at the Chinese

University of Hong Kong. As a fieldworker interested in doing research in the Hakka homeland, with a local *danwei* (work unit) willing to sponsor me, I was warmly welcomed by the local cadres. With acceptance by both church and state, I made later visits on my own.

For my extended fieldwork in 1996, I moved with my anthropologist wife, Rebecca Ruhlen, and our seven-year-old son, Patrick, into an empty house in Little Rome, having received temporary household registration from the county. The presence of my family greatly shaped our neighbors' attitudes toward me—I was not merely an observer intruding on their everyday lives with my camera, but also a husband and a father, watching over my son as he ran through the village with the other children.[16] In many subtle ways, my experiences as a fieldworker were similar to those of a "native anthropologist" (Narayan 1993) because I am Catholic and regularly attended mass, because I was a householder, and also because as an Asian-American, I looked like other people in Little Rome. For example, when I made trips to Hong Kong and Singapore during our residence in Little Rome, I was asked to serve as an "advocate" for the community by presenting fund-raising documents to external church organizations and explaining the community's needs to church liaisons in Hong Kong. Nonetheless, I was clearly not a native; I talked to neighbors (and they talked to me) in Mandarin; gradually I built up my understanding of Hakka.

With people, commodities, and ideas moving in and out of Little Rome, I readily saw the difficulty of treating the village as a bounded community—a methodological concern that Gupta and Ferguson argue is transforming the field science of anthropology. I planned to do my fieldwork on transnational processes by focusing on their transformation of a local community and then discovered that the idea of locality itself had to be addressed. I started out by mapping the village—drawing a map of the physical space, and matching it with the social space of the households that occupied each house. These survey data, however, were not the main source of information that I used to explore the localization process. Instead, I focused on particular events—a wedding, a funeral, building a road—to map out the localization process. These events structure what Anthony Giddens refers to as *time-space distanciation*: "the conditions under which time and space are organized so as to connect presence and absence" (1990: 14). Methodologically, this implies a focus on observing and documenting events that illustrate how time is compressed and how space (a social conception) is separated from place (the physical setting). Both fieldwork and analysis were thus structured to follow Sally Falk Moore's diagnostic event approach.

The diagnostic event approach is "simply a time-oriented perspective on both continuity and change" (Moore 1987: 729). It situates ethnographic observations within the larger global and historical processes, enabling the fieldworker to connect limited, partial, but specific observations from a particular fieldsite to the larger world by making explicit the social, political, and economic ties of a community to the larger system. Connecting observations of smaller-scale social processes to larger-scale historical process reveals the multiple layers of actors, forces, and meanings that comprise an event. Methodologically, this approach requires the fieldworker to look for diagnostic events, everyday events experienced by people that "reveal ongoing contests and conflicts and competitions and the efforts to prevent, suppress, or repress these" (Moore 1987: 730). I assert that complex, unbounded transnational processes require a diagnostic event approach in order to reveal the connections among the actors, forces, and meanings that characterize the localization process. Although the actors in this process cannot be isolated from the fields in which they participate, the diagnostic event approach reveals the battle lines of normative indeterminacy (ibid.: 729). These events are historical moments, connected however remotely to shifting large-scale historical processes, and they reflect Little Rome's residents' local concerns and interpretations of their social context.

A diagnostic event perspective has deep methodological implications. First, the unit of analysis is not individual villages (Catholic, Hakka, multisurname, or otherwise), families (or households), weddings, funerals, or community projects. (I do not make any claims that the wedding, funeral, or other events described here represent Chinese weddings, funerals, or other cultural practices in general.) Although I collected demographic information about Little Rome, my focus was to document (through videography, photography, interviews, and participation) preparations leading to a particular event, the conduct of the event, and the closing and after-effects of the event. Hence, I was not overly concerned with such issues as sample size or sample composition, although these factors are critical for demonstrating (and knowing) the reliability and validity of the conclusions that fieldworkers make from participant-observation-based research. In this study, the main conclusions I reach are not about Hakka families or Chinese Catholic weddings per se, but about what such social forms and events reflect—namely, the "ongoing dismantling of structures or of attempts to create new ones" (Moore 1987: 729). In essence, my unit of analysis for understanding the localization process was the events themselves. I chose these events not because they represented some larger static category, but because they were the best documented, the events that I knew the best. What is striking is the centrality of the same process—the localization process—in such disparate social events as a wedding, a funeral, the building of a church, and the building of a road.

Second, the diagnostic event approach keeps the fieldworker close to what is actually experienced. In the field, events unfold before us, and our job as fieldworkers is to painstakingly record as much detail as we directly observe. Through discussions with informants, we also reconstruct important parts of the events that happened outside our field of view, or before we arrived at the fieldsite, in order to better understand what these events mean to the people involved. Knowing my interest in a particular event, such as a wedding or the arrival of overseas relatives, people would tell me to come and see what was happening (also implying that if I brought my equipment to take photos and make a video for them, so much the better). I would then sit down with those outside and inside the event in an attempt to gather more of the relevant information. I did not have to orchestrate many of these post-event discussions—people's normal conversation filled in the blanks. Friends and neighbors made small talk about these events, expressing approval of a newlywed couple's success ("Her dowry was so big!") or disapproval of local cadres who hovered over people for contributions to a project ("Don't listen to them when they come asking for money—tell them you're a poor academic, not a rich businessman"). The events were important not only to myself as fieldworker, but also to my neighbors as community members. Holiday celebrations of Christmas and Chinese New Year punctuated the routine of daily life, marking the passage of time as well as helping to pass the time.

Third, events provide an alternative way of "bounding" inquiries that is less dependent on cultural constructions, local or otherwise, of boundaries and social groups. Olwig and Hastrup point out that conceptions of bounded communities, linked to geographical places, not only are a product of methodological concerns about fieldwork but also are linked to our own culture's notions of rootedness, where "movement as an aspect of social life in general . . . has been regarded as a special and temporary phenomenon" (1997: 6). Likewise, Appadurai (1996) asserts that the main focus for understanding social groups should be how locality is constructed in places where rootedness is not assumed to be normative. This was a key consideration in my approach to Little Rome, where people often came from far away to participate in an event such as a funeral or the opening ceremony of the church.

Praying Together

Growing up Catholic, I was constantly reminded that "the family that prays together stays together." Churchgoers in Little Rome often gathered before mass to chant the rosary together, just as my family did in my childhood. When I sat in the pews of the church in Little Rome, this powerful demonstration of faith always moved me. Such practices of faith by my neighbors there and in other rural Hakka Catholic communities at first struck me as "old-time Catholicism," that mythical Catholic setting that I heard about as a young altar boy from a grizzled old priest in a New York parish and from my parents at home. Looking more closely at the practice of mass and other ritual activities and learning more about the structure of the church and the community, I came to realize that this was not simply a recommencement of traditional Catholic practices in public after decades underground. The Little Rome church's use of an updated mass liturgy in Hakka, the participation of lay women readers, and a parish council that helped the priest make plans and decisions—all these were characteristic of post–Vatican II churches. Participants knew that the priest could place the host in their hands, but most preferred to kneel at the communion rail and have him place it directly in the mouth. They did some things in the manner that the older generations remembered from their youth, while changing other things that made for a more localized church. Keeping some elements of old-style Catholicism connected the living generations to their Catholic ancestors and grounded their Catholic practices in the lived space of Little Rome.

After hearing story after story about "the bitter times" of the Maoist period, when the Little Rome church was forced underground, I also realized that being reconnected to the universal Church was very important to people in Little Rome. After resurfacing in 1983 and reestablishing links with overseas relatives, friends, and clergy (especially those from Hong Kong), they gradually learned about the many changes in the church that they had missed because of their isolation during the Maoist period. Shifting to a post–Vatican II liturgy, then, held special symbolism as a statement that they were truly Catholic, part of the Holy Church on earth. Including the Pope in Eucharistic prayers, reading papal encyclicals painstakingly written on a blackboard at the church entrance, listening to the Vatican's shortwave radio broadcasts—all these elements of their Catholic practices connected the people of Little Rome to their fellow Catholics throughout the world. Repeated calls by the state to modernize (*xiandai-*

hua) China seemed to be understood by people in Little Rome also as calls to modernize their faith.

Being Catholic was not seen as contradictory to being modern—in fact, quite the reverse. For people in Little Rome, to be Catholic is to be modern, to be global in a local world. Modernizing Little Rome has not been detrimental to their community, because the church kept the community intact in the face of dislocations associated with the deterritorialization of people and the influx of outside ideas and commodities. Praying together means staying together for the transnational community of Little Rome.

CHAPTER 2

Chinese Religious Culture

I remember they had a procession. Maybe it was Tin How [Tianhou]—it
might have been the Goddess of the Seas—or it might have been Gun Yam
[Guanyin]—they took a statue out and it reminded us very much of our
Blessed Mother processions. And I remember some of us feeling very
uncomfortable saying, "What is the difference then between taking
the Blessed Mother statue out on procession?"

—*Maryknoll sister who served in China*[1]

Catholicism, like other foreign ideologies and religious traditions, simultaneously adapted to and transformed Chinese society. It did so by building upon
a thriving religious culture and within specific historical contexts. In 1918,
when American Maryknoll missionaries arrived in Republican China, they
encountered a China in social and cultural flux. Some even say that this time
period, so crucial to the Christian missionary enterprises, was characterized by
a Chinese cultural crisis (Hunter and Chan 1993: 5). China in the early twentieth century was in the process of localizing a wide range of foreign ideas and
practices introduced by missionaries and traders, and by Chinese who returned
from study or work overseas having learned about social Darwinism, chemistry, and Marxism-Leninism.[2] Paul Cohen has described this process of localization through a model of the Chinese littoral and hinterland, where the outward-looking littoral provides a better arena for the introduction of foreign
cultural ideas than the more inward-looking hinterland. Foreign cultural elements like Catholicism, however, can only be introduced in the littoral, resulting in what Cohen characterizes as "two largely separate and distinct cultural
environments evolving side by side" (Paul Cohen 1974: 199). At the heart of
these different cultural environments are competing cultural authorities that
attracted people to employ new hybrid strategies in pursuing their visions of
the future. New strategies that include cultural elements from outside China,

such as Christianity and chemistry, blend local and nonlocal sources of cultural authority; they are in essence the localization of a nonlocal tradition.

In this chapter, I continue the discussion of charisma and further explore how charisma can be used to understand the localization of religious traditions in China. I first discuss what I propose is the dominant theme in Chinese religious culture—the interaction of the centralizing Chinese state with local religious organizations, centered on the paradigmatic figures of the sage and the rebel. Using this framework, I then discuss how Chinese popular religious traditions and gender ideologies reflect this negotiation of authority. This negotiation of authority between religious and political authority is clearly evident in the localization of the Indian Buddhist tradition—a process that can also be seen as the transformation of Indian Buddhism into a Chinese religion. Understanding this uneasy relationship between "church and state" is crucial to understanding Catholicism in China.[3] The underlying question examined in this chapter is, What makes a religion a Chinese religion?

Chinese Religious Culture

Geertz's classic definition of religion is a "system of symbols which acts to establish powerful, pervasive, and long-lasting moods and motivations in [people] by formulating conceptions of a general order of existence and clothing these conceptions with such an aura of factuality that the moods and motivations seem uniquely realistic" (1973: 90). Using that definition, I define religious culture as the aspect of a culture that is created, informed, explained, and practiced using a religious system of symbols. Chinese religious culture is not a homogenous, systematic whole, but an arena that provides the *doxa* (following Bourdieu, the culturally shaped range of imagined possibilities) through which new religious movements and nonindigenous religious traditions are understood. For Japan, this has been described by James Foard as *endemic religion*: "a kind of minimal religious practice that absolutely every Japanese participates in to some degree and which helps bind the Japanese together" (quoted in Keyes, Hardacre, and Kendall 1994: 10). The problem is that it is difficult to pin down precisely what is meant by a Chinese religious culture—to what extent do all Han Chinese share a coherent religious culture? Julia Ching suggests that Chinese religions cannot be separated from the wider Han Chinese cultural heritage: "This inseparability between religion and culture has led many to the conclusion that the Chinese have no religiosity of their own. But it also explains why much common ground can be found among the religions of China" (Julia Ching 1993: 221–22). Religiosity in China has a long multiethnic history. At the two ends of the pluralistic spectrum of Chinese religious culture are the polar attractors of sagehood (*sheng*) and spiritual power (*ling*) (see Dean 1998: 40).

In characterizing Chinese religious culture, Catholic theologian Hans Kung paints a picture in broad strokes of religions in China around the figure of the sage. According to Kung, the Chinese sage is the embodiment of the paradigm of a third religious river system, standing in contrast to the Semitic prophet and the Hindu mystic. The wise sage, unlike the Semitic prophet voicing a message from God or the Hindu mystic renouncing the world, is active in the direct leadership and administration of society, promoting harmonious values. Kung also highlights what he considers to be an undeniable Chinese characteristic: "The great value set on age and its wisdom is a constant of Chinese history. This was reinforced by the absence of the Western dualism of state and church, nobility and clergy" (Julia Ching and Kung 1989: xv). What Kung proposes is a Chinese system of religiosity grounded in the dispersed charisma of the ancestors and the state administrative systems (see Shils 1975).

However, Kung neglected the other embodiment of Chinese religious culture: the rebel. In the long annals of Chinese imperial history, dynastic records are punctuated with the rebellions arising out of soteriological movements (Fairbank 1983; Overmyer 1976; Naquin 1985). The first recorded religious rebellion centered on the deity the Queen Mother of the West (*xi wang mu*) during the Han dynasty:

> [In 3 B.C.E.], there was a great drought. . . . The common people carried in procession the wands of the Mother Queen of the West. They passed through commanderies and kingdoms and went west through the Han-gu Pass to the imperial capital. The common people there also met and collected, sacrificing to the Mother Queen of the West. Some by night took fire up on top of the buildings, beat drums, and cried out, exciting and frightening one another. [They] were excited and ran, each holding a stalk of straw or hemp, carrying them on and passing them to one another, saying, "I am transporting the wand of the goddess's edict." Those who passed along and met on the roads were as many as thousands. Some let down their hair and walked barefoot. Some at night broke door-bars and some climbed over walls, entering houses. Some rode chariots or on horseback, galloping fast, or making themselves post-messengers to transmit

and transport the wands. They passed and traveled thru twenty-six comman-
deries and kingdoms and came to the imperial capital. (Dubs 1942: 235)

The Queen Mother of the West is still a central deity in modern Daoism
(Lagerwey 1987; see also Overmyer 1986: 34). More recently, the Hakka-led
and Christianity-inspired Taiping Rebellion (1851–1864) put much of
southern China in turmoil and left the Qing dynasty vulnerable to Western
intrusion (Spence 1996). In dealing with such soteriological movements, the
state has used the time-tested strategy of co-opting popular religious movements. James Watson (1985) gives a detailed account of one method, the
standardization of the Tianhou mentioned by the Maryknoll sister, a deity
popular on the coast of southern China and among Southeast Asian diaspora
Chinese, through her incorporation into the imperial pantheon. This pattern
of state co-optation has shaped the structure and cultural forms of Chinese
popular religion.

Popular Religion and Chinese Religious Culture

Traditional Chinese religion has been described from both emic and etic perspectives as the *sanjiao*—the three teachings of Confucianism, Daoism, and
Buddhism. The inadequacy of this model for understanding Chinese religious culture, however, becomes clear in an examination of the dominant
mode of Chinese religiosity—what has been called "popular religion." Fieldwork observations of Chinese religious practices yield a bewildering array of
ideologies, deities, and myths that do not fit neatly into the intellectual categories of Confucianism, Daoism, and Buddhism. Temples that have been
labeled "Daoist" in the Hakka homeland, for example, have an altar with an
icon of the bodhisattva Guanyin. Popular religious practices, whether historical or contemporary, are largely syncretic and locally based. This phenomenon of syncretism in Chinese popular religious practices may even be considered a hallmark of Chinese religiosity: "What is of interest in the Chinese
case is the second sense of 'syncretism,' which is the *self-consciousness* of
historical syncretism [the historical fact of parts of a cultural system having
different origins], the intellectual defense of the *desirability* of historical
syncretism, and even the delight in, as it were, wallowing in historical syncretism" (Jordan and Overmyer 1986: 9). Daoist, Confucian, and Buddhist
ideas, deities, myths, and rituals are commonly blended together by local
practitioners to create new traditions. Popular religious practices like lineage-

based ancestor worship can be combined with elite intellectual systems, such as in the conversion of a lineage ancestral hall into a Confucian temple in Gansu (Jing 1996). Such novel blendings of traditional cultural repertoires are not dangerous to Chinese religiosity, as Myerhoff (1978) would suggest for such blendings that highlight the "invented" nature of ritual. Instead, the combination of primordiality and novelty by religious entrepreneurs is precisely what leads to success in local religious marketplaces.

This is most clearly evident in a case study by Kenneth Dean (1998) of one cult in southern China, the cult of the Three-in-One (*sanyijiao*). A blend of Confucian ethical thought, Buddhist meditative practices, and Daoist inner alchemical practices, the Three-in-One originated in Fujian from an attempt in the sixteenth century by Lin Zhao-en, a local scholar, to popularize Confucian ideas. Throughout its history, the Three-in-One (like Catholicism) has been both tolerated and persecuted—at times labeled a heterodox "White Lotus"–related movement, and at other times ignored by the state.[4] Julia Ching cites the Three-in-One as a challenge to imperial authority because Three-in-One initiates are prompted to establish a personal relationship with heaven (*tian*) in a tradition "where only the emperor as Son of Heaven had the prerogative of worshipping Heaven, where ordinary citizens only dared address themselves to the minor deities of the city, the locality, or the household" (Julia Ching 1993: 217). After being persecuted during the mid-Qing dynasty, the Three-in-One underwent a revival in the late Qing and Republican period but was again forced underground during the Maoist period. In the postsocialist period, the Three-in-One has again flourished in Fujian; the group organizes ritual events and even holds academic conferences attended by local cadres, but it has yet to obtain official recognition. Nevertheless, Dean estimates that half a million people are involved in Three-in-One ritual activities. One activity that has helped their cause is renewed contacts with other Three-in-One temples in Taiwan and Southeast Asia. Cadres from the local consultative congress (*zhengxiehui*) are eager to welcome donations from overseas Chinese for the development of Three-in-One temples and other social projects. Likewise, as I discuss in detail in a later chapter, Catholics in Little Rome are caught in the sometimes conflicting relationship between the official support of local cadres and overseas capital.

Like other popular religious traditions (such as *qigong* traditions in contemporary postsocialist China), the Three-in-One features an inner alchemical tradition that is a central part of everyday religious practices. This tradition is based on the "heart method" developed by Lin Zhao-en, a nine-step meditative practice that transforms the self by empowering individual control of *qi*. Three-in-One initiates can develop powers to improve their own health and physical condition and can use their own *qigong* to heal others. In his examination of Three-in-One communities in Fujian, Dean found a range of emphasis in their religious practices; while some practitioners focus on the immediacy of *ling*, showing the efficacy of the heart method through healing or other physical demonstrations, others focus on the *sheng* aspect, emphasizing self-cultivation and ethical concerns.

Dean explains how, over time, local Three-in-One communities negotiated the practice of popular religions with the Chinese imperial center (and, in modern times, the PRC state). With the political center's monopoly over the correct definitions of proper ritual (*li*), local deviations in religious practices can be seen as challenges to state authority. Dean's contribution to the understanding of the Chinese state's preoccupation with religion lies in the nuances he ascribes to elite and popular negotiations over ritual practices: "Rather than simple opposition expressing an essentialized local community or a totalistic counterhegemony, these changing localized [ritual] forms must be explored in context, as the *temporary consolidations of a host of transverse flows, many arriving from the outside*, well beyond the reach of the imperium" (Dean 1998: 9; my emphasis). For religious traditions from outside the Chinese state to survive and flourish in China, then, they must adapt to the paradigm of the sage—namely, incorporation into the state administrative system.

Although Dean dismisses the relevance of charisma and its routinization in Chinese religious organizations, I would suggest that a reexamination of charisma and authority are essential in understanding how religious organizations and practices embody the temporary consolidation of multiple transverse cultural flows. If religious practices such as rituals enable different levels of power formation, there must be an authority that convinces ritual participants of the potency of such events. Rituals are interpretive events that, if convincing as demonstrations of *ling*, generate charisma for the people who lead popular religious organizations (for new religious groups) or for the office (for religious groups that already have an institutional structure). For the Three-in-One, Dean describes how social and cosmic forces combine to channel power to participants. The sources of attenuated charisma (social forces) combine with the intense charisma drawn from cosmic forces by Three-in-One initiates. Dean's descriptions of transverse flows are competing sources of charisma, such as the state, the ancestors, and global capitalism. Focusing on the appeal of such diverse sources of charisma clarifies the competing authorities involved in what at first glance looks like a simple opposition between a local community and the state center. The harnessing of the intense charisma of the sacred, whether through the control of cosmic *qi* in the Three-in-One or through the direct access to the holy in Catholic mass, is what happens when the state incorporates local religious organizations into an administrative structure. Such attenuated charisma in the offices of state religious bureaucracies, however, can be revitalized or called upon to again provide a source of competing authority, as local communities create interpretive moments through the performance of ritual. The sage, in effect, creates the space for the rebel.

Gender and Chinese Religious Culture

Another way to see how the disciplining of intense charisma shapes Chinese religious culture is to examine the transformation of Avalokitesvara into the Chinese bodhisattva Guanyin. Gender shapes the precarious equilibrium of the paradigms of the sage and the rebel in Chinese popular religious practices. Female deities, who are central figures in popular religious movements, embody a potentially undisciplined *yin* power in opposition to a Confucian *yang* hegemony. As previously discussed, the first historically recorded popular millenarian movement centered on the Queen Mother of the West. Gendered symbols, building upon cultural concepts such as the *yin-yang* dialectic, thus shape popular perceptions of charismatic authority in Chinese religious culture.

The importance of bodhisattvas, celestial beings who have returned from a state of nirvana in order to guide human beings, separates the Mahayana Buddhist tradition from the Theravada tradition prevalent in India and Southeast Asia; Avalokitesvara has especially served as an important vehicle in the inculturation of the Buddhist tradition. Avalokitesvara is the celestial bodhisattva of compassion who saves those who remember it and recite its name. Although the bodhisattva Avalokitesvara was originally depicted as a chief attendant to Amitabha Buddha, later writings describe it as more omnipresent and omnipotent. It has taken a bodhisattva vow to assume any form and to grant boons in order to save all sentient beings. The earliest scriptural reference to a female Avalokitesvara is in Kumarajiva's fifth-century translation of the Lotus Sutra. In comparing Kumarajiva's translation with the original in Sanskrit, Diana Paul discovered that Kumarajiva left out certain verses in his Chinese translation. Verse 31 extols the virtue of a world where there are no women and sexual intercourse is absolutely unknown.

Verse 33 describes Guanyin as a ruler without equal in the three worlds. These two omissions highlight the rejection of Indian paradigms that conflicted with traditional Chinese culture: the Chinese unity of secular and spiritual authority in the person of the emperor and the notion of monastic celibacy as an attack on the Confucian norm of filial piety. Such changes were typical of the process by which the translators adjusted the Buddhist sutras to fit the Chinese palette.[5]

The feminization of Guanyin also has its roots in Chinese mythology, taking advantage of the widespread popularity of the Queen Mother of the West (Xi Wang Mu). The mythological development of the Queen Mother of the West, from a therianthropic figure to a beautiful, regal woman, has been discussed in detail by Yuan Ke (1988).[6] In Chinese folklore, the Queen Mother of the West is associated with the drug of immortality and her ability to guide people's souls to heaven. In contemporary times, the Queen Mother of the West is still a central deity in the Daoist pantheon (Lagerwey 1987: 39–43). Matsunaga (1969) concludes that the spread of Guanyin devotion tapped into the popularity of Chinese matriarchal deities (*niang niang*) like the Queen Mother of the West who granted children to women. In addition, the simple means of gaining salvation through Guanyin and Guanyin's power of guiding recently deceased souls is similar to powers attributed to the Queen Mother of the West. Therefore, the widespread popularity of Guanyin should be seen in the context of the tradition of the Queen Mother of the West. Also, Guanyin may have symbolically displaced the Queen Mother of the West because of the historical context of official patronage of Guanyin temples combined with the persecution of the Queen Mother of the West cults (Cahill 1984). The feminized bodhisattva Avalokitesvara had a Chinese audience that was already prepared for such an image by the indigenous Queen Mother of the West tradition.

The immense popularity of Guanyin also results from the numerous "precious scrolls" (*baojuan*) central as a scriptural source in Chinese popular religion (see Overmyer 1976). As a bodhisattva, Guanyin serves as a powerful source of charisma to be tapped by leaders of popular religious movements. As a powerful *female* bodhisattva, Guanyin symbolically stands in opposition to the male, Confucian hierarchy of imperial times. The transformation of the male Avalokitesvara into the female Chinese Guanyin can thus be seen as the adaptation of the Indian Buddhist tradition to fit Chinese religious culture. Although the Chinese Buddhist tradition, as in the historical example given above, was shifted to fit the ideals of the sage, in the gendered symbol of Guanyin there has been the potential for tapping into her intense charismatic authority to generate the rebel. The role of Mary in the Chinese Christian tradition must be seen in light of the Chinese religious traditions of Guanyin and the Queen Mother of the West.

Charisma and the Localization of Marian Devotion

As a source of charismatic authority, the Virgin Mary has commanded more widespread devotion in different cultures than any other Roman Catholic saint. Her personification has both influenced and been influenced by the changing social and historical conditions of her devotees. The Virgin Mary has been used as a powerful source of charismatic authority by elite groups to legitimize their higher position and by lower elements of the social hierarchy to mobilize revolution and resistance. The power of her symbol, reinterpreted and appropriated by people throughout history, lies in her unique personification of the feminine within the Catholic tradition as the Virgin Mother of Jesus Christ.

Although there are few canonical scriptural references to Mary, a vast literature and tradition has developed and become accepted by the Catholic Church.[7] She has been portrayed by the Catholic hierarchy as virgin, bride, mother, and, in her most powerful role, queen. Her role in Catholic tradition expanded with the institutional growth of the Catholic Church and the consolidation of Church authority in papal supremacy (Perry and Echeverría 1988). The image of Maria Regina was a powerful symbol for the popes in their struggle with the Byzantine emperors and kings of Western Europe, as shown in her use as a shielding figure during the first crusade launched by a militant Church on the Day of the Assumption in 1095. In the twentieth century, Mary as queen continued to be a source of charismatic authority for popular lay groups like the Legion of Mary. As a queen, Mary has her own army in the Legion of Mary. This lay organization follows the hierarchy of a Roman Legion, from legionaries assembled in military formation to a leadership that derives its authority from Mary as queen. By the mid-twentieth century, this group had established a network of politically active *praesidia* on every continent, including China. Because of the anticommunist pronouncements at Fatima, the Legion of Mary was specifically targeted by the Chinese Communist Party and denounced by the *People's Daily* in 1951 as "an international, secret, reactionary fascist organization, . . . an imperialist tool for aggression against China."[8]

Mary's role as mother is part of her appeal to women as they deal with human problems such as infertility or a sick child. One study of Rachel (in Judaism), Mary, and Fatima (in Islam) found that a feature common to the hagiographies of these three women saints is the ordinary human situations they experience in their lives: "The critical expertise of the female saint is that she translates personal matters into universal symbols, at the same time that she transforms cosmology and theology and rules and rites into personal matters" (Sered 1991: 139). Like Guanyin, Mary thus serves as a bridge between the mundane needs and hopes of human beings and the strength and majesty of a transcendent spiritual power.

Marian devotees have participated in her charisma largely through her relics, shrines, and apparitions. With her assumption into heaven, Mary left no body to venerate or locale to worship as her tomb shrine; but she has appeared more often, to more people, and in more locales and forms than any other saint and has thus been transformed into a localized patron adapted to the needs of her devotees. Mary's embodiment as the physical presence of the holy in her local manifestation can unify a local community with an extended network of ecclesiastical hierarchy and can be used to strengthen the position of local, less powerful groups. Her ideal power, moreover, assumes "a vertical model of dependence [that holds] the individual in a tight bond of personal obligation" (Brown 1981: 118). As a universal saint with local manifestations confirmed by the dogma of the ecclesiastical hierarchy, Mary is unique in both her universality and her particularity. As a result, she can be used as a powerful source of charismatic authority.

One example of the localization of the cult of Mary is the Virgin of Guadalupe in Mexico, proclaimed the "Patroness of the Americas" by Pope Pius XII in 1946. Anthropologists have determined that her cult represents the colonial encounter between the Spanish and indigenous peoples in Mexico, both in the Catholic hierarchical acceptance of her manifestation (Kurtz 1982) and in the iconography that represents an amalgamation of the preconquest Aztec goddess Tonantzin and the Virgin Mary (Campbell 1982). Guadalupe emerged as the national patron after her abatement of a plague in 1736–37 and was a powerful source of charismatic authority in mobilizing indigenous peoples and creoles against the French-influenced government of New Spain in the Hidalgo Insurrection of 1810–11 (Turner 1974; cf. William Taylor 1987). Guadalupe was a powerful symbol for creating an imagined community because she linked family, politics, and religion, colonial past and independent present, and indigenous and creole populations (Eric Wolf 1958).

Thus it can be seen how the symbol of the Virgin Mary, as a powerful source of charismatic authority, has been localized and can unite people into a coherent social group. In his examination of religion in Chinese society, C. K. Yang has concluded that the "essential function of religion [is] to provide a collective symbol that would . . . make it possible to coalesce a large multitude into a community" (Yang 1961: 81). As a source of charismatic authority, Mary can both reinforce and challenge the claims of traditional authority—and as the Virgin Mother of Jesus Christ she has charisma that can not be fully attenuated or dispersed. The widespread distribution of various manifestations of Mary, from Lourdes and Guadalupe to a Marian pilgrimage site in Sheshan (near Shanghai), attests to the role of Marian devotion in creating local specificity in Catholicism. For these reasons, Marian devotion continues to be an important part of Chinese Catholic devotion.

Buddhism: A Historical Antecedent for Localization

Although Buddhism today is a crucial component of traditional Chinese culture, it was once considered a foreign religion and constantly held in suspicion by the state. Therefore, there are similar processes at play in both the historical sinification of Buddhism and the contemporary experience of Catholicism in China. Chinese debates over the localization of the Indian Buddhist tradition have flowed through history, up to the twenty-first century. Hu Shih, a renowned protagonist of the May Fourth Movement, describes five paradigmatic aspects of the Indian Buddhist tradition that conflict with the Han Chinese Confucian worldview.[9] First, according to Hu, Buddhism teaches an apparent negation of life (as enacted by the self-immolation of monks) that runs contrary to the Confucian sacrality of individual life as an inheritance from one's ancestors. This leads to the second conflict, the vow of celibacy, which contradicts the duty of a person to continue the ancestral line and the Confucian emphasis on posterity. Third, the Buddhist ideal of mendicancy conflicts with the Chinese work ethic. Fourth, the otherworldly Buddhist worldview conflicts with the this-worldly Chinese perspective. Finally, Hu Shih asserts that the "whole Indian imaginative power, which knows neither limitation nor discipline," was too much for the Chinese mind, which emphasizes rationality (Hu 1937: 229). For Hu Shih, Buddhism was the root cause of China's failure in the early twentieth century to meet the challenges of Western imperialism because it hampered the development of science and technology through its reorientation of Chinese culture away from its original, rational foundation.

When Buddhism arrived during the late Han dynasty (25–220 C.E.), the itinerant Buddhist monks and their Chinese converts had great difficulty translating, in both words and ideas, the Buddhist scriptures brought overland to China. Many Buddhist ideas became localized early in Chinese history through the translation of Buddhist sutras into Chinese, often through the use of traditional Confucian and Daoist terms (Ch'en 1964). However, localizing the structure of the Buddhist sangha (the organization of monks and nuns) and ritual practices took more time. During a millennium of tempering forged through cycles of official patronage and persecution, the Buddhist sangha, rituals, and ideals were gradually adjusted to address many of the ethical concerns of Confucian thought. As the Buddhist tradition gained in popularity before its high point in the Tang dynasty, 618–907 C.E. (see Ch'en 1964), the relationship between the sangha and the imperial state became a major issue needing resolution. During the Eastern Jin period (317–420), the relationship between the sangha and the emperor was addressed by a leading monk named Hui Yuan, who spelled out the symbiotic relation between the state and the sangha in a treatise titled "A Monk Does Not Bow Down Before a King." According to Hui Yuan, the religious goals of the sangha fully complement the political goals of the state: "Therefore, they who rejoice in the way of Sakya invariably first serve their parents and respect their lords. . . . If their lords and parents have doubts, then they retire, inquire of their wishes, and wait until [the lords and parents] are enlightened. This, then, is how the teaching of Buddha honors lifegiving and assists kingly transformation in the way of government" (Hui Yuan in De Bary and Bloom 1999: 427). By the Song dynasty (960–1127 C.E.), the Buddhist tradition was an integral part of Chinese religious culture, as expressed in its inclusion in the *sanjiao*—the three "religious" traditions of Confucianism, Buddhism, and Daoism.

Many Buddhist ideas were made local by adapting to Chinese religious culture, but all can be seen as connected with the this-worldly emphasis in Chinese culture—an emphasis that stresses the maintenance of order through the centralizing authority of the Chinese state (see Ch'en 1964). A historical example illustrates the localization of the Buddhist tradition through its co-optation by the state. By the time of the Northern Wei dynasty (386–534 C.E.), the Buddhist tradition in China had achieved national importance, as evidenced by its first-time appearance in an imperial dynastic history (Ch'en 1964). The non-Han rulers of the Northern Wei dynasty were politically divided between those who favored maintaining their Central Asian identity and those who favored some degree of sinification. When those who wanted to maintain their non-Han identity were in power, the strong patronage of Buddhism promoted unification under a non-Han Chinese ideology, and the Buddhist sangha thrived. When the third emperor (Emperor Wu, 424–51) rose to the throne, he sought to represent himself as sinified (i.e., civilized), favoring Confucian ministers and Daoist clerics who later convinced him to first curb and then actively persecute the Buddhist sangha in 446.

In the restoration of 453, the pro-Buddhist faction again took power. The head of the Buddhist sangha, named Tan-yao, sought to strengthen the relationship between the imperial state and the Buddhist sangha by deepening the commitment of the sangha to the administration and expansion of the dynasty. In particular, he worked to establish the sangha's economic independence, shifting its activities to include the administration of land and people.[10] The Buddhist community, especially the great landholding Buddhist establishments, played an important role not only in its own territorial expansion but also in that of the Chinese empire (Gernet 1956). The economic expansion of the Buddhist community continued in the Sui and Tang dynasties and extended to practices like accumulating money and precious metals and lending money, grain, and silk with interest—a clear departure from the Indian Buddhist ideal that prohibits monks from engaging in commercial activities (Ch'en 1973). This lasted until the Tang dynasty persecution of 842–45, which stripped the Buddhist community of its economic base. Tan-yao's model therefore set the pattern for state-sangha relations during the reunification of China under the Sui dynasty and the flowering of Buddhist thought and culture under the Tang dynasty (Wright 1990).

The localization of the Indian Buddhist tradition meant incorporation into the Chinese state. Structurally, the sangha was refashioned to play a more active role in administering society:

> Such features as the granting of ordination certificates by the government in order to limit the size of the clerical community, the subordination of monk officials to the civil authorities, official ordination through examinations administered by the government, compilation of a registry of monks, all were distinctive of the sangha in China. (Ch'en 1964: 485)

In postsocialist China, the same active role of helping social administration is manifested in the Buddhist state administrative structures of the PRC. The Indian Buddhist tradition was transformed into a Chinese tradition through accommodation to the Chinese political order, the dominant theme in Chinese religious culture.

State Administration of Religion in Postsocialist China

In postsocialist China, the charismatic authority inherent in religious organization has been attenuated through the state administration of religion but can reassert itself in religious movements, such as the 1999 mobilization of Falungong (a popular religious movement) in Beijing. China's postsocialist religious policy is based on Document 19, issued in 1982 by the Central Committee of the Chinese Communist Party. Document 19 is the central document for the official state ideology, which represents Chinese religious culture as constituted by five state-recognized religions: Buddhism, Daoism, Islam, Catholic Christianity, and Protestant Christianity. This document marked a transformed political stance on religion and led to a massive revival of religious practices throughout China, including those in Little Rome. Religious practices not recognized in Document 19 are considered superstition (*mixin*), something to be eradicated; according to the document, the state will conduct "a determined crackdown on all criminal and antirevolutionary activities which hide behind the facade of religion, which includes all superstitious practices which fall outside the scope of religion and are injurious to the national welfare as well as to the life and property of the people" (from Document 19, in MacInnis 1989: 22). In other words, the state considers criminal the religious practices most documented by anthropologists of Chinese religion: the system of "gods, ghosts, and ancestors" that includes such deities as the kitchen god and local earth gods (see, for example, Jordan 1972; Arthur Wolf 1974; Feuchtwang 1974; Faure 1986). Specialists on Chinese religions, on the other hand, exclude Islam and Christianity from both the category of Chinese religions and from the scope of popular ritual life, because these world religions are not considered "Chinese."

Studies have described Chinese popular religion as a loose system of gods, ghosts, and ancestors that provides local Chinese communities with a translocal cosmology (Freedman 1974). People venerate ancestors, placate ghosts, and appeal for favors to gods. Ancestors and ghosts can become gods (Harrell 1974), and ineffectual gods can be discarded in favor of more efficacious ones (Lang and Ragvald 1993). Various accounts portray the gods, ghosts, and ancestors in this hierarchical system as both sages and rebels—as sages, they comprise a spiritual bureaucracy that mirrors the earthly imperial bureaucracy (Feuchtwang 1978); as rebels, they are murderers, thieves, or females—the opposite of idealized Confucian sages (Shahar and Weller 1996).

Even after forty years of socialism, traces of this system of gods, ghosts, and ancestors still exist in the Hakka homeland. Popular religion has reemerged to mark the social and physical landscape of postsocialist China. As I later describe in more detail, many ritual practices of ancestor worship have resurfaced rapidly and in force, and villages throughout China in the postsocialist period are busy rebuilding ancestral temples and refurbishing ancestral tombs (Zhang Quanqing 1997; Jing 1996). People are also rebuilding shrines to earth gods, and they continue to worship many other deities in the public Buddhist and Daoist temples. John Lagerwey, who conducted extensive fieldwork in these temples in southern Fujian and northern Guangdong, traces one network of southern Fujian temples that are linked through the circulation of a god named Dingguang gufo. Lagerwey found that village communities were linked through this "wandering god network" into a wider social hierarchy that was culturally integrated through a local, western Fujian–based mythology.[11] Intercommunity links that can be explained by geography, water control, and land use parallel links in the religious realm through the wandering god network and the idiom of geomancy (*fengshui*). Lagerwey's finding is important because it details the processes through which the religious system itself maps out an imagined community, one that may or may not be congruent with the aims of the state (see Anderson 1991).

One such imagined community that the PRC state has targeted as antistate is Falungong, a popular religious movement centered on *qigong* practices. In her study of the rising popularity of *qigong* associations like Falungong, Nancy Chen (1995) has concluded that such groups are fluid, spanning a continuum between state-recognized groups incorporated into the state bureaucracy and groups unrecognized by the state that follow charismatic leaders. Chen divides *qigong* associations into three types: *ying qigong* (hard *qigong*), a martial art; meditation, where *qigong* is used to help individuals harness their own bodily *qi*; and healing practices. The third type of *qigong* associations, ones that focus on healing, are seen by the state as the biggest challenge to state authority because of their resemblance to popular soteriological religious movements: "Individual masters of great charismatic authority visit the parks, instantly drawing waves of followers seeking relief or cures. Lineages and networks of followers emerge to reveal accumulations by such masters of political capital in *guanxi* (personal relations) and power" (Ibid.: 354). From the Chinese state's perspective, its distrust of such popular religious groups was validated by Falungong's April 1999 demonstration in Beijing.

On April 25, 1999, in the largest demonstration since the 1989 student demonstration in Tiananmen, more than ten thousand people gathered in silent protest outside Zhongnanhai, the walled compound in Beijing where the top Chinese leaders live. The protesters came from all over northern China to petition for state recognition of the cult. The protest was initiated by an earlier incident in Tianjin, where Falungong practitioners had been assaulted by police while protesting the publication of an article critical of Falungong. The protest in Beijing terrified the top leadership of the Communist Party because it demonstrated that popular religious groups like Falungong were well organized and could mobilize large groups of people. Practitioners represent a wide variety of Chinese society, and more important, the top leadership later discovered that many party cadres and members of the army were active practitioners of Falungong. By July 22, 1999, the PRC had proscribed participation in Falungong and actively persecuted Falungong leaders.

Falungong, or Falun Dafa, as it is referred to by its founder, Li Hongzhi, is a system of *qigong* beliefs and exercises that enable practitioners to develop "moral character" (*xinxing*) so as to tap into the power of the supreme cosmic quality that Li refers to as *zhen-shan-ren* (truthfulness, benevolence, and forbearance). Falungong's beliefs and exercises are designed for healing, stress relief, and health improvement, with the ultimate goal of personal enlightenment. Founded in 1992, Falungong was initially recognized by the state-sponsored Chinese Qigong Research Association in 1993, but was later expelled in 1996 for Li's cosmological ideas (Eckholm 1999). Before its proscription, Falungong remained connected with the state through the Sports Administration Office (Holland 1999). Falungong has since attempted to regain full state recognition, but while in a quasi-recognized state the group developed rapidly inside and outside China; Falungong leadership claims one hundred million adherents throughout the world, eighty million of them in China. Under pressure from the state, Li Hongzhi moved to New York in 1998, where he continues to propagate his *qigong* theories and cosmology.

There is a strong transnational aspect to Falungong. Now based in New York, this popular religious organization maintains an extensive virtual presence. Its sophisticated Web page (www.falundafa.org) offers a wide array of free publications and is linked to videotapes and other material available for purchase from Amazon.com. After the crackdown by the PRC in July 1999, Falungong also initiated a transnational public-relations initiative that has succeeded in mobilizing media coverage, U.S. congressional debates, and the U.N. Human Rights Commission. Because of Falungong's origin in

Chinese popular beliefs, the PRC cannot accuse foreigners of "cultural imperialism," as it can with Catholicism; instead, the PRC has claimed that Li Hongzhi is being used as a "pawn of anti-Chinese forces." In global discourse, the PRC is absolutely correct—the case of Falungong is being used by such figures as U.S. congressional representatives to support their political claims in other arenas such as PRC admission to the World Trade Organization. As will be discussed in the case for Chinese Catholicism, the global discourse on religion in China is shaped as much by external agendas as it is by actual domestic practice.

The growth of Christianity in the postsocialist period must be seen in light of this flourishing Chinese religious culture. Hunter and Chan document what has officially been referred to as "Christianity Fever" and the growing concern among top CCP cadres about the strict administration of religion. They conclude that both Christianity Fever and the state's concern about Christianity result from the uncertainty of the transition away from a centralized economy and the increased penetration of the Chinese rural heartland by transnational processes. Like the popularity of *qigong* movements, the appeal of Christianity lies in the ability of believers to tap into a spiritual power that can generate wealth or improve health. Paradoxically, another appeal of Christianity for people in postsocialist China is its association with Western modernity—an association that is further supported by overseas capital and philanthropy (see Hunter and Chan 1993). Although Hunter and Chan's study of Christianity in China focused on macropolitical discourse, Chinese theology, and national trends (with an emphasis on Protestant Christianity), their findings correspond to a surprisingly large extent with my findings in a rural Catholic community: the popular practice of Christianity taps into a latent charisma that provides an alternative authority to that of the state or global capitalism. Because popular religious traditions have the potential for generating the rebel (see Hunter and Chan 1993), the Chinese state is highly suspicious of religious organizations that are not disciplined through incorporation into the state administrative system. As a result, the state's problem with Christianity is not its foreign origins per se—rather, Christianity is seen as a potential threat by the state only when it, like other popular religions, remains outside the state bureaucracy.

CHAPTER 3

Building a New Church

Little Rome is a transnational community, with its members scattered throughout the world. Transnational processes intersect in the daily lives of people in Little Rome, from the media and entertainment that inform their imaginations to the labor diaspora that draws them to other regions and countries. At the heart of this deterritorialized community, however, are its structures of faith. With its strong overseas connections, Little Rome has always embodied a structural tension between the sovereignty of the Chinese state and the social and economic benefits of participating in the global scene. This tension has been an integral part of the community's history since its nineteenth-century founding. In the late 1990s, this structural tension was clearly illustrated in the community's construction of a new church. The local Catholic church is the center of life in Little Rome, both physically and socially. Next to the PRC state, which penetrates the local community through an array of local extensions of the government bureaucracy, the local church is the principal structure around which Little Rome is built.

Building a Village Church in Guangdong

Seven-thirty A.M., Sunday, April 6, 1997. Unlike most Sundays, on this day the residents of Little Rome in Jiaoling County put away their farming tools. They dressed in their Sunday best to welcome the hundreds of guests who came to celebrate the opening of a new Catholic church. In fact, the whole county had been welcoming guests from around the world, since the day before was *qingming*, when people return to their *laojia* (hometowns) to participate in ancestral worship (see Lagerwey 1996: chap. 7). According to my neighbor Mr. Deng, who had helped his brother in Taiwan get airplane tickets in order to attend the church opening, and Father Liang, the village pastor, who had arranged tickets for many other visiting overseas donors, the three flights from Hong Kong that week had been completely full.

The Catholics in Little Rome had been preparing for the church opening for many months. In the winter of 1995, when county building inspectors had determined that the existing church structure was unsafe for public use, the pastor and the Parish Council (*jiaotang guanli weiyuanhui*), with the approval of the bishop, had decided to build a new church. In February 1996 the church building committee had published an appeal for capital contributions from friends, relatives, and other Catholics, both inside China and overseas; the cost of building a new church was estimated at one million renminbi (RMB) (around US$120,000). Ground was broken in June 1996, and after speedy construction, the church structure was completed in December and then approved for public use by the county inspectors in January 1997. More than two hundred major contributors from overseas and within China were invited to attend the opening as "honored guests" (*jia bin*)—overseas Catholics who contributed more than 3,000 RMB and mainlanders who contributed at least 100 RMB.

The mass was scheduled to start at 8:30 A.M., but by 7:30 the church was already crowded with honored guests, other Catholics from the region, and villagers. Ceremonial assistants (mostly women villagers) wearing red badges with ribbons, stood at the church gate and throughout the compound to help the police keep order. Three red placards expressed a warm welcome to visiting provincial, prefectural, and county cadres, Bishop Zhong and other visiting priests and sisters, and overseas guests. Inside the church compound, a member of the parish council had set up a table to collect last-minute donations, which he carefully noted in a ledger. Many people milled around a stone monument that listed donors to the building fund. Most people gathered in groups to chat with visiting friends and relatives. Another crowd gathered around a little girl in a white dress, who danced to hymns sung by members of the church in nearby Jiaoling City.

Inside the old church, the priests and altar boys were preparing for mass; the sisters did the same in the convent and then joined the priests in the old church. Bishop Zhong was the principal celebrant, but ten other priests had joined him to concelebrate mass, including an American Maryknoll priest working in Hong Kong, a Taiwanese priest originally from the area, and other priests from Hong Kong, Indonesia, and elsewhere in Guangdong. Ten village altar boys helped the priests prepare. Twelve sisters and three novices from the diocese were also present. Among them was a daughter of Little Rome, Sister Maria C., who just a few months earlier had taken her final vows with the first class of religious sisters since the reopening of the diocesan convent. Some of the younger sisters and novices were inside the crowded church distributing memorial cards with a picture of Mary to the guests already seated, while ushers danced around them trying to seat more guests. The choir had already assembled in the second-floor choir loft of the new church. Government cadres and honored guests were drinking tea in the rectory, waiting for the mass to begin.

The mass in celebration of the church opening began with a procession from the old church to the altar of the new church. An altar boy carrying a cross led the procession, followed by pairs of altar boys with incense, the sisters in black habit, the concelebrating priests, and Bishop Zhong, carrying his bishop's staff. The choir sang the entrance hymn as the procession squeezed through crowds of people to the altar. More than fifteen hundred people were in the church compound to participate in the events (or just to see what was happening); since there was not enough room for everyone to stand inside the new church, many remained outside throughout the celebration. A camera crew hired by Father Liang, the village pastor, moved through the crowd, videotaping the event. After the bishop blessed the laity and the new altar with holy water, the church opening ceremony followed the usual order of mass. The readings, responsorial psalm, and gospel stressed that the building of a new church would help Catholics live a full Christian life in Little Rome.[1] The gospel, in particular, alluded to how the contributors to the building fund were fulfilling God's will with their philanthropy: "Zaccheus stopped and said to the Lord, 'Behold, Lord, half of my possessions I will give to the poor, and if I have defrauded anyone of anything, I will give back four times as much.' And Jesus said to him, 'Today salvation has come to this house, because he, too, is a son of Abraham. For the Son of Man has come to seek and to save that which was lost.'" The bishop reiterated these themes in his homily, as he welcomed and thanked all the people who participated in the church building process. The bishop also stressed that the church was an important place for Catholics to pray and learn about God and Mary's love for humanity, so that people could live in society according to God's will.

After the homily, four village girls wearing veils decorated with fresh flowers presented the symbolic community offering of bread and wine. The usual Sunday morning money collection was not taken. After the Liturgy of the Eucharist, involving all the priests, communion was distributed and followed with a closing prayer. The procession re-formed to leave the church, stopping at the main door for a group picture. The clergy then changed out of their vestments to prepare for the remainder of the ceremony. Helpers descended upon the front of the church to set up tables between the altar

Figure 2 Final blessing at the church opening ceremony, April 1997. A visiting Maryknoll priest (far right) participated in the Mass.

railing and pews for honored guests and government cadres. Other helpers left to prepare the lunch banquet that would follow in the old church. The host was removed from the tabernacle, signifying the secular nature of the next stage of the ceremony.

Father Liang began the ceremony by introducing the eighteen government representatives and honored guests from Hong Kong, Taiwan, and Indonesia, all seated in front, as well as other honored guests sitting in the pews. The congregation sang the Chinese national anthem and then chanted the "Hail Mary." Seven speeches followed, mostly stressing how the achievement of building this church had brought glory to China or the Catholic Church (depending on whether the speaker was a government cadre or overseas Catholic). The following people spoke in the order listed: township chief; chair of the Guangdong Patriotic Church Association; Bishop Zhong; a priest, born in Little Rome, now living in Taiwan and active in village philanthropy; the chair of the Jiaoling County United Front (a government bureau); a lay Catholic surgeon from the United States, also born in Little Rome and active in village philanthropy; the chief of the Jiaoling County Religious Affairs Bureau, also from Little Rome.

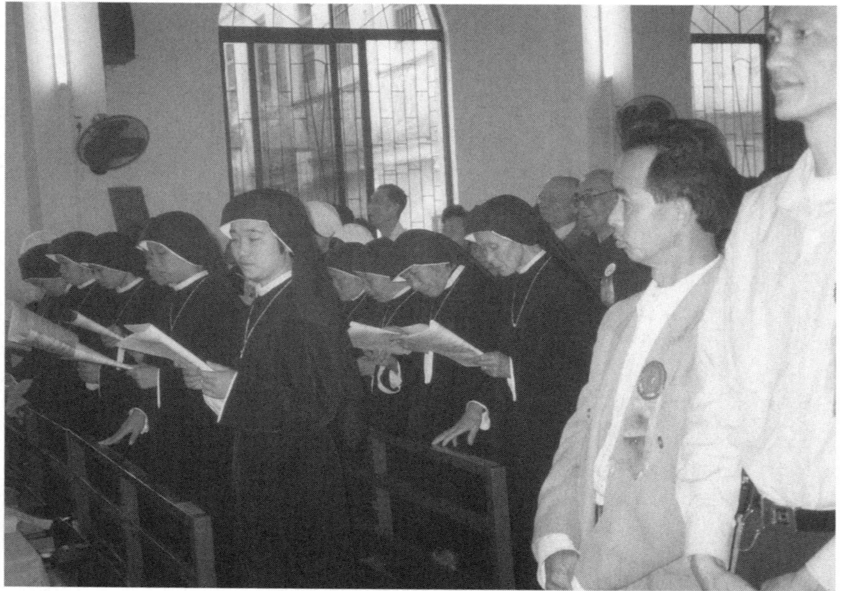

Figure 3   Church opening ceremony, April 1997. The men on the right wearing the red "honored-guest" ribbons are religious affairs cadres. Sister Maria C. of Little Rome is the first sister in the front row, across the aisle from the cadres.

The audience listened carefully to all the speakers, clapping respectfully as each one finished. The speeches took about an hour and a half, and then Father Liang closed the ceremony with an invitation for the honored guests to attend the lunch banquet.

Other volunteers had spent the entire morning in the old church preparing the lunch, which consisted of typical Hakka banquet dishes.[2] Forty banquet tables seating eight people each were covered with white tablecloths and set with drinks such as sodas and rice liquor. Men prepared the food in the kitchen, and women brought out the dishes as they were ready. The cadres were seated with many of the clergy at different tables, and the honored guests sat with friends and relatives from the village. More tables were set up in the convent for visiting guests who were not honored guests. People mingled easily, taking the opportunity to visit with relatives who had come from afar. Once all the dishes had been served, Father Liang and the township chief stepped to the front and made a toast, again thanking all who had helped to

Figure 4   Speeches at the church opening ceremony, April 1997. The speaker, originally from Little Rome, was a retired surgeon living in New York. He was active in the capital campaign to build the new church.

build the new church. The atmosphere was free and easy, and many older Catholics who normally do not drink alcohol became tipsy.

Following the banquet, a large group took the priest from Taiwan and the surgeon from New York to the village elementary school to meet with the principal, the school chair (*xiaoxue dongshizhang*), and the county school supervisor. Both men had made substantial donations to the school in the past; their names were engraved on a stone monument at the school entrance (although the priest from Taiwan was listed only as "Mister," not as "Father"). They went to a meeting room to have tea and discuss further projects for the school. The two guests listened to reports about the school and its future plans, and shared ideas with the local educators, such as for expanding the school library and providing computer education.

"All Things Have a True Origin":
Celebrating the Churches of the Past

While raising money for the new church, the leaders of Little Rome reminded residents and potential donors about the importance of past churches in the history of Little Rome. A visible symbol of the new church's link to the past was a large black wooden plaque over the altar, inscribed in calligraphy, that read, "All things have a true origin" (*wan you zhen yuan*). According to missionaries' historical accounts, Emperor Daoguang wrote the statement in the mid-nineteenth century as a tribute to the Catholic Church (Hervel 1887, as translated by Downs 1962: 10), and Catholics in Meizhou have always prominently displayed a plaque with this inscription in their churches. Members of the church construction committee told me that an ancestor of Mr. Peng (a retired teacher and my landlord) had inscribed the original sign hung in the first church in 1872. When American Maryknoll missionaries rebuilt the church in 1931, a more recent Peng ancestor inscribed a new sign. According to Mr. Lai, a lay church leader, when Red Guards were harassing the community at the height of the Cultural Revolution and destroying any trace of religiosity they could find, treasured church items like the plaque were entrusted to different Catholics in the community; the large plaque was hidden by using it as construction material, with the calligraphy obscured. In 1983 the plaque was recovered for the reopening of the church. For the 1997 church opening ceremony, the calligraphy was refinished and the plaque transferred to the new church.

Like the history of past churches, the identity of Little Rome has been shaped by its transnational links. Before 1850, Little Rome had been a two-surname village more typical of other Hakka villages. A local historian reports that the two surnames moved into Jiaoling two to three hundred years ago, when it was "a desolate area, overgrown with brambles, weeds, and graves" (Shi 1985: 15). One man (surnamed Tang) sojourned in Malaysia, converted to Catholicism, and returned home in the 1860s. He built a chapel (*gongsuo*) in part of his house and invited Father Bernon, a French missionary of the Mission Étrangères de Paris (MEP), to visit from Meixian. This chapel served as a mission station for the priests and catechists who would come up from Meixian and did not house a priest.

To gain converts in their nineteenth-century efforts in Guangdong, the MEP missionaries relied heavily upon this pattern of conversion, in which a person (usually male) who converted to Catholicism overseas then returned to his natal home and convinced his family to become Catholic (Wiest 1977). These "returning Christians" served as catechists, translators, and language teachers first for the French and then for the American missionaries working in the Hakka areas. The MEP priests relied upon these returning Christians to spread the faith. Most of the returning Christians had originally converted to Catholicism under other MEP missionaries working in Southeast Asia. In fact, the MEP often asked their converts to return to their natal homes specifically to help spread the faith (Wiest 1977: 66). The grandfather of my landlord, Mr. Peng, had himself been a language teacher to the American Maryknoll missionaries in the 1930s.

As the number of Catholics increased, Father Bernon found the chapel in the Tang house too small and so separated the worshippers by gender. After 1866 (when the Taiping Army had retreated from the county), he moved the men's chapel to the Wu house on the northern end of the village and built a multistory women's chapel on property adjoining the house of Mr. Tang, the original returning Christian mentioned above. According to a retired Little Rome cadre who wrote a history of the community for the county gazetteer, the height of the women's chapel created dissension among this fledgling Catholic community. Mr. Tang had advised Father Bernon not to build a multistory building because it would block the good geomancy of the Tang family. When Tang returned to the village after work in Guangxi province and discovered that the French missionary had not heeded his advice, Tang stopped going to mass and rebuilt the Tang house into a taller structure. By this time, however, Catholicism was firmly entrenched in the village, with new converts from neighboring Meizhou counties (especially Wuhua and Meixian) settling on lands purchased by the MEP.

As the population of Little Rome grew, Father Bernon expanded construction in the village. He laid out the roads to intersect in the village center and then built more houses around them. Father Bernon also built the first church; the largest structure in the village then, it could hold over a thousand people and was completed in 1872. In Chinese style, it was divided into two parts, upper (*shang*) and lower (*xia*), separated by a wide uncovered atrium. The lower part housed the main entrance, facing south, with a multistory building attached. The upper part housed the altar area. By 1887 a wall had been built to protect the village, complete with cannons, gunports, and four large gates in the cardinal directions. From this Catholic stronghold the MEP expanded further, building other mission stations throughout the county.

Maryknoll took over the mission area in 1925, and in 1929 the American priests and sisters turned the attached multistory building into a convent. That same year the main highway was constructed, connecting Fujian to Meixian (and ultimately to the waterways that flow down to Shantou). In 1931, Father Hilbert, the Maryknoll pastor, rebuilt the church itself, moving

Figure 5   "Our new bus road near [Little Rome]. The mission is in the background." Written on the back of the photograph by the Maryknoll priest who took the picture in 1934. Courtesy of Maryknoll Missioners.

the main entrance to the north, facing Little Rome's main street. He also had a ceiling added to the atrium in order to enclose the upper and lower structures under one roof. Little Rome elders remember that Father Hilbert also built an activities center and basketball court for the young Catholics. And in 1937 he built a rectory and church in the nearby county seat. Residents of Little Rome consider the 1997 church built by Father Liang to be the third village church.[3] Realizing the importance of youth interest for the future of Catholicism in Little Rome, Father Liang also expressed a desire to rebuild the activities center and basketball court.

As Little Rome expanded during the late Qing and early Republican period, connections to overseas relatives became increasingly Catholicized. The village population grew at the same time that Chinese overseas emigration was on the rise, and many people from Little Rome joined this exodus. Émigrés to different parts of Southeast Asia, especially Indonesia and Singapore, found other Catholic communities there and established a steady flow of remittances to support the Catholic activities of Little Rome. Donations from Little Rome's overseas relatives helped Maryknoll build the Kaying Cathedral in Meizhou City, the prefectural capital, in the 1940s. Ironically, the Kaying Cathedral is now the site of the Meizhou CCP headquarters.

Figure 6   Main road for vehicle traffic between Fujian and Guangdong, 1996.

Raising Money Locally and Globally

The church opening ceremony, as seen in the geographic representation of its participants, clearly manifested the transnational nature of Little Rome. However, it also revealed the structural tension between the need both for local leadership and administration and for overseas support. The selection of speakers stressed the localness of the event: three were county cadres, one was prefectural, and one was provincial, and only two speakers were from overseas (Taiwan and the United States). The contributions recognized the clear necessity of overseas community members. This "balance of power" was at the heart of the project from its inception.

In February 1996, the Parish Council and diocese organized the Little Rome Church Construction Committee. The thirteen formal members of the group (all men, except for the two sisters in the Little Rome church) included community leaders, Parish Council members, and those with many overseas family and friends. This original committee headed all the groups later involved in raising money for the church construction. After the priest from Taiwan visited, he established the Jiaoling County Church Construction Capital Development Committee there, which was further divided into five regional sections charged with raising money in specific areas: Hong Kong, Southeast Asia, Africa,[4] the United States and Canada, and Taiwan.

Villagers and overseas committee members pledged enough money to begin construction in June 1996, and by April 1997 when the new church opened the village had enough money to discuss building a new convent.

First, although the overwhelming majority of donors are from the mainland (84 percent), most of the money came from overseas donors (79 percent) (see Table 1). This pattern is characteristic of fund-raising projects in the Meizhou area and throughout southern China, where large-scale migration overseas has long been common. From at least the turn of the twentieth century, when Sun Yatsen called on overseas Chinese to provide economic and political support for the rebellion against the Qing government, local activists have relied on their friends and relatives overseas. Today, even lower levels of the PRC are working hard to raise overseas support for local development projects, by establishing government offices (*zhengxiehui* and *lianyihui*) that provide contacts for visiting relatives (Wang 1991; Yen 1995) and produce vast numbers of publications consumed by overseas Chinese. Large community efforts, like paving a road or building an ancestral hall, simply cannot be accomplished without the participation and philanthropy of overseas friends and kin.

Second, the majority of funds come not from organizations (i.e., missionary groups or regional churches), but from individuals (76 percent). These individuals—like the surgeon from New York, the priest from Taiwan, the son of a Catholic high school principal from Indonesia, the government clerk from Hong Kong, or the wife of a banker from Malaysia—all have connections to the village that are confirmed and renewed at special ritual events like the church opening ceremony. Ties to these nonlocal members of the village community are also maintained through more mundane events throughout the year, such as telephone calls, letters, remittances, and visits to the ancestral homeland/natal home. (*Tan qin*—visiting relatives in China—is an official immigration and public security bureau category for ethnic Chinese who hold foreign passports.) In short, although transnational organizations facilitate and shape links between localities, it is individuals, like Hannerz's "cosmopolitans," who actually embody the connections (see Hannerz 1996, 1992).

Third, four key leaders were responsible for bringing in other overseas donors. These individuals accumulated 71 percent of the gifts from overseas. The priest from Taiwan, with the help of my neighbor Mr. Deng's brother, contacted other Taiwanese Catholics originally from Jiaoling and applied for

TABLE 1

Contributions to Church Construction, by Region

Region	No. of donors	Percentage of donors	Amount donated (RMB)	Percentage of donations
China	225	84	151,990	21
Taiwan	14	5	107,448	15
Indonesia	9	3	130,708	18
Hong Kong	7	3	152,378	21
Thailand	7	3	44,217	6
United States	4	1	115,092	16
Mauritius	2	1	21,420	3
Malaysia	1	<1	3,240	<1

N O T E : This list only includes overseas donors who gave at least 3,000 RMB (US$360) and mainland donors who gave at least 100 RMB (US$12). Thus some donors, especially overseas donors, are not included in the tabulation.

funding from Catholic foundations. Their efforts collected 27 percent of the overseas gifts. Another priest originally from Jiaoling, who lived in Indonesia, built up a network of Hakka Catholics associated with a successful Catholic school in Indonesia. Although he was deceased by the time the church was built, his network of Hakka Catholics collected 21 percent of the overseas gifts. The surgeon from New York collected 14 percent of the overseas gifts, and a Thai woman whose natal home is Little Rome collected another 8 percent. These four individuals returned to Little Rome every year or two and remained in close contact with the community.

Fourth, despite the strong support and involvement of foreign friends, relatives, and Catholics, most donors were local, as was the project's management and leadership. The administrative regulations governing foreign involvement in Chinese religious activities clearly reflect the government's recognition of the importance of foreign philanthropy. According to two 1994 State Council Documents, foreign organizations and individuals are allowed to participate in and support the activities of recognized religious organizations in China, but only as approved by the appropriate religious affairs bureaus (at the county level and above).[5] Guangdong provincial regulations further specify procedures for accepting substantial donations from visiting foreign Catholics; for example, the local church must report them to the provincial Patriotic Church Association and provincial Bishop's Conference. The reason for these regulations is to maintain domestic control of religious organizations. In Little Rome, the participation in the church opening ceremony of different levels of government cadres symbolically highlighted the state's involvement and the local control of the event.[6]

In Guangdong province as a whole, local support has long been an important feature of capital projects, even during the Maoist period, when the national government in Beijing was seen as the center for the redistribution of national resources (Lardy 1980). Self-raised funds have always been critical for public works projects in Guangdong province (Loo 1998). During the Maoist period, the proportion of self-raised funds and foreign investment to nationally allocated funds was higher in Guangdong than in other provinces. Since 1985 in the postsocialist period, self-raised funds and foreign investment have surpassed nationally allocated funds as the most important source of capital investment resources. This economic reality, combined with the official ideology toward religion, has forced religious communities in Guangdong to rely on their own initiative in funding capital projects like the church construction.

Fifth, the importance of the Hong Kong Church in the fund-raising project illustrates the special link between the local church in Jiaoling County and the Hong Kong Church. Money donated from Hong Kong constituted the largest percentage of gifts, and over half (56 percent) of the amount from Hong Kong was from the worldwide branch of a Catholic charity. In other words, as an institution, the Hong Kong Church was deeply involved in the support of the Little Rome church. The Little Rome church also uses liturgical texts from Hong Kong for mass, which requires lay readers to have a knowledge of traditional characters. (Since the establishment of the PRC state, however, simplified characters have been used throughout China, and only simplified characters are taught in the state educational system. As a result, lay readers must either learn to read traditional characters on their own or pursue higher levels of education to serve as lectors. This made the recruitment of women lay readers, the group targeted by Father Liang for participation in ritual leadership positions, even more difficult.) Hong Kong Catholics often visit Little Rome, either as individuals or as representatives of organizations like Maryknoll, reinforcing the Catholic link with a personal relationship. Members of the Hong Kong Church were instrumental in reopening the Little Rome Church after the Maoist period and took part in the reopening ceremonies in 1983. In 1985, Cardinal Wu of Hong Kong, a

Hakka originally from Meizhou prefecture, was the first Hong Kong bishop officially to visit the mainland. In 1986 he returned to his home diocese of Meizhou (stopping, of course, in Little Rome) in a visit that personified the growing role he foresaw for the Hong Kong Church as a bridge between the mainland and world churches.

Little Rome and the Hong Kong Connection

Since its establishment as a British territory after the Opium War, Hong Kong has been a stronghold for foreign Catholic groups conducting missions in China. Throughout the colonial period at least fifteen Catholic missionary groups used the territory as a haven and a launching point for activities on the mainland. Although missionary groups are still active in postcolonial Hong Kong, the Hong Kong Church itself now has a large influence on missionary work in China. The Hong Kong Church maintains a commitment to two basic missions: its prophetic role in Hong Kong society, and its role as a link to the church in China. As a major provider of social services in Hong Kong, from schools to welfare centers, the Hong Kong Church tries to fulfill its prophetic role as the conscience of modern materialistic Hong Kong, encouraging social activism at all political levels. Meanwhile, in the absence of political relations between China and the Vatican, the postcolonial Hong Kong Church can uniquely serve as a bridge—linking the Chinese Catholic Church with the universal Roman Catholic Church. The elevation of Bishop Wu to the College of Cardinals and the 1996 appointment of two other Hong Kong bishops, Bishop Joseph Zen Ze-kiun and Bishop John Tong (director of the Holy Spirit Study Centre, an institution that focuses on exchanges with China) further reinforced the presence of the Roman Catholic hierarchy in Hong Kong in preparation for its return to China.

THE CATHOLIC CHURCH AND THE RETURN OF HONG KONG

In the closing days of June 1997, the Hong Kong Catholic Church also took part in the ritualized return of Hong Kong to China. On June 29, 1997, the last governor of Hong Kong, who happened to be Catholic, attended his final mass in British Hong Kong. Reporters from every possible news organization descended like locusts on the Cathedral of the Immaculate Conception to bring this event to the world, but only one television camera was allowed inside the church and had to set up unobtrusively in the choir loft. Bishop

Figure 7   Hong Kong Governor Chris Patten at his farewell mass at the Hong Kong Catholic cathedral, June 1997. He is standing next to Bishop Zen.

Zen,[7] the successor to the soon-to-retire Cardinal Wu, and other priests gathered at the entrance to greet one family of parishioners: Governor Chris Patten; Hong Kong's First Lady, Lavender Patten; and their three daughters. As they made their way to the front pew, the organ started the entrance hymn, "The Church's One Foundation."[8]

The scheduled "Thirteenth Sunday in Ordinary Time" Mass was replaced with the "Feast of Saints Peter and Paul" to honor and say farewell to the governor and his family. Governor Patten himself came to the altar as lector for the First Reading. After the responsorial psalm, Lavender Patten read the Second Reading, which I cite in full below:

> I am already being poured out like a libation.
> The time of my dissolution is near.
> I have fought the good fight, I have finished the race,
> I have kept the faith.
> From now on a merited crown awaits me;
> on that Day the Lord, just judge that he is,
> will award it to me—and not only to me
> but to all who have looked for his appearing with eager longing.

> But the Lord stood by my side and gave me strength,
> so that through me the preaching task might be
> completed and all the nations might hear the gospel.
> That is how I was saved from the lion's jaws.
> The Lord will continue to rescue me from all attempts
> to do me harm and will bring me safe to his heavenly kingdom.
> To him be glory forever and ever. Amen.[9]

The main celebrant read the gospel and delivered a homily on the social responsibility of Catholic Christians, avoiding the political issue on everyone's mind, the future of postcolonial Hong Kong.

The mass continued through the Liturgy of the Eucharist; just before the final blessing Bishop Zen came to the lectern to say some words about the return to China and to introduce the governor. Governor Patten first jokingly apologized to the crowd that he would not be able to attend the coffee hour following mass because he had to attend Prince Charles's final bestowing of knighthood in Hong Kong. During his farewell speech, he thanked the community for providing him and his family with moral support during his difficult but highly rewarding tenure as Hong Kong's governor. The main theme of his speech was to reassure the community about the bright future of Hong Kong: the democratic principles developed during the British rule of Hong Kong had been firmly planted, and with perseverance, Hong Kong would continue to flourish. This was the clip that CNN included in its coverage of Hong Kong's return to China.

During his tenure, Governor Patten had attended masses throughout the territory and established many ties to people in the Catholic community. He was also represented as the champion of democracy in Hong Kong, much to the ire of the PRC government, which repeatedly criticized the governor and Britain for violating the specifications of the Joint Agreement—a trend that Hong Kongers feared would be reversed with the handover to the PRC on July 1. The second reading suggested that the governor accomplished all this because "the Lord stood by [his] side and gave [him] strength."[10] The Catholic community—and, as the governor's popularity indicated, the Hong Kong community in general—agreed that the last British governor of Hong Kong had indeed fought the good fight and finished the race.

The Church's honoring of Governor Patten at his final mass begs the question: Which fight is the good fight? Was the governor being honored for furthering the interests of the powers-that-be (i.e., the government and business elites of Hong Kong), the powers-that-used-to-be (the British colonial government), the powerless of Hong Kong, or the powers above (the interests of the Church)? It is clear from the vilification heaped upon him by the Chinese government that Governor Patten had not been championing the cause of the powers-that-would-be.

With Hong Kong's elevation to a diocese in 1946, the restructuring of the Catholic hierarchy with Vatican II, and the simultaneous growth of the Hong Kong economy, Hong Kong's Catholic Church shifted during the post–World War II period from a mission church (run by foreign missionaries) to an indigenous church (run by people in Hong Kong). The first Hong Kong bishop ordained was Bishop Francis Hsu (Xu Chengbin) in 1967, nearly three hundred years after the first Chinese bishop had been ordained.[11] With indigenization, the administration of the schools, hospitals, and other social organizations sponsored by the Catholic Church gradually became a Hong Kong affair. Today, these social organizations are largely supported by government subsidies and private charitable organizations (Kwok 1997).

The Catholic community's most visible and important social influence in Hong Kong has been in the schools, hospitals, and other arenas of social services sponsored by the Church. In 1997, Christian churches administered 40 percent of Hong Kong's schools (Kwok 1997); the Catholic Church itself administered 39 kindergartens, 154 primary schools, 77 secondary schools, and 34 adult education and other special schools (Charbonnier 1997). The period of greatest growth in the number of Christian institutions occurred during the massive influx of refugees from China after liberation and the later Cultural Revolution, when the near quadrupling of the Hong Kong population overwhelmed government facilities. Before the 1960s, most of these social services were administered and financially supported by foreign missionary groups.

The Hong Kong Catholic Church is most tightly linked to the Hong Kong elite through the Church's administration of social service organizations. Because some of the Church's schools are among the top-ranked schools in Hong Kong (including St. Joseph's, La Salle, Wah Yan, and Sacred Heart Canossian), they have produced many of Hong Kong's government and business elite, as seen in their alumni's continued support today. Few of these elite are Catholic; in fact, there are more students in Catholic schools than there are Catholics in Hong Kong.[12] Of the 290,000 students attending Hong Kong Catholic schools in 1997, only 7.4 percent were Catholic; 30 percent of teachers were Catholic. However, alumni continue to support and provide social access to Catholics, and Hong Kong Catholics are publicly reminded of these links in church publications.[13]

There are other ways in which the Hong Kong Catholic Church has both historically and, according to some analysts, up to the present day been closely associated with the colonial hegemony and the Hong Kong elite (e.g., Kwok 1997). Before World War II, churches received favorable land grants; today, the property owned by churches would yield fortunes if sold. The relationship between church and state is made most explicit in Hong Kong colonial ceremonial protocol: the Catholic bishop is accorded a status just below the governor, chief of the armed forces, the executive secretary, and Chief Justice in official functions (Ibid.: 8). Indeed, Cardinal Wu attended the official turnover ceremonies on June 30, 1997, in this formal capacity. Christians as a whole are overrepresented in politics. Though Christians comprise only 10 percent of the population, they occupy 22.5 percent of the positions in government agencies (Kwok 1997). However, it is in the area of education that the Church is most closely associated with colonial power. Schools administered by the Church, in their preparation of young people for roles among the government and business elite, maintain colonial hegemonic practices. Kwok concludes:

> While the churches do a lot of good for society, and are also aware of the faults and failures of the colonial system . . . by maintaining vested interests and social privileges, they also play a part in supporting and preserving the status quo. For most, "Don't rock the boat" has become the 11th Commandment. (Kwok 1997: 11)

BECOMING POSTCOLONIAL

The Hong Kong Catholic Church, driven by the changing wind of Vatican II, became more local with the appointment of Chinese bishops as leaders of the Hong Kong diocese, starting with Bishop Hsu in 1969. Because of the short tenure of these Chinese bishops, changes to the organizational structure of the Hong Kong Church were not implemented until after the election of Bishop Wu in 1975. The Hong Kong Church was restructured to meet the demands of a larger population after the war, with a special emphasis on localizing the leadership and staff and decentralizing financial and operational authority (Ticozzi 1997; Lee 1997). The restructuring included elevating Catholic lay leaders to positions of authority and expanding leadership committees.

With the signing of the Joint Declaration in 1984 and Bishop Wu's elevation to cardinal in 1988, the Hong Kong Church prepared for its special role as a bridge church, linking the Chinese Catholic Church with the Church in the rest of the world. In addition to the missionary groups and individuals that maintain informal contact with churches in their former mission territories, many other Catholic organizations (such as the Holy Spirit Study Centre and the magazine *Yi*) foster exchange between Hong Kong and mainland Catholics. The 1996 appointment of two other Hong Kong bishops further reinforced the presence of the Roman Catholic hierarchy in preparation for the reunification of Hong Kong. However, the Church's bridge mission is fundamentally different from its earlier service as a foreign missionary center. The bridge today, between the universal Church and the Chinese Church in the PRC, is represented by Chinese Hong Kong Catholics. Some Hong Kong Catholic leaders have also suggested that their bridge mission is to serve as a link between the public and underground churches in the PRC.

However, with the uncertainty felt by Hong Kong Catholics in 1997, the bridge mission was not the only concern of the Church. The Hong Kong Catholic Church also sought to strengthen its presence in local communities by fostering greater social activism among Catholics—by establishing the Hong Kong Church as a "prophetic" church. In a qualitative survey of the Hong Kong Catholic leadership, Sze found that this group intended to increase its social activism both within and beyond the Church in ways that would promote "postmaterialistic values": "a gradual shift from emphasis on economic and physical security above all, toward greater emphasis on belonging, self-expression, and the quality of life . . . , and to accord a high priority to self-expression both in their work and in political life" (Sze 1996: 157). As a whole, this group welcomed the postcolonial shift as beneficial to Hong Kong in the long run, but had reservations about the intentions of the PRC government and was dissatisfied with the colonial legacy of the Catholic Church. Those surveyed believed that the postcolonial Church should refrain from direct political involvement, unlike the PRC Church, and instead should promote issues of social justice in Hong Kong society.

FIGHTING FOR THE POWERS ABOVE

Considering the context of the Hong Kong Catholic Church leading up to reunification, I suggest that "the good fight" referred to in the scripture reading at the mass described earlier was the work that Governor Patten and other Hong Kong Catholic leaders did to lay the groundwork for their prophetic mission. Owing to social changes in Hong Kong as well as changes in the culture and structure of the Catholic Church, the Hong Kong Church itself has also shifted toward a counterhegemonic position, as demonstrated by its prophetic role in society. Although the space for exercising its role was created through a partnership with the Hong Kong elite, the Catholic Church's promotion of postmaterialist values has not always been in line with the practices of the Hong Kong elite. The resulting tension is brought to the fore in its attempt to form a bridge to the Chinese Catholic Church.

BACK TO LITTLE ROME

With the 1997 return of Hong Kong to Chinese sovereignty, however, residents of Little Rome did not expect the relationship between the Chinese and Hong Kong Catholic churches to become any closer. The PRC's policy on relations with the Hong Kong Church is summarized by the slogan "the three mutuals" (*san hu*): mutual nonsubordination (*hu bu lishu*); mutual noninterference (*hu bu ganshe*); and mutual respect (*huxiang zunzhong*) (*Zhongguo tianzhujiao* 1997: 5). These three mutuals were not specially formulated for the return of Hong Kong. Rather, they have been the official policy on relations with the universal Catholic Church and other transnational religious organizations since the reorganization of religious affairs following the *gaige kaifang* (reform and opening) policy of Deng Xiaoping. This policy has allowed renewed contact with other Catholic organizations outside China, including the Hong Kong Church. As long as administrative control is maintained by state-recognized clergy and lay leaders, then—at least in Guangdong—the state permits exchanges between Catholics on the mainland and elsewhere.

How then do Catholics in Little Rome perceive their Hong Kong connection and its impact on their daily lives? Surprisingly, most people reported that they foresaw little change with the 1997 turnover. The Catholic leadership in Little Rome felt that relations could be no closer as long as the "one country, two systems" approach was maintained—for while the three-mutuals policy safeguards the Hong Kong Catholic Church, it also maintains the status quo for relations between the Chinese and Hong Kong Churches. Little Rome church leaders contend that internal processes of the Chinese state have the greatest impact on their practices, and the primary factor in fostering closer relations with the universal Church will be the turnover of local cadres. The Catholics of Little Rome believe that restrictions on their relations with the universal Church will gradually lessen as older, less-educated cadres retire from local religious affairs bureaus and are replaced by younger, more outward-looking cadres.

For lay Catholics, not much has changed with the return of Hong Kong because travel restrictions into Hong Kong are as strict as ever; Hong Kong remains unreachable, though people can experience its traces in Shenzhen,

Guangzhou, Zhuhai, and other areas of the Pearl River delta. Although the prefectural government organized activities to celebrate the return of Hong Kong (and maintained a large billboard counting down the time to July 1, 1997), residents of Little Rome did not participate in many events beyond watching the extensive coverage on Chinese Central TV. In fact, one mother of a teenage daughter entering the county's top high school said the students had to pay an extra fifty renminbi (US$6) for "celebrating the return of HK to China." She complained that she was unaware of a single event organized by the high school and that her daughter had not participated in anything. She saw the fee cynically, as another example of how cadres milk the people for money.

A Transnational Village Community

In Little Rome, the Chinese state's goal to maintain sovereignty over its territory, a major guiding principle in the development of the Chinese state, is the most evident aspect of China's experience of postcolonialism. However, the global diffusion of Little Rome community members, and their uneven prosperity, constrain the state's efforts on this score. The balancing of the exclusive maintenance of local sovereignty and the inclusive reaching out to overseas Chinese and organizations—as seen in the church opening ceremony—lies at the heart of all transnational processes in China. The experiences of McDonald's in Beijing, the diffusion of Chinese laborers and capitalists throughout the Pacific Rim, and the mass media in Shanghai all reflect both the Chinese state's conundrum and its complicity in transnational processes (see Yan 1997; J. Watson 1997; Ong and Nonini 1997; Mayfair Yang 1997).

Therefore, the analysis of any transnational process must include the impact of the state and of state-to-state relations. Transnational processes make national borders less of an obstacle but do not make states themselves wither away. The claim that they do is the weakest link in Appadurai's otherwise excellent model of transnational processes and modernity (1996, 1995). In today's world, the production of locality, a key social process in Appadurai's model, takes place only within the boundaries of a sovereign state. The apparatuses of state hegemony, such as passports, visas, national currency, customs, and airport taxes, may not constrain the "work of the imagination," but they do effectively constrain the person. In fact, states are necessarily complicit not just in allowing but even in promoting transnational processes, provided they do not work against state agendas (see Lozada 2000). To make matters more complex, the state itself cannot be seen as a unitary actor but must be approached in its multiple layers and competing parties (Herzfeld 1997; Ferguson 1990; Shirk 1993). Just as various levels of the Chinese state were given a voice at the church opening ceremony, different levels of the state must be compared to fully contextualize the local transformation of transnational processes.

Moreover, multiple transnational processes intertwine in any social event. In focusing on the Catholic link between Hong Kong, Little Rome, and other relevant regions, I have not discussed some of the other transnational processes occurring simultaneously. One is the regional and international migration of laborers and students.[14] Another is the unceasing flow of media that feed the imaginations of Little Rome villagers: videos, music CDs, television, and so on. A third is the influx of consumer products from abroad—XO cognac from France, Tang orange drink, Motorola cellular telephones, Japanese motorcycles, and other goods.

Nonetheless, being Catholic colors what it means to be a modern Chinese citizen for people in Little Rome and shapes how other transnational processes unfold in the community. The local church serves as the guide for organizing community life in Little Rome. The physical contours of the church are located in the heart of the village and dominate the skyline; socially, the church also lies at the heart of the village, dominating community identity. Since Little Rome's establishment in the 1860s, its participation in transnational Catholicism has defined its relationship with the larger political organizations that surround it.

As the Chinese state incorporates transnational processes in constructing its imagined community, so must villages continually construct themselves as rural communities.[15] In Little Rome, the community is held together not through state political penetration but through the symbolic and institutional reaches of the Little Rome Catholic Church. As a "natural village" (*ziran cun*), Little Rome existed in its own right before Liberation, unlike "administrative villages" (*xingzheng cun*), which were bounded into a single unit only by the CCP administration. From an anthropological perspective, no village is strictly natural; specific historical events create village communities. The cadre discourse on natural and administrative villages, however, highlights the processes of community formation, in which the accretion of local historical narratives naturalizes villages. As I explain in the next chapter, history has inscribed the place that is Little Rome with meaning through its built landscape.

CHAPTER 4

Faith of Our Fathers

The built environment of today's Little Rome, home to a vibrant community planning for tomorrow, is also a living monument to the past. Various reminders make past events part of the present in Little Rome, from people's memories of imprisonment and persecution during the Maoist period to the buildings, walls, and roads that are part of their daily lives. Nothing from the past, however, is as strong as their memories of being Catholic. In choosing to become Catholic, they and their ancestors indelibly shaped what it means to be part of Little Rome today. In this chapter, I discuss how the "traces of passage" (Steedly 1993) that their ancestors left behind embed history in the landscape. Here I use three historical events, from the imperial Qing era (1644–1911), the Republican era (1911–49), and the Maoist period (1949–76), to illustrate how transnational processes have always been an integral part of the narrative of Little Rome. These events weave several transnational processes into what people in Little Rome see as a coherent theme of being Catholic in China.

Urban and Rural Catholicism in China

The history of Christianity in China reflects cycles of official tolerance or even support, as well as harassment or persecution. During periods of tolerance, Christianity in China flourished in urban centers, from its first documented arrival in 578 C.E. When the lotus flower of Chinese Buddhism was in full bloom during the Tang dynasty, Christianity was introduced to China through Persian traders and Nestorian missionaries who gained imperial patronage by Emperor Tai-zong (618–649) (Covell 1986: 22–24).[1] His imperial edict from the oft-cited Nestorian tablet read: "The Way has no unchanging name, sages have no unchanging method. Teaching is established to suit the land, that all living may be saved" (A. C. Moule, cited in Covell 1986: 23). In line with the cosmopolitanism of the Tang period, the

Nestorian Church introduced an assimilated form of faith that appropriated Confucian, Buddhist, and Daoist concepts in Christian apologetics. In 845 C.E., however, the Nestorian Church was dissolved, when Emperor Wu-zong laicized its two thousand monks along with Buddhist and Daoist monks.

Among the earliest Roman Catholic missionaries to arrive in China were the Jesuits during the late Ming dynasty. Following the lead of Matteo Ricci, a Jesuit missionary who settled in China in 1583, the Jesuits maintained an urban-focused missionary strategy of slow, methodical teaching, hoping to convert Chinese elites and ultimately the ruler (Spence 1984; Minimaki 1985). The Jesuits initially entered Chinese society in the robes of Buddhist monks. When they discovered that Buddhism lacked prestige and authority in the Ming and Qing periods, they instead donned scholars' robes to enhance their appeal to the Chinese elite. Ricci presented himself to the Chinese court not as a man of religion but as a Western man of letters (Gernet 1985: 15–24). Ricci and other Jesuits then grounded themselves in the Confucian classics, used Confucian-style philosophical debates to present Christianity, and introduced Western science and technology to win the support of the Chinese literati. An important legacy from Ricci was his translation, with advice from Chinese intellectuals, of the word "God" as *tianzhu*, or "Master of Heaven." Catholics still use the term today, and Catholicism is called *tianzhujiao*—"the teachings of the Master of Heaven"—as distinct from Christianity, known as *jidujiao*, "the teachings of Jesus."

Through their involvement in the imperial court, the Jesuits introduced a wide range of technologies and ideas to the Chinese intellectual and political elite. A striking example of the secular ideas introduced by the Jesuits is their work in weapons technologies. Jesuits Adam Schall (1591–1666) and Ferdinand Verbiest (1623–88) wrote definitive treatises on gunnery and designed cannons for both the Ming and Qing imperial courts. The foundry established by Verbiest is said to have produced more than half of all cannons built during Emperor Kangxi's reign (1632–1722) (see Waley-Cohen 1999: 119). As a result of such activities, the Jesuits became an integral part of the Chinese imperial court. However, the Vatican rejected their missionary strategy in the Rites Controversy, disbanding the Jesuit order in 1773, after which all Jesuits gradually left the service of the Chinese court (Mungello 1994). After their restoration in 1814, in the early twentieth century the Jesuits searched for a way to revive their intellectual apostolate in light of the success of Protestant missionaries in establishing colleges and universities in China (Yeh 1990). When Ma Xiangbo requested Jesuit support in opening a modern university, "an old project long nurtured by the Jesuits was about to be realized: to repossess on a new basis the apostolization of the leading elite, and to impede, without delay, the Protestant intrusions on the Catholic monopoly" (Brou 1928: 285).

Ma Xiangbo was born in 1840 into a family that had been Catholic since the time of Ricci and that traced its ancestry to the Song scholar Ma Duanlin. He was educated in the traditional Chinese classics as well as in Latin, mathematics, and French at Le Collège St. Ignace and was later ordained a Jesuit priest. Although most of his career was in education, Ma Xiangbo left the priesthood to engage in various modernization projects as a Qing official. Ma explored economic development opportunities for Liu Mingquan, the governor of Taiwan (Paul Cohen 1974).[2] Li Hongzhang, a high-level Qing imperial official, later made Ma his secretary for foreign affairs and sent him to the United States to negotiate loans. In 1898 national reform leader Liang Qichao commissioned Ma and a French missionary, Father Garnier, to establish a modern university in Shanghai. However, with the failure of the 1898 reforms, Ma did not succeed in opening the university until 1903. Cai Yuanpei, another national reform leader, had asked Ma Xiangbo to teach him and some of his students Latin, to help them better understand Western thought. From this impetus, Ma sought help from the French Jesuits to establish a university with three priorities: the teaching of science; an emphasis on both Chinese and Western culture; and the avoidance of religious disputes (Hayhoe 1983: 329). Ma named the school Aurora University (*Zhendan daxue*), a name that reflected his hopes for its future. The early curriculum was divided into four sections: language and literature; philosophy; mathematics; and natural sciences. Ma also stressed military training and the examination of contemporary political issues. A critical feature of Ma's educational system was weekly training in public oratory, for which all students would be gathered together to debate contemporary issues (Li Zhengfu 1960: 362–63). Many CCP revolutionaries attended Aurora in its early years (Gu 1987).

In 1905, political conflict between the students and Jesuit administrators prompted Ma Xiangbo and many students to depart and form Fudan University, one of China's top universities today. According to Hayhoe, while Ma was on leave from Aurora University owing to illness, the Jesuits seized the opportunity to assert their curriculum, administrative style, and selection of students. For example, they changed the language of instruction to French because, themselves largely French, they believed that a "French curriculum would give respectability to the school, . . . and that it made the content of education more remote from the burning national issues of the day"

(Hayhoe 1983: 332). Furthermore, Hayhoe asserts that the Jesuits strongly desired to purge anti-Qing student activism from the campus. Gu Yulu, however, attributes the split between the students and Jesuit administrators primarily to student demands for English instruction, which the Jesuit faculty, lacking English fluency, could not provide (Gu 1987). The resulting contest of wills between students and faculty escalated into a debate over Chinese versus foreign control of the university—and ultimately triggered the departure of Ma and many of his students and the formation of Fudan.

Father F. X. Legrand described the characteristics of urban Catholic intellectual organizations that marked Aurora University in a 1949 description of the intellectual apostolate in China. As Legrand points out, the academic integrity of the Catholic school was first and foremost. He cited Chinese rationalism and their conviction of the incompatibility between religion and science as the most pressing obstacle to the legitimacy of the Catholic tradition in China. As a result, the instruction in Catholic institutions in China, especially in the sciences, needed to be free "from poisonous errors and stupid prejudices" (Legrand 1949: 63). Accordingly, Aurora's "University Goals" in 1935 showed concern for maintaining a high academic standard:

> Moreover, lessons are drawn from famous French and American institutions, and day by day we plan for modernization. Aurora faculty selection is very different [from other missionary colleges] in that we are attentive to indigenous scholars. Professors' lectures are regularly demanded to contain the most current scientific education (Zhendan Daxue 1935: 9; my translation)

Second, Legrand advised that a Catholic school must do "nothing to antagonize its patrons" (Legrand 1949: 65). During its formative years, Aurora had not only the support of Ma Xiangbo and reformers like Cai Yuanpei and Liang Qichao, but also sponsorship from members of the non-Catholic local elite such as the industrialist Zhang Jian (later minister of commerce) and Li Bingshu (*Far Eastern Review* 1936a: 391). Aurora consistently ensured that it was properly recognized by the Chinese government and complied with current government regulations. In 1904, Aurora was approved by the governor-general of Nanjing. After the fall of the Qing, Aurora was readily approved by the Chinese Republic in 1912. With the rise of the Nanjing government in 1927, Aurora's Board of Administration was accepted in 1931 and the university as a whole was registered in 1932. As stated in its university goals in 1935, Aurora's responsibility in training and educating youth for national public service or a private career in China was why "the academic regulations and requirements of Aurora University conform in every aspect to the regulations of the Ministry of Education and are adapted to the needs of society" (Zhendan Daxue 1935: 9).

Third, Legrand stressed that the Catholic school "itself should refrain from all religious propaganda, exercising no pressure or coercion" (1949: 66). Aurora, unlike other missionary schools such as the Protestant St. John's University, also in Shanghai, did not offer academic courses in religion. Although the goal was to make the Catholic tradition attractive through the social gospel and the conduct of its believers, Aurora asserted that it did not

> discriminate against other non-Christian publicly educated youth. This conviction of absolute freedom was incorporated from Aurora's traditional policies. For this reason, a religious academic requirement was not established, and there is indeed no pressure on students to participate in religious rites. The activities that most students participate in can be said to be uniquely different from those found in most missionary schools (Zhendan Daxue 1935: 9; my translation).

From Legrand's writings and the self-assertions of Zhendan, Ma Xiangbo and the Jesuits established Zhendan as a continuation of the intellectual apostolate, as exemplified by Ricci and his Jesuit successors. Jacques Gernet concludes that Ricci's policy was

> to adapt to the milieu of the literate elite, to impress them with the sciences of Europe and thereby acquire among them the authority indispensable to men who had come to preach the true God in China, and to become initiated into their traditions of wisdom in order to be in a position to refute them or make use of them, depending upon whether they appeared to disagree with or support the truths of Christianity (Gernet 1985: 22).

Aurora University cultivated a twentieth-century Chinese elite that included Nanjing government officials, military officers, and the Shanghai bourgeoisie—a top-down approach that paralleled Ricci's earlier cultivation of the Ming literati elite. Although these two elite groups were of vastly different social composition, their goal was the same: to cultivate people of influence who would respect the Catholic clergy and establish an alternate social hierarchy. As with Yenching University, where Philip West (1976) compares founder Leighton Stuart and Ricci, Aurora at its core was a Christian product, searching for an "exportable Christianity" that stressed the social dynamic of Christianity and also respected the fruits of Chinese civilization.

This practice within the Catholic hierarchy of creating and training an indigenous elite group was consistent with the Church's missiological strategy of using indigenous intellectuals to represent the Church and for family-based conversion. Unlike the Protestants, who emphasized individual conversion, the Catholic Church preferred to "educate a family into the faith rather than encourage an emotional conversionary experience by individuals" (Lutz 1988b: 33). Although Aurora University serves as an example of Catholic missionary efforts among urban intellectuals, the Church's emphasis on establishing primary schools, especially in the countryside and in towns with little educational infrastructure, was based on the importance of family conversions. These schools extended the reach of churches in the countryside, promoting the development of rural Catholic strongholds, like Little Rome, which maintained the historical continuity of Catholicism in China. During periods when Catholic missionaries lost the support of the urban Chinese elite, such strongholds served as an "unbroken line of Catholic local communities that had existed from the time of Ricci" (Hanson 1980: 23). For example, under persecution from Qing Emperor Yongzheng following the Rites Controversy, Catholic communities in Guangdong's urban areas died out, but many believers retreated to isolated Catholic communities that survived in the countryside (Wiest 1988).

Catholicism in the Hakka Homeland

Catholicism came to the Hakka homeland in the 1840s, before the repercussions of the Treaty of Nanjing reached the local level. A returning Christian from Malaysia introduced Catholicism to his relatives in a town in nearby Meixian county, just south of Little Rome (Downs 1962). French Missions Étrangères de Paris (MEP) missionaries accepted an invitation from this returned Christian in 1849, during a period of persecution by local officials reacting to the Treaty of Nanjing. As a result, the MEP presence in the Hakka homeland was at first intermittent, and missionary work was conducted in secret. By the time MEP priests arrived in the area that would become Little Rome, local officials had become tolerant of their presence. Father Bernon, who established the Catholic church in Little Rome, did retreat to the upper hills when Taiping rebel troops occupied the area, but returned to Little Rome upon their suppression in 1864.

A period of tolerance followed until local anti-foreignism, transforming into anti-Qing sentiment, developed at the turn of the century. The first of this chapter's three events, a legal case, is from this period when antiforeign sentiment was on the rise. This period climaxed nationwide with the Boxer Rebellion, and a period of tolerance returned, surviving the fall of the Qing and the establishment of the Republican government. The second historical event, a local protest against the establishment of a Catholic school in Little Rome, happened during the Republican period, when American missionaries were stationed in Little Rome. The next cycle of persecution followed the establishment of the People's Republic of China, climaxing during the anti-rightist campaign and the Cultural Revolution. With the ascendance of Deng Xiaoping, a period of tolerance returned that continues today. The third event briefly addresses the struggle of the church after it was forced underground until its emergence in the post-Mao era.

The macrohistorical representation of these cycles does not mean there were no individual instances of tolerance and persecution. It is only meant to illustrate the prevailing sentiment. During the periods when state penetration into local areas was strong, such as in the Maoist period, the prevailing sentiment was the official national policy. But in the current period of relative tolerance in the early twenty-first century, "underground" Catholics in other areas of China still face harassment and imprisonment by local governments (see Madsen 1998).

Old Walls: Revolutionary Heroes and Foreign Missionaries

Little Rome used to have a wall surrounding it, with four gates facing the cardinal directions. People knew the wall had been built before the turn of the twentieth century, because some latecomers—those whose ancestors arrived after about 1900—had built their houses outside the wall. By 1996, Little Rome had expanded far beyond the original wall, and only a portion of the western wall still stood. Neighbors told me that the wall was built to keep out bandits, but one older neighbor remembered hearing that it had been built because of an incident between the French missionaries and some locals. This older neighbor was the primary source for the historical information published in the 1992 county gazetteer (a compendium of local history published by county governments).

Before the Opium War, the early Catholic presence in Guangdong was under the jurisdiction of the Portuguese bishops of Macao. However, with the rise of the British and the French as European powers in the eighteenth century, and their increasingly aggressive expansion in China during the nineteenth century, Catholic missionary activities largely fell under the control of Catholic France. The establishment of French imperialism and French dominance of Catholic activities in China was symbolically expressed by the imposing Sacred Heart Cathedral (*Shi shi*) in Guangzhou, completed in 1888 after twenty-three years of construction. The events that led to the construction of the cathedral reveal how closely MEP activities were linked to French imperialist strategy in China. According to Wiest, French missionaries' involvement in their converts' lawsuits fueled a growing nationalist sentiment, as each case of foreign encroachment demonstrated Qing imperial impotence (Wiest 1977).

The incident associated with the building of the Little Rome wall comes from this period of French dominance over Catholic missions in China. When the French missionaries arrived in Little Rome, they purchased land throughout the county to build churches and mission stations and to provide for their poorer converts. Such purchases, however, did not go unopposed. One particular incident of local opposition to missionary expansion in Jiaoling, recorded in a "Christian case" (*jiao an*), has become well known locally through its use by the county government to demonstrate nascent revolutionary ancestors.

In 1887, Father Canac, the pastor of Little Rome, wanted to purchase land in Fuling village, about fifteen kilometers southwest of Little Rome. Only seven residents of this village of several thousand people were Catholic, but Father Canac saw a chance to expand into the area and sought to build a new mission station in the village. According to the court records, one convert, Chen Rongxing, sold to the missionaries land that allegedly was his to sell; but other lineage members contested his right to sell the land to the French missionary. Chen Tingfeng, a local leader who held the imperial degree of *juren*, asserted that the land transferred to the French missionaries was not Chen Rongxing's own land but lineage fields reserved for ancestral tombs. Nonetheless, the transfer was approved by the county government—under false pretenses, Chen Tingfeng claimed. In 1894, despite local opposition, Father Canac started construction of a church, allegedly further encroaching upon lands owned by non-Catholic villagers. The county government ignored Chen's demand that it halt construction, and as a result he led a group of hundreds of people to storm the construction site and then built a new ancestral tomb on this ground.

After the incident, Father Canac demanded that the county government send troops to quell this "bandit disturbance." Because of Chen Tingfeng's local status as an imperial degree-holder, neither the county nor the higher-level district office acted on Father Canac's request for intervention. Dissatisfied, Father Canac reported the matter to the provincial authorities in Guangzhou, and it eventually became an international incident that was handled by the Foreign Affairs Bureau (*Zongli Yamen*) in Beijing, with diplomatic pressure from the French representatives. With the intervention of higher-level investigators, Chen Tingfeng was required to pay reparations of 2,000 yuan, return the original land to the Catholics, and contribute 950 taels of silver to another local Catholic to build an orphanage. During this tense period, Father Canac had the wall built around the village. This is where the documentation of this "Christian case" ends in the national archives of the Christian case bureau.

The version in the 1992 gazetteer, however, continues the story, which ends with the eventual martyrdom of Chen Tingfeng. The fines assessed by the Chinese government did not put an end to this incident. The county magistrate who earlier had supported Chen was replaced with an official who, the local gazetteer reports, had "established close relations with Father Canac." Owing to some confusion caused by the crowds visiting the county seat for the Dragon Boat Festival in 1898, Chen was accused of instigating another uprising (in a scenario, as interpreted by the 1992 county gazetteer, that involved subterfuge by Father Canac). The county magistrate then asked for troops to quell the disturbance. Although Chen escaped, other relatives and associates were executed by the troops that occupied Fuling village, and lineage property was confiscated.

History, Myth, and Experience

The story of Father Canac and Chen Tingfeng is only one of many more well-known events in a large body of historical literature—the Christian cases (*jiao an*)—that chronicles in imperial litigation records the Chinese experience of contact with Christian missionaries riding the wave of an expansive, imperialist West in the nineteenth century. Historians studying the late imperial period have long used the Christian cases to illustrate, for example, how local elites resisted missionary intrusion into local structures of authority (Paul Cohen 1963) or the early development of a secular Chinese state through the ideas of sovereignty and rule of law (Thompson 1996). Some point to the Christian cases as evidence of the incompatibility of Christianity and traditional Chinese society (Gernet 1985); others, such as Entenmann (1996) and Sweeten (1996), have used them to show that Christianity was in fact an integrated cultural part of local imperial Chinese society. Because these cases involved litigation between local individuals, who were embedded in supralocal networks like missionary societies, official categories such as degree-holders, and government administration, they provide enormous detail on local life in the late imperialist period.

Historians of China disagree on whether local opposition to Christian missionary activities was caused by Chinese cultural predispositions or by foreign missionaries' infringement on the privileges of the local elite. Regardless, the expansion of Western missionary efforts had a lasting impact on village life at the turn of the twentieth century. The presence of the missionaries in rural communities gave local people access to a new set of resources. Christian cases in nearby Jiangxi province are less indicative of antiforeignism arising from local perceptions of Christianity than they are of conflicts between locals over land, money, or other resources (see Sweeten 1996).

From this perspective, the case of Chen Tingfeng and Father Canac is not an example of a local elite resisting the intrusions of an overbearing French missionary, as portrayed in the local gazetteer. Rather, it is an intralineage dispute, in which one individual, Chen Rongxing, circumvented the elite members of his lineage by gaining access to the resources of the French missionary. As mentioned earlier, poorer Catholics from neighboring counties could move onto MEP-purchased land in Little Rome. They were able to escape landlessness or limited resources for social advancement by turning to the French. This use of missionary resources, however, does not necessarily indicate a purely utilitarian approach to becoming Catholic (the "rice Christian" phenomenon discussed extensively in missionary literature). Their continued practice of Catholicism in times of persecution demonstrates their deep attachment to the faith. Nonetheless, local people did find new mechanisms for upward mobility under the patronage of foreign missionaries.

In his analysis of the Boxer Rebellion, which took place in northern China in the same period as the Chen-Canac incident, Paul Cohen describes how the presence of European missionaries, whether through direct contact or indirect gossip and stories, fueled local imaginations of things foreign. Although the Boxer ideology was a popular xenophobic attack on foreigners as well as elements of Chinese society who collaborated with them, Cohen explains that the Boxer Rebellion gathered force partially as a result of drought, famine, and other socioeconomic factors not directly linked to missionary activity. According to the emic view, missionaries caused the drought and famine by upsetting the relationship between local people and the gods. People thought that converts were turning away from the worship of local deities and often blamed drought and famine on this neglect. Thus both cosmological and sociological disturbances catalyzed the Boxer Rebellion (see Cohen 1997).

The Chen-Canac case shows that similar dynamics took shape in the

Figure 8   1933 Corpus Christi Benediction at Little Rome. Courtesy of Mary-knoll Missioners.

south as well, despite the absence of Boxer activity in Jiaoling county. The arrival of missionaries in rural China created new opportunities for people, new structures that shaped local social practices. Such changes had to be accommodated on both the cosmological and the social level and inevitably caused tension between people negotiating new structures.

Walls Around the Church

If they could afford it, people in Little Rome built walls around their houses; the house of God was no exception. In the 1990s the church compound had a tall wall, with shards of glass embedded on the top to discourage people from climbing over it. During the Republican period, when Little Rome expanded beyond its original walls, the walls around the church compound served as the final barrier protecting the American missionaries assigned to Little Rome. Although the Republican period was not characterized by offi-cial anti-Christian policy, tensions arising from issues of sovereignty and the foreign missionary presence were part of the environment as China became a modern nation-state.

People in Little Rome particularly recall strained relations between the local elementary school and the church. In one incident that arose from issues of educational sovereignty, the walls around the church compound provided security against attack.

Like their Protestant counterparts, Catholic missionaries saw the establishment of Church-sponsored schools as a way to attract new converts and to educate a future generation of Chinese youth who would be more sympathetic to the Church. When Maryknollers took over the Hakka mission from the French MEP, they brought along the idea that every parish should have an elementary school, which arose from their American experiences (Wiest 1988: 186). Father Francis X. Ford, who took charge of the Hakka mission and later became its bishop, wrote in 1922:

> The parochial school in America is the backbone of the Church. Without it, non-Catholic influences would weaken the faith of the growing generation. In China, the situation is yet more serious. . . . [O]ur Catholic schools in China are not only safeguards against pagan corruption, but positive nurseries of manly virtues and refined habits. So much so that pagan parents are anxious to send their children to our schools and conversions both of parents and pupils result. More important, Catholic schools are our only source of vocations without which it is hard to vision the conversion of China. (Wiest 1988: 186)

Catholic missionaries preferred to focus not on higher education, but on primary schooling, where young or aspiring Catholics could be instructed in the Catholic faith. Primary schools targeted entire families and thus were seen by Catholic missionaries as more necessary for missionary work than institutions of higher education.

Maryknoll missionaries first went to China in 1917 but did not establish a permanent presence in Little Rome until 1925. The Little Rome parish priest at that time was Father Shi Bingchun; he worked under the jurisdiction of MEP bishop Rayssac in Shantou. When the Maryknollers arrived in Little Rome and Father Malone took over the parish, they promptly set up a language school so their missionaries could learn Hakka, a catechist training program, and a small elementary school, even though the village already had a well-established public elementary school. Father Ford asserted that Little Rome needed a private Catholic school because "the principal of the pagan school is a renegade Catholic, the product of non-Catholic education" (quoted in Downs 1962: 22).

In the fall of 1925, therefore, a school was established with a hundred students from the Catholics in the village.[3] According to the entry in the county gazetteer, over one thousand displeased people gathered in a village next to Little Rome to "regain educational sovereignty" (*shouhui jiaoyuquan*). According to a report from Mr. Wang, a resident of Little Rome, the county government organized workers, farmers, traders, and military representatives into a group to hold a demonstration in response to the establishment of a Catholic school in the village. The people surrounded the village, carrying signs and shouting slogans about the invasion of imperialist culture. Mr. Wang told me the story as follows:

> During the meeting, they made public the dangers of the invasion of imperialist culture, shouted slogans, and started a demonstration. Many hundreds of middle-school students wearing white uniforms encircled Little Rome. The panic-stricken American missionaries sealed the gates and did not receive the representatives of the group that came forward. Some brave students and representatives climbed the walls to negotiate with the missionaries, ordering them to sign a contract that they would not open a school. (My translation)

According to Father Ford, the incident was instigated by the "pagan principal" mentioned above who resented the possible loss of pupils and tuition to the Catholic school and stirred others into action. Father Ford's version of the incident:

> The student associations united with him [the principal] and gave us several demonstrations and a few speeches, and the superintendent of education paid us a call to tell us not to teach religion in our school as we thereby prejudiced the minds of the boys in our favor before they were of an age to decide their own beliefs. We reminded him that Confucius was a believer in the duty of parents to guide their children, but he assured us that Confucius was a back number, and that the modern world would not stand for any religion at all.
>
> Unsatisfied with our stubbornness, he called a meeting of the soldiers, students, and labor guilds of the whole prefecture, and over a thousand of them marched down on us to convince us by force. We hastily removed the Blessed Sacrament from the chapel, barred the doors of the buildings, and warned the group of Catholics not to offer violence in the hope that the affair might blow over peacefully. But the mob had been fasting since breakfast and had walked for miles in a hot sun and were in no mood for calm thoughts. They broke down the outer doors, entered the chapel, and threw stones at our only set of colored windows; inside the school, they smashed the door and windows and ripped to pieces the holy picture on the wall—and then they made for our house.
>
> Luckily, the passage is very narrow and those in front were in danger from the crush behind. After useless attempts to break in the door, the leaders called

them off. The very act of smashing things seemed to be all the vent they needed for their energy, and they withdrew. . . . It is not a question either of our being foreigners, although that undoubtedly added zest. As a matter of fact, the present pastor is a Chinese priest and it was he who opened the school. (In Downs 1962: 22–23)

At the time of this incident during the Republican period (1911–49), Chinese education was dominated by structures established by Christian missionaries. Following a mission strategy of the era, many missionaries believed that if the Chinese people could be liberated from pagan superstition through education in Western rationality, they would rapidly convert to Christianity (Hutchinson 1987). As a result, mission boards from all over Europe and America funded schools and universities, introducing a Western-style pedagogy and curriculum to many who previously had had little access to modern educational resources. These mission schools had a great impact on the development of the modern Chinese educational system (Lutz 1971; Yeh 1990). More important, they trained generations of Chinese leaders, leaving deep impressions (favorable and unfavorable) of Christianity and Western culture.

There were two trends in missionary education. Some educational missions, starting with the Jesuit efforts in the Ming-Qing courts, focused on elite education, an effort that has been well documented (Malatesta 1985; Spence 1984). The Catholic effort to educate the elite continued in the Republican period, as embodied in Furen University in Beijing and Aurora University in Shanghai. Protestant groups were especially active in creating colleges and universities (Pott 1936), and their graduates became national and local leaders (Yeh 1990; West 1976). The other trend focused on popular education. Missionaries opened primary schools for those who previously had had no access to elite Chinese education, targeting girls and the poor. The Little Rome school described above was one of many schools opened by the American Maryknoll missionaries in China. Like the land made available by the French missionaries, these Catholic institutions served as an alternative path to social and economic advancement for the people of Little Rome, many of whom sent their children to these schools, studied there, or staffed them. For example, one villager from Little Rome first taught at Maryknoll schools, before going to Beijing to become a professor at Furen University. Numerous other older adults living in 1990s Little Rome had received their high school education at the St. Joseph's Minor Seminary in Meixian.

Before the Opium War, the traditional Confucian education system prepared candidates for entry into the Chinese bureaucratic system. Students were educated by tutors or in local schools organized by lineages and other local groups. In the late Qing period, reformers organized their own *shuyuan* (schools) in an attempt to reinvigorate traditional education by including elements of what they saw as Western education (*xi xue*). The slogan used by such reformers, "Chinese learning for essence, Western learning for utility" (*zhongxue wei ti, xixue wei yong*), reflects the beginning of a nationalistic agenda in modernizing the Chinese educational system. In the Republican period, education was very much at the forefront of domestic political agendas. In 1927, national education standards were established for schools at all levels, and missionary schools and universities were required to meet the criteria established by the new Nanjing government of the Guomindang Party. This was the context in which the demonstration to regain educational sovereignty against the private school in Little Rome occurred—as part of a series of nationwide demonstrations from 1925 to 1928.

The demonstrations against the Catholic private school were part of a rising tide of nationalism, and the people of Little Rome were caught in the middle. The structural resources provided by the missionaries gave Catholics a means to improve their material and social capital. It also made them a target of local nationalism. As in earlier antiforeign movements, the people of Little Rome were marked as different, and therefore suspect, because of their Catholicism. With the rise of modern nationalism, however, the ante went up. For local nationalist activists during the Republican period, being Catholic was no longer simply a turning away from the gods; the profession of faith led people to suspect Catholics of betraying the state.

As the ante went up, so did the prizes. Missionary-sponsored education gave villagers from Little Rome access to educational opportunities outside the region and abroad—experiences that became highly prestigious as people throughout the nation sought to modernize China. During the Republican period, many villagers from Little Rome studied at the high school–equivalent St. Joseph's minor seminary in Meixian. Some became priests, but many continued their education in other disciplines in Hong Kong, Shanghai, and Beijing. Some went abroad, to get advanced degrees such as M.D.s and Ph.D.s, while others emigrated to Hakka Catholic communities in Malaysia, Indonesia, and other South China Sea areas. One such individual was Little Rome's bishop, Paul Lan, who received a theological doctorate in Rome and, much later, played a large role in the public reemergence of the local Catholic Church in the post-Mao period.

The conflict over educational sovereignty illustrates some of the processes coming to the forefront with the development of a modern nation-state system in China. Shue (1988) argues that although there is a great deal of continuity with the imperial past in the structures and practices of local government, in the twentieth century the political structures of the modern nation-state penetrated local daily life more deeply than before. James Ferguson (1990) describes the greater penetration of the modern nation-state through hegemonic control at several different and often competing administrative levels. This model is apparent in the case of China in the Deng-era slogan, "Control less, in order to control better" (Shue 1988: 75). As the modern Chinese nation-state developed, political discourse became more secularized, and political practices were explained more in sociological terms than in cosmological ones. This shift, however, did not allay the local leaders' suspicion of the Catholics in Little Rome. Rather, alleged betrayal of the Chinese state through foreign connections became the rallying cry of local movements against the Catholics in Little Rome.

A Martyr Church and a Patriotic Church: Surviving the Hard Times

The establishment of the People's Republic in 1949 put an end to missionary activity and Catholic educational institutions in China. When the Church went underground after the expulsion of the Maryknoll missionaries and the arrest of local priests, local cadres began using the church building as a warehouse. During collectivization, the church served as a canteen, and other buildings in the compound were used as offices for local cadres. Later, during the Cultural Revolution, students from the nearby high school formed a Red Guard unit and further defaced the church building in their campaign to wipe out the "Four Olds" (old ideology, thoughts, habits, and customs). However, with the Deng era reforms, the church was returned to the community for use as a house of worship and was reconsecrated on Assumption Day in 1983. Like the church building, the church as community also endured the campaigns of the Maoist period and reemerged in the Deng period. Church leaders in Little Rome saw their church as a "martyr church": a church purified by ordeal, in the form of persecution and harassment.

The Catholic stance against communism, and the strong affiliation of Catholics with the Guomindang, did not help their chances of institutional survival with the new CCP government. For example, in the Jiaying (Meizhou) diocese[4] Bishop Ford organized a special day of prayer on May 2, 1948, that made clear the Catholic hierarchy's opposition to communism

Figure 9   A Catholic family in Little Rome in 1997. The man standing in the center lives in Taiwan and was visiting his father (seated, center) and his other siblings.

(Wiest 1988: 385). In 1950, similar anticommunist activism led to the arrest of Bishop Ford and Sister Joan Marie Ryan for espionage (described in detail in Wiest 1988: 395–400). After a lengthy, highly publicized trial, Bishop Ford and Sister Joan Marie were found guilty and were imprisoned in Guangzhou. Bishop Ford died in prison the following year, and Sister Joan Marie was deported. The memory of Bishop Ford, however, lives on in Little Rome and throughout the Meizhou diocese. When a stone tablet listing contributions to the building of the new church in Little Rome was erected in 1997, the villagers wanted to include Bishop Ford's name on the list commemorating priests who had served in Little Rome. His name, however, never made it to the stone memorial. Officially, the prefectural religious affairs bureau felt it was not appropriate to list him because he had not served as a parish priest there.[5] Unofficially, local leaders in Little Rome believed that Bishop Ford was still a controversial figure for local cadres, even forty years after his death.

St. Joseph's Minor Seminary, like other Catholic educational institutions, lost its private status and was nationalized when the CCP consolidated its

Figure 10 A 1930 photograph of a Catholic family in Little Rome. Courtesy of Maryknoll Missioners.

presence in April 1949. Father Paul Zhang (from Little Rome), who had become St. Joseph's schoolmaster in 1948, stayed at the middle school until 1951, when the seminarians were sent home for land reform (Wiest 1988: 222). Father Zhang died shortly before the Cultural Revolution but is remembered in Little Rome; the library of Fudan Elementary School is named after him (although his title as priest is not included). His bones were also reburied at the Catholic cemetery of Holy Mountain near Little Rome, and his tomb serves as the focal point for Catholic rituals held at the cemetery.

Foreign missionaries and Catholic leaders were persecuted all over China. The largest campaign against Chinese Catholics began in 1950 in Shanghai, an urban stronghold of Catholicism (Hanson 1980). The campaign reached a climax in 1955 when the Shanghai cadres arrested Bishop Gong Pin-mei and many other priests, sisters, and lay leaders.[6]

One Little Rome resident was caught up in the Shanghai persecutions. In 1949, Joseph Lai was a high school student at St. Joseph's. He wanted to become a priest and in 1951 was sent with two other seminarians to Guang-zhou so that he could continue on to the Hong Kong seminary. When the three could not obtain passports to go to Hong Kong, they were instead sent to the Shanghai seminary (then at the Xujiahui [Zicawei] compound). During the 1955 roundup of Catholics, Joseph and the other seminarians underwent one year of reeducation (i.e., indoctrination in official Communist ideology, *jieshou jiaoyu*), and then were sent home for forced labor. For twenty years, the college-educated Joseph (fluent in English and Latin) was allowed to do nothing but farm. In the meantime, he married and had two children. With Deng Xiaoping's ascension to power and the shift to reform policies, Joseph taught high school English until his retirement in 1995. Because he married, he could not continue his training to be a priest, but Joseph is still an active Catholic leader in Little Rome. One of the three classmates sent in 1951 to Guangzhou returned to the Shanghai seminary when it reopened in 1982 and was ordained a priest in 1986, more than thirty years after he started his training.

In 1957 the Chinese Catholic Patriotic Association (*tianzhujiao aiguohui*) was established as the official institutional framework for the Catholic Church in China. The following year, Chinese bishops began to be consecrated without the approval of the Vatican, a practice that exacerbated tensions between the Vatican and the Chinese government and within Chinese Catholic communities. The Meizhou diocese, however, was not recognized by the state through incorporation into the state administrative structure until 1983, when Anthony Zhong Quanzhang became bishop. The church in Little Rome and other parts of the Meizhou diocese remained underground for thirty-two years, starting with the arrest of Bishop Ford. It resurfaced and was incorporated into the state's administrative structure only during the cycle of tolerance of the Deng era, when the Catholics of Little Rome could again practice Catholicism in a manner consistent with their tradition. In other words, the church resurfaced on its own terms and thus was acceptable to the Catholics of Little Rome.

When Bishop Ford was arrested, he entrusted the diocese to his vicar general, Father Paul Lan. During the church's underground period, Father Lan was in effect the bishop of the Meizhou diocese and is remembered by people in Little Rome as "Bishop" Lan.[7] After Bishop Ford's arrest, Bishop Lan was jailed and then placed under house arrest in Meixian to undergo reeducation. According to secret reports smuggled from the underground priests to Hong Kong, only two of the nine priests remaining in the Meizhou diocese cooperated with the Communist authorities during the Maoist period;

the rest, especially Paul Lan and Paul Zhang, endured imprisonment and labor reform. When released from prison in 1956, Paul Zhang was sent back to Little Rome, and when possible he conducted mass at people's homes. After being released in 1958, Paul Lan was first kept in Meizhou City but was then sent back to Little Rome; in 1966 he was again imprisoned in a labor reform camp for the duration of the Cultural Revolution. In 1976, Bishop Lan was released and returned to Little Rome.

Many lay Catholics in Little Rome suffered similar treatment from the local authorities. One lay leader in 1990s Little Rome was sent to prison at the age of nineteen, during the 1958 antirightist campaign. His father had been imprisoned since 1956. Two of his neighbors were with him in prison, and one died there. He himself remained in prison for seven years. This leader told me that in a sense he was fortunate to have been in prison during the famine of the Great Leap Forward, because he ate better than free people in Little Rome. A neighbor's father had been in prison for ten years because of his activism in the Little Rome church and because one of his sons had fled to Taiwan. Most villagers, though, endured these difficult times by being confined to agricultural labor, like the teacher Joseph Lai. Public Catholic activity ceased, and private activity was confined to small prayer groups and house masses conducted in secret.

The bitterest memories among people of Little Rome were of friends and family reporting on one another during the antirightist campaign. During the Cultural Revolution (1966–76), dossiers were released to the public that revealed reports and criticisms individuals in Little Rome had made about their neighbors. People in Little Rome discovered that the reports of one lay activist, made in the heat of the various campaigns, had caused many of his peers to be sent to prison. Lifelong friendships, some tied by their children's marriages, dissolved when these reports were released. By the 1990s public forgiveness was the rule, yet distrust still lingered between some families as a result of the Maoist-period betrayals.

The reforms of the Deng era gradually restored people's sense of community in Little Rome. Between 1980 and 1983, the many residents who had been assigned "hats" (i.e., categorized as counterrevolutionary undesirables) had them removed and their civil liberties returned, including Bishop Lan. As a result, when Deng Xiaoping initiated a new central policy on the practice of religion, Bishop Lan went to Beijing in 1980 to participate in the reorganization of the Chinese Catholic Church. On the national level, the reorganization resulted in the establishment of two national structures, the Chinese Catholic Bishop's Conference (*zhujiao tuan*) and the Catholic

Administrative Council (*tianzhujiao jiaowu weiyuanhui*), in addition to the earlier established Patriotic Association.

When Bishop Lan returned to Meizhou, he continued his involvement in the reorganization of the Catholic Church, both in Little Rome and throughout the diocese. With new national structures in place, Bishop Lan, with the strong support of the priests and the laity who had remained loyal to Catholic tradition, reorganized the Catholic community throughout Meizhou. In 1983, Bishop Lan and a lay Catholic leader took charge of the newly established Little Rome Church Administrative Council. At the same time, Meizhou was reestablished as a separate diocese (during the underground period, the former mission diocese was not recognized by the PRC state), and Father Anthony Zhong elected bishop. Bishop Zhong's selection as head of the diocese reflected the prefectural authorities' recognition that the formerly underground Catholics' approval was needed to legitimize the new structures; their preferred candidate, one of the priests who had cooperated with cadres during the Maoist period, was not acceptable to the Catholics who had survived the difficult times. In 1988, during a period of acceptance among the local Catholic community, a local Patriotic Association was finally established in Little Rome. The Patriotic Association was acceptable because administratively it was clearly subordinate to the other two organizations, which were structured like post–Vatican II Catholic hierarchies throughout the world. In 1992 this fact was officially recognized by the central government with the announcement of the Bishops' Conference as the leading Church organization, and with the national implementation of Vatican II liturgical reforms. Structurally, therefore, the Chinese Catholic Church at the national level and at the local level in Little Rome became like that of Catholic Churches in other nations.

Local History, Social Memory, and Catholic Identity

In 1992 the Jiaoling County Gazetteer (*difang zhi*) was published as the local culmination of the "national politics of remembrance" (Jing 1996). The last county gazetteer had been published in 1880, the first in 1633. Why in the 1980s and 1990s was there a nationwide campaign, directed from the center of the PRC, to collect and publish local historical and sociological information? Jing concludes that this movement was meant to promulgate an official history that would gloss over the past political mistakes of the Maoist era and promote stability in the new postsocialist era. However, the past is not so easily glossed over, and there are many reminders, in a wide variety of media, of what happened earlier.

In her exploration of Karo social experiences in Indonesia, Steedly writes that a "history inscribed in landscape is emplotted less by chronology than by coincidence" (1993: 143). The landscape of Little Rome is itself a disorganized transcript of people's historical experiences. The spaces that people live in and pass through are replete with stories of what happened there, in what Steedly calls "signs of habitation." In everything from stories to official histories, specific places ground historical narrative, making it real (or at least possible). The remnants of the old wall around the village, the walls and buildings of the church compound, and most important the church itself give concrete evidence of the past lives of local Catholics (Jing 1996; Herzfeld 1991; Appadurai 1981). Absent structures also serve as indices of change, traumatic and gradual. When older people in Little Rome saw photos I had digitized from the Maryknoll Photo Archives (taken between 1920 and 1950), they invariably began reminiscing about people and places long gone by pointing out a concrete object in the photo. When shown a picture of young boys gathered around a fountain in front of the rectory, one neighbor first pointed out the small fountain, remembering that it had been built by an American priest, and then started telling us stories about the pranks they used to play as kids hanging out at the church compound. The absence of the fountain today, like the absence of the Maryknollers associated with it, becomes an index of change, of growing up, surviving, and getting old in Little Rome.

Place names are a key sign of habitation and concisely tell stories to those who live in and pass through local space. The village elementary school whose principal made life exciting for Bishop Ford in the 1920s was then called Fudan Elementary, but after liberation it had a series of names: The Second District Number One Central Elementary School, the Long'an Elementary School (the name of the administrative district), the Victorious Hall Elementary School (a modification of the real name of the village, in which a religious term was replaced with a homophone more martial in meaning), then Facing the Sun Elementary School (as the village was known during the Cultural Revolution), and finally, once again, the Fudan Elementary School since 1985. Many houses in Little Rome also have names, prominently displayed over the main doorways. They are the given names of the ancestor who moved to Little Rome. Also, at the site of capital-intensive constructions, such as the main road through town and the new church, stone monuments list the names of the people who contributed money to the project. Even the absence of some names (such as Bishop Ford's) tells a story to those inside the community who remember.

The stories that places tell, with the many meanings that people give to them, are central to how the local appropriates the global. In the dispute of the 1890s described above, the object of contestation was land. The missionaries who arrived in China to import a foreign cosmology and ritual system spent enormous amounts of time and money constructing buildings. Once a space becomes a place, it is animated by the experiences of the people who use it; like commodities, places develop a social life through both mundane and spectacular social exchanges. Buildings like the churches built by the French and American Catholic missionaries accrete stories grounded in local experiences and meaning.

These narratives, however, are very much like the Karo voices that Steedly describes—multiple, fragmented, and interrupted. The built landscape of Little Rome itself, let alone the stories it tells, is a hodgepodge of interruptions and fragments. Its orderly layout during the late Qing period (if indeed the histories describe it accurately), with its walls and gates facing the four cardinal directions, is a testament to the ever-increasing entropy of unregulated rural construction. As the village expanded, walls came down and new walls were built. As children became adults, families separated (*fen jia*), dividing houses or building new ones, and streets took new paths around the construction. No master narrative was at work in the expansion of Little Rome before the Maoist period—however much one would have helped in maintaining order and hygiene—and none is being implemented in the postsocialist era. Even during the high point of collectivization, when Little Rome was part of a highly bureaucratized economic system, the local cadres had to work with what was on the ground, and any streamlined master plan became fragmented with a deluge of quick fixes that made things work temporarily.

The house of God that the French and American missionaries built gradually became a Hakka church, through processes accelerated by the nationalist project during the Maoist period. The building of the new church described in the previous chapter is highly symbolic of the transformation of what was once a foreign religion into the localized faith of their fathers (and mothers). The French and American missionaries who sought to indigenize the Catholic tradition deliberately built churches that looked like other local buildings. At least in Little Rome, they built churches with Chinese characteristics.[8] In postsocialist China, each new church was built in a style seen by foreign Catholic visitors as unfamiliar (some said deplorable, with the use of a white tile ubiquitous to new constructions in postsocialist China). Its authenticity, however, remains undisputed by visiting foreign Catholic clergy, validated by the experiences of Bishop Lan and the other Catholics of Little Rome during the Maoist period. The people of Little Rome see themselves as a martyr church (as do the foreign priests and sisters who maintain contacts with the community). The experiences that animate the built landscape of Little Rome, that give rise to the narratives that ground the community identity, also validate their Catholicism.

It is tempting to juxtapose the historical events described above with the description of Little Rome in the latest county gazetteer, and thus to portray the continued remembrance of such experiences as the active maintenance of an unofficial discourse that resists the homogenization of the official history. There is some truth in this perspective, in that the people of Little Rome keep alive the stories about Bishop Lan and Father Zhang that are ignored in the gazetteer. Based on the textual evidence of past conflicts that Catholics in Little Rome have had with the state and some of their neighbors, an argument can be made that the people of Little Rome are contesting their history with the state as a way of holding on to their identity.

But the people of Little Rome are not waging battles with the local bureaucrats over the building code; they are not fighting to build new houses with cadres who want to preserve monuments to the past (cf. Herzfeld 1991). In fact, they are working with the state to raise money to build new roads, a task that the state supports but cannot afford. Moreover, the general ignorance of what is published in the gazetteer precludes any inference that the Catholics of Little Rome are waging a contest with the state about what is local history. Few people in Little Rome have actually seen the entry in the gazetteer about Catholicism in Jiaoling county, even though one of the older lay leaders in the community himself contributed the information for that section. (The gazetteer is not easy for local people to buy; it is not sold in any bookstore in the county seat and can only be purchased directly from the county office.)

The stories are kept alive because they tell the people of Little Rome who they are—not primarily in relation to the state, but in relation to each other. It is their shared social memory, especially of the Catholic faith held by their ancestors and themselves, that makes a community like Little Rome a coherent social unit.

CHAPTER 5

Practicing Catholicism in Little Rome

Catholic ritual life, whether in Little Rome or anywhere else in the world, can be divided into two categories: sacraments (life-cycle rituals) and holy days (calendrical rituals). Baptism is the first of the sacraments, the rite of passage marking entrance into the church. For residents of Little Rome, it more immediately signifies membership in the community. This first sacrament is also a ritualized recognition of the authority of the church by those being baptized. Holy days like Christmas and Easter are special interpretive moments that give shape to the community and structure the calendrical year. Because of the institutional cohesion of the Roman Catholic Church throughout the world, the sacraments practiced in Little Rome are identical, in ritual speech and movements, to Catholic baptisms conducted in such disparate places as a village in Sardinia, Italy, and a city parish in Boston, Massachusetts. This shared ritual repertoire is central to Little Rome's claim to a share of the transnational authority of the universal Church in that it demonstrates the authenticity of its citizens' Catholicism.

While the Catholic Church maintains a formal institutional structure that radiates outward from the center at the Vatican, the most powerful attachment that Catholics throughout the world have to this global imagined community involves shared local ritual practices. Holy days like Christmas are celebrated at the same time throughout the Catholic world. However, practicing Catholicism can mean very different things, because of individual experiences that are embedded in specific social and historical contexts. Being Catholic during the Maoist period was (and in other areas of China, still is) risky business. In 1996 in Dublin, Ireland, being baptized may have been a normal part of life for children, but in China baptism and other public demonstrations of Catholic identity were still not performed automatically or with complete ease of mind. In this chapter, I describe one baptism and one Christmas celebration that show how ritual identifies who is a part of Little Rome. I also describe daily and Sunday mass in contemporary Little Rome because they are key parts of routinized social life in this Catholic village.

Baptism in Little Rome

The weather in Little Rome in May 1997 was already stifling, warranting long afternoon rest periods for the farmers. The first rice crop had already been transplanted and was growing tall, and people's farming duties were relatively light. In this interlude between transplanting rice seedlings and harvest, most people who farmed in Little Rome were tending gardens, caring for pigs and chickens, and doing assorted repairs they had put off during the busy times. On one afternoon during this slow period, sixteen people gathered in the church to be baptized. The group included one young married man, three older women, four young married women, seven preschoolers (four girls and three boys), and one male infant. I knew many of the adults who were being baptized and had been asked to attend and take photographs of the event.

Earlier that morning, the adults had passed an oral exam given by Father Liang. This exam was administered strictly, from a Hong Kong–published catechism book that presented Catholic doctrine in question-and-answer format. The young married man, my neighbor Mr. Lai, had received individual catechism lessons from one of the catechists, Mr. Wang. Mr. Lai was a bartender in a karaoke bar in the county seat and mostly worked nights. The fact that he made time to meet with the catechist is not surprising; his wife (who converted when they married), his parents, and his grandparents were staunch believers, and the lineage was well represented in church activities. I knew one of the older women because she was the leader of one of Little Rome's five production teams.[1] She and the other women had received catechism lessons from Sister Wang, meeting regularly during the year in one of the classrooms on the ground floor of the convent. The children had been taught separately by Sister Wang, who also ran catechism classes (*daoli ke*) for older school-aged children during summer vacations. The preschool-aged children and infants were not tested.

People slowly gathered in the new church for the baptismal rite, with those to be baptized sitting in the front pews. Friends, relatives, and godparents (*daifu*, godfather; *daimu*, godmother) sat in the pews behind them. As people gathered, Sister Wang prepared items such as the water and chrism (holy oil, *sheng you*) to be used during the ritual, and Father Liang checked to see if everyone was present. Standing in front of the pews on the ground level (not on the altar, which is only used for mass), Father Liang opened the service with a prayer that started like all other Catholic rituals throughout the world: "In the name of the Father, the Son, and the Holy

Figure 11   Summer catechism class run by Sister Wang, July 1995.

Spirit. The Lord be with you." The remainder of the opening prayer stated that the purpose of this gathering was to perform baptism on people who would publicly declare their belief in the teachings of the Holy Catholic Church. The first declaration of faith was made by the group being baptized, followed by a declaration by the godparents that they would teach and support their godchildren in the performance of their duties as Christians.

This was followed by the Liturgy of the Word, readings from the Bible that showed the biblical source for the sacrament of baptism. Before Father Liang started the reading, he noticed that an infant to be baptized was missing and asked someone to fetch the family. The infant was the grandson of a Catholic leader, Mr. Zhou, who lived across from the church; a couple of weeks before, I had attended this infant's "coming-out" ritual of *man yue*, celebrated in a restaurant at the county seat.[2] Mr. Zhou's daughter had married a non-Catholic man surnamed Shen who works in Taiwan. Ms. Zhou rushed into the church with her infant and joined everyone in listening to the gospel reading. The readings were followed by prayers of intercession (the Prayer of the Faithful, identical in format to that used during mass), asking that God guide those about to be baptized.

After reading the prayers of intercession, Father Liang turned to a table

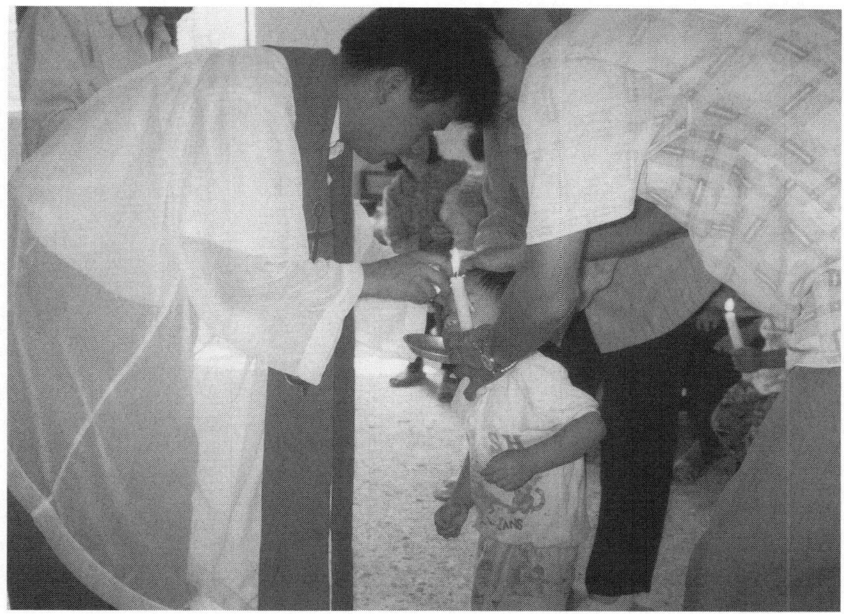

Figure 12   Baptism in Little Rome, 1997.

by the entrance to the altar to bless the water to be used for the baptism. Symbolically, the water is used to cleanse and anoint those being baptized. After blessing the water, Father Liang led the adults in the baptismal group to the altar rail, where they knelt and together recited a group prayer for the forgiveness of sins. At this point, Sister Wang lit the candles held by the group, and, as they were called by the catechist, Mr. Wang, people came forward individually to be baptized.

The same procedure was repeated for each person. As each name was called, that person stepped forward holding a lit candle, with one godparent (for men, it was the godfather; for women, the godmother). Father Liang first asked each person his or her Christian name (*sheng ming*). Repeating the Christian name, Father Liang asked whether the person was willing to be baptized, and each person responded yes. Using an eyedropper, Father Liang sprinkled some holy water on the person's forehead, stating, "I claim you in the name of the Father, Son, and Holy Spirit" (the standard Catholic baptismal formula). The newly baptized person then returned to the pew, and another name was called out.

Once everyone had been baptized, Father Liang anointed the newly baptized with chrism, as is the custom throughout the Catholic world. With the newly baptized kneeling in the pews, he went from one end to the other anointing their foreheads with some chrism, followed by Sister Wang, who gently wiped off the excess oil. At this point, the baptismal rite was completed, but Father Liang continued with the confirmation ritual for the eight adults who had just been baptized. The adults all came forward to kneel at the altar rail. With their godparents behind them resting a hand on their godchildren's shoulders, each person received the sacrament of confirmation from Father Liang. First, Father Liang placed his hand on the person's forehead and spoke a blessing. Next, Father Liang anointed the person on the forehead with chrism (the same oil that had been used during the baptism), performing the rite of confirmation. After being confirmed, each person returned to a seat in the first pew.

Father Liang then returned to the center, just in front of the first pew, and led everyone in singing the Lord's Prayer. Once this was complete, he recited a final blessing and concluded the ritual events for the afternoon. He then informally explained to the newly baptized their responsibility to attend mass, receive communion, and perform penance. After this announcement, he distributed votive cards (pictures of Mary with a prayer on the back) inscribed with each person's name, a medal of Mary, and a crucifix to be worn around the neck. Once the gifts were distributed, everyone gathered in front of the altar for a group picture, which I took and later made copies of for everyone who wanted them. Some people asked me to take individual or family pictures in front of the altar. My neighbor Mr. Lai asked me to take a picture of his wife and son; Ms. Zhou asked me to take numerous pictures of her and her infant, her mother and her family, and other group pictures. At the weekday mass later that evening, the adults who had been baptized all made their first confession before the start of mass and then came forward for their first communion, without any special ceremony, along with everyone else receiving communion.

Everyday Ritual Life in Little Rome

The people who were baptized and confirmed were initiated into full participation in the ritual life of Little Rome. This ritual life is more than just weekly attendance at mass and at life-cycle rituals; it is, directly and indirectly, a major part of the social processes of everyday life. There is always something going on at the church that draws people. For especially active Catholics in Little Rome (who are known as fervent Catholics, *rexin de jiaoyou*), the faith community *is* the social community through their physical participation in day-to-day activities; the faith community comprises about 15 percent of the people in Little Rome.[3] For most residents, however, the faith community *generates* the social community through long-standing alliances between families whose symbolic leaders (the older generations) and backbone (married women) have formed special bonds through participation in the church.

The typical weekday and Saturday began with a morning prayer service. If Father Liang was not tending to administrative matters with Bishop Zhong in Meizhou City or with other communities in churches (*jiaotang*) or chapels (*gongsuo*) for which he is responsible in other counties, he presided over a morning mass. At 5:30 A.M., Mr. Lai, a catechist who lived in the church compound, rang the church bell as a signal that the service would start in fifteen minutes. At 5:45, people filtered in as Mr. Lai led a series of chanted prayers. This sequence of prayers, listed in prayer books from the church, was not a typical prelude to mass in the United States but did consist of the same prayers found in American Catholic prayer books.[4] In a loud voice, Mr. Lai led each prayer with its first line, then everyone else joined in. During this prayer sequence, Father Liang sat in the pews with everyone else, near the confessionals; as needed, he would step into one to hear a confession. At the start of the third-to-last prayer, Father Liang came forward to prepare the altar for mass and change into his vestments. Mass was then conducted in the standard manner used in post–Vatican II Catholic churches throughout the world. In Little Rome, for example, the Pope is specifically referred to as the head of the universal Catholic Church in the Eucharistic prayers. At the close of mass, the congregation ended the service with another sequence of prayers, different from the earlier one. On average, between forty and fifty people attended this early service, most of them elderly (*laorenjia*).

Another mass was held on weekdays at around 7:15 P.M. On Monday, Wednesday, and Friday, Mr. Lai led the congregation in chanting the rosary.[5] Half of the congregation (those sitting on the left side of the church, mostly men), usually following Mr. Lai, chanted the first half of each prayer, while the other half (those sitting on the right side, all women) usually followed Mrs. He in chanting the other half of each prayer. (At the end of each decade—one of the five divisions of the rosary—they switched: the women began the prayer and the men finished it.) On Tuesday and Thursday, Mr. Lai led the congregation in chanting a sequence of prayers similar (but not identical) to the morning sequence. During this period, Father Liang again sat by the confessional to hear confessions from parishioners. After mass, which usually took about forty-five minutes, Mr. Lai led the congregation in another sequence of prayers that ended the event. On average, between eighty and one hundred people attended these weekday evening masses, many more middle-aged and young adults, teenagers, and children than attended the morning masses. Because the Saturday evening mass is a vigil mass—that is, it counts as the required Sunday mass—between three hundred and five hundred people attended. During school vacation in the summer, many more teenagers attended this mass as well.

Catholics throughout the world are required to attend Sunday mass when it is available, and Little Rome was no exception. The Saturday evening mass and Sunday morning mass that fulfill this requirement were well attended. Sunday mornings in Little Rome started with people gathering at the church for the prayer sequence before the start of mass. Many more people came early to perform confession, and I observed that Father Liang often remained in the confessional as long as possible before going to the sacristy—the room where priests and altar servers prepare for mass located at the side of the altar. The Sunday mass was structurally identical to the daily mass but more elaborate. On Sunday, two readings instead of one were performed, plus the gospel and the responsorial psalm. The altar servers were two teenage boys wearing full cassocks, whereas on weekdays one elder came alone to the altar to perform these tasks. Also, there were additional prayers and much more singing. The resulting effect was to stress the importance of Sunday mass above daily mass; masses performed on Sunday and other major holy days in the church calendar were called "the Lord's days" (*zhu ri,* or days of obligation).

Sunday mass is also the only one in which ushers collect money from the congregation. On Sunday, Mr. He (a retired cadre and lay leader) and Mrs. He (the wife of Mr. He's younger brother, and the same woman who leads the chanting) passed baskets through the congregation for donations. After mass, the money was given to Sister Wang, who as the treasurer for the Parish Council kept accounts for the Little Rome church. A neighbor once told me that this was why she preferred to attend the Saturday vigil mass— no collections! The Chinese Catholic Church, according to state regulations (State Council Documents 144 and 145), must be self-supporting and not rely on foreign Catholic organizations for income. Exceptions to this regulation are made only for capital campaigns, such as the building of a church, and by approval of the various religious affairs bureaus from the county level upward.

On Sunday morning in Little Rome, vendors set up stalls along the main road. In addition to the stores that crowd the main road by the church, these stalls, run by Little Rome residents, featured items not usually sold in the village, such as Western-style suits and fresh fish. The stalls and the larger crowds of people made Sundays in Little Rome more lively than the other days of the week; relatives, such as out-married daughters who had left the village, often returned for mass and lunch, to catch up on the news around the village, and to play mah jong. However, in the annual cycle of Little Rome, nothing is as lively as Christmas.

Celebrating Christmas in a Chinese Village

The second rice harvest in the early weeks of November 1996 marked the end of the "busy time" (*nong mang*) for farmers in Little Rome. The pace of work may have slowed, but people were still busy preparing for social events. The three months between the second harvest and the first planting is high season for rituals in Little Rome, spanning both Christmas (*shengdanjie*) and the Chinese Lunar New Year (or Spring Festival, *chunjie*). It is also the wedding season (funerals, of course, cannot be so conveniently scheduled). The Lunar New Year is undoubtedly China's most important holiday; businesses and schools slow down or close for nearly a month. Translated into American terms, the Chinese New Year has the fun of Christmas combined with the headaches of Thanksgiving. The headaches are caused by what is known in China as the Spring Festival movement (*chun yun*)—when it seems that half of China is on the move and passengers are willing to pay much higher prices than normal for train, plane, and bus tickets in order to get home for the holidays.[6] In Little Rome, however, people insist that Christmas is the high point of the holiday season; for Catholics, it is more exciting (*renao*) than the Chinese New Year.

Even before guests arrived for Christmas visits, things were happening all over Little Rome. One young woman from the village (a high school English teacher) married a colleague a week before Christmas. Another family held a housewarming party to celebrate moving into a newly built house. People were busy preparing for large feasts. Women worked together in groups making labor-intensive treats such as *jianban* (sweet fried glutinous rice balls). Others were preparing a traditional Hakka rice wine (*niangjiu*), which is served warm to guests. The church choir had intensified its rehearsal schedule at the completion of the harvest, meeting three times a week to practice Christmas songs. Because of the construction of the new church, many people volunteered to patch the cement courtyard in the church compound, while others cleaned the old church (still in use) and set up the nativity scene near the altar (minus Baby Jesus, who would be set in place during the Christmas Eve Mass). Church staff were busy making arrangements for the Christmas Eve Mass; the previous year, some rival middle-school groups had come to watch the festivities on Christmas Eve and had gotten into a fight, so the preparations this year included arranging for the county police to be present.

People in the village were also calling on their neighbors, delivering Christmas cards by hand to friends and relatives. Exchanging Christmas cards has become very popular in China, and the Catholics of Little Rome were not immune to such fads. In the major cities of China like Beijing, Shanghai, and Guangzhou, department stores set up Christmas decorations and play Christmas music to attract customers; such decorations were absent in the rural county seat of Jiaoling City. Though many of these non-Christian consumers may not recognize the more religious decorations such as the nativity scene, they do know about Christmas trees and Santa Claus (*Shengdanjie laoren*). Christmas cards are readily available for people to buy, even in Jiaoling City. Some people exchanged cards they bought in Jiaoling City, with pictures of Santa Claus, Christmas trees, and snowmen. However, many purchased their cards from the major printing company in the Catholic archdiocese in Shanghai (Guangqi Press), which depicted Jesus and Mary.

Frequently overseas relatives return home at Christmas for an extended visit to their hometown. Tina Li, a college student whose family had moved to Germany, returned to Little Rome to see her relatives and her boyfriend (in China, when a couple is referred to as boyfriend and girlfriend, *nan pengyou and nu pengyou*, the expectation is that they are planning to get married). When Tina's family lived in Little Rome, their house was next door to the Dengs; Tina was in elementary school then. The transnational romance had been difficult for Tina and my neighbor Christian Deng. He had a good job with the county water treatment plant, and she was working on a college degree in Germany; after living in Germany and graduating from college, Tina was not likely to return to Little Rome to work on the family farm. Christian spoke little German so had few prospects for a career in Germany beyond working in Tina's family's Chinese restaurant. Neighbors empathized with the couple, calling them the "shepherd boy and weaving maiden," in reference to a traditional love story about a mythological couple who only meet once a year. But Christmas was a happy time for Chris and Tina, for they were together.

The son of another neighbor (Tina's cousin) also lives with Tina's family in Germany. Although he had a holiday from school in Germany, he could not make the trip home to visit his widowed mother and younger sister. Many people working in other parts of China also could not go home for Christmas because of their work schedules; the Chinese state does not recognize Christmas as a holiday. As a result, those who did return to Little Rome from other parts of the province were mostly women and children.

The Christmas Eve Mass was the ritual focal point of the Christmas celebration. More than fifteen hundred people participated in the mass. People without relatives in the area who came from other parts of Jiaoling and neighboring counties were assigned to spend the night with local residents in their homes. (I hosted a young family of three from neighboring Pingyuan county.) Some visitors were hosted by the church staff; before mass, all the visitors ate together at the church compound. By 7:00 P.M., the church compound was full of people, including younger children playing and adolescents conversing in small groups.

The people involved in the procession all met in the rectory on the other side of the church compound. The choir met in the conference room, and Sister Wang used the hallway to arrange the middle-school children for the procession into the church. The children wore school uniforms (the ubiquitous sweatsuits in local school colors seen throughout rural China) and carried candles and handfuls of glitter that they were to sprinkle as they marched into the church. The altar boys in red and white cassocks were in the foyer preparing their incense (placed in a brass bowl dangling from a chain, similar to what I used when I was an altar boy). The altar boys led the procession with a large crucifix and incense, followed by the children, and the choir sang "Adeste Fideles" in Hakka. Father Liang was at the end of the procession, carrying a small statue of Baby Jesus. The procession entered the main door of the church and made its way to the altar. The choir was seated to the left of the altar, the children to the right, and Father Liang set the statue of Baby Jesus in place in the nativity scene.

The mass itself was celebrated in the same order as every other Christmas Eve Mass in the Catholic world. Like many other priests who gave homilies that evening, Father Liang explained the importance of the Christmas event, the birth of Jesus, and that Catholics should hold the light of Christmas to shine throughout the year. Because many of those participating in the ser-

vice were non-Catholics who were simply curious about the Christmas celebration, Father Liang announced that communion was only for those who
had been baptized and studied catechism. Since so many people took communion, Sister Wang helped Father Liang distribute the host. At the close of
mass, the church was left open and lighted for people to gather in front of the
nativity for individual prayers, and Christmas music was played over the
church sound system.

Christmas Eve was the ritual high point of the celebration, and the social
high point was Christmas Day. Christmas Mass was held the following
morning in Little Rome, and in the afternoon Father Liang went to the
county seat to hold another Christmas Mass. In Little Rome, people hosted
banquets for friends and relatives, to which they invited both their Catholic
and their non-Catholic friends and colleagues, and there was much drinking
and partying. I was reminded of my own Christmas dinners in New York (an
area where Catholics are also a minority), where we invited close Jewish
friends to our Christmas dinner. On Christmas evening, the church had
scheduled a veneration of the host; but many of the Catholics in Little Rome
stayed at home to celebrate. In Little Rome that evening, the lights stayed on
late into the night.

Although people claimed that Christmas was the high point of the year in
Little Rome, the Chinese New Year (February 7, in 1996) was also very festive. Because it is an official holiday, many more young adults were able to
return home from their workplaces in other parts of China, and so there
were many lively reunions among former classmates. Children were out of
school, so Little Rome was full of people of all ages. As at Christmas, many
women were busy in the kitchens preparing large batches of traditional
goodies to exchange with other people. The men decorated the houses and
hung traditional banners (*chun lian*) over doorways.

Nearby villages, however, were in an even bigger frenzy than Little Rome.
In addition to the feasts for relatives and friends who would visit their
homes, people in the fifty-five households of nearby Dalubei were also
preparing for a New Year communal ancestor worship at the lineage segment's ancestor temple. On the afternoon of New Year's Eve, the Shen segment gathered to worship their ancestors. Lines of tables with food offerings
prepared by individual households were already set up in front of the altar,
which held their ancestral tablets. When everyone was ready, musicians
started playing and people came forward to light incense and candles that
were placed on a table immediately in front of the ancestral tablets. When
about half of the people had cycled through, a lion dance group came

through the main doorway of the ancestral temple, danced around the food offerings up to the tablets, and then left through the main doorway. After the incense had been offered, people (mostly women) came forward to burn paper money while the men and young adults watched from the sides. After everyone had finished their offerings, a group of men grabbed long bamboo poles with multiple rolls of firecrackers draped at the end and ran outside into the courtyard to set them off. This deafening explosion of fireworks lasted over fifteen minutes. Then the women removed the food offerings from the tables and put them into baskets to carry home. As people returned home, each household again set off rolls of firecrackers. Roman candles and other fireworks could be seen and heard throughout the night, with an especially loud barrage taking place at midnight and at sunrise the following morning, New Year's Day.

For the next fifteen days (especially the first four days) in Little Rome and other communities around the county, people held banquets and feasted (the fifteenth day, *yuan xiao*, traditionally marks the end of the New Year season). Children were dressed in new clothing as they visited family and friends to receive their New Year's gift of money (*hong bao*). One of the few Chinese phrases that my son still remembers is the greeting that children gave to adults to receive their *hong bao*, "*gongxi facai, lishi nalai*" (Congratulations and good fortune—where's my gift?). Mass was held at the church on New Year's Day, but attendance was usually smaller than at regular Sunday mass. On the third day of the New Year, many of the women of Little Rome traveled to their natal homes to visit their kin, as is the custom throughout China. From the perspective of ritual life in Little Rome, Christmas is the high point of the liturgical calendar, though Easter and Assumption Day are also important holy days.

Political Structure of the Little Rome Church

The Little Rome church is part of two parallel organizational lines associated with the Chinese Bishop's Conference and Patriotic Association. One line is administrative, corresponding to the Bishop's Conference, and is the structure most used in the daily conduct of church activities. The administrative structure in Little Rome centers on the Parish Council (described in Chapter 2). This body meets frequently, whenever a special event approaches, such as All Souls' Day, Christmas, or the church opening. Father Liang presides over this council and in this role reports both to the county Religious Affairs

Bureau in matters pertaining to public safety and to Bishop Zhong for matters pertaining to pastoral duties.

The other line at the county level is political, the county Patriotic Association. It is not involved in the day-to-day supervision of Catholic activities and meets far less often—only three or four times since its formation in 1988. The Patriotic Association approves structural modifications (e.g., changing the administrative charter for the Parish Council) and personnel changes. In 1997 the leadership of the county Patriotic Association passed from an elderly retired Catholic physician to the young Father Liang. The members of the association are Catholic lay leaders throughout the county; many members of the Little Rome Parish Council are also members of the county association.

The central figure in Little Rome of the 1990s was undoubtedly Father Liang. Although two cadres were responsible for public safety in the village, when new projects or a social event was being organized, Father Liang was always at the center of discussions.[7] He was the first person from the Meizhou diocese to be ordained a priest after the church resurfaced in the postsocialist period. A native of Wuhua county, about 150 kilometers southwest of Jiaoling county, Father Liang grew up in a village similar to Little Rome—a rural Catholic stronghold high in the mountains. After graduating from high school, he went to the regional seminary in Wuhan (reopened in 1983) under the sponsorship of the Meizhou diocese. After being ordained in 1991, he first served in the church at Meizhou under the direct guidance of Bishop Zhong and was later assigned his own parish in Little Rome in 1994.

Father Liang was a very energetic and determined man. When I asked him why he became a priest, he said that he saw his vocation as an opportunity to serve society. He wanted to rebuild and modernize the entire Catholic infrastructure of the county, beginning with the church compound in Little Rome. When a church building was condemned, he was quick to organize committees and develop fundraising outreach to relatives, individual Catholics, and Catholic organizations overseas. The success of this very demanding capital project was due in no small measure to the work of Father Liang. His next planned project was to rebuild the convent by adding a social center for children and young adults. With his imported motorcycle (a gift from a foreign priest) and his pager, he resembled the young entrepreneurs who are beginning to abound in the Hakka homeland. His agenda, however, was very different; Father Liang was committed to his pastoral work in Little Rome and the nearby county seat and was also responsible for Catholic communities in neighboring Pingyuan county. During the year, he and one of the catechists, Mr. Wang, made trips to many Catholic communities deep in the more remote areas of the county, going as far as southern Fujian. The diocese's three other older priests relied heavily on Father Liang's young legs to reach the communities in the diocese.

Two older sisters, Sister Ye and Sister Wang, had trained under the Maryknoll missionaries in Little Rome. With Bishop Lan, these two sisters were instrumental in reorganizing the church when it resurfaced in the early 1980s, and continued through the 1990s to be vital in the pastoral care of Little Rome. Both had extensive kin networks in Little Rome—Sister Wang was the older sister of the catechist Mr. Wang—and because of their age were allowed to remain in their natal home when the church resurfaced. Priests and sisters are usually assigned to positions outside their own hometown, as is customary throughout the Catholic world; one of the young sisters from Little Rome who took her final vows in 1997 was assigned to a church in Fengshun county, about two hundred kilometers south of Little Rome. Sister Ye was older (in her late sixties), and was more active in the initial resurfacing of the Little Rome church with Bishop Lan; the somewhat younger Sister Wang, in her early sixties, was the treasurer of the parish council and more active in church administration. Both continued to teach catechism to the children and women of Little Rome and maintained the household of the church compound. Another woman, a "Catholic virgin" (see Wiest 1977), who had studied to be a sister under Maryknoll but did not take final vows, also did many jobs around the church but did not wear a habit and was less involved than the sisters in formal events. She was addressed by the same colloquial term, *guniang*, as the other sisters; formally, Sisters Ye and Wang are *xiunu*.

The church's two catechists, Mr. Lai and Mr. Wang, were heavily involved in day-to-day church activities. Mr. Lai lived in the rectory and was a former middle-school teacher who returned to Little Rome to join the church staff. He lost his teaching position because of a combination of poor health and political background—his father, a former teacher at St. Joseph's, was labeled a "religious worker" during the antirightist campaign. Mr. Lai led the congregation in chanting prayers before and after mass and was also the secretary of the Parish Council and county Patriotic Association. Mr. Wang was a farmer whose primary duty in the church was teaching catechism. As a youth, he had been imprisoned because of his key role in the church; his father was also a catechist for the Maryknollers. Although he had been denied a formal education because of these political problems, Mr. Wang was a self-taught intellectual, familiar with a wide range of Western theological and philosophical discourse in Chinese translations. He was a prolific writer whose articles appeared in almost every issue of the national magazine *Catholic Church in China* (published in Beijing).

In addition to the priest, the two sisters, and the two male catechists, there was also a cook, an older lay Catholic man; these six people constituted the official church staff of Little Rome. They worked with a wide array of lay leaders, mostly men, who mobilized support for various activities, both communitywide, like All Souls' Day, and family-specific, like weddings and funerals. Some of these lay people had an official place in church administration through their participation in the Parish Council. Others held functional positions, such as the two women who were lectors and the retired teacher who served as music director, and participated in the planning of church events in their liturgical capacity. A few were recognized as lay leaders through their mobilization of Catholic activities off the church grounds. One such activity was a prayer group that chanted prayers for the deceased; another group conducted informal prayers and lessons based on imported materials—devotionals printed in Hong Kong, Taiwan, or the United States, or transcribed material from the Vatican's short-wave radio broadcasts. One older man whom everyone considered especially devout received prayer cards and other relics from Catholic areas, and he often shared with other elders prayers that other Catholics outside China claimed could help heal illnesses. When I traveled to Hong Kong, he asked me to bring back Marian devotional literature and other materials from the Catholic Center there.

The core of people involved in Catholic activities, both ritual and nonritual, was a group of older women; they constituted the majority of volunteers and people attending ritual activities in Little Rome. In an article written for the national Catholic journal, Mr. Wang described the central role of women in the resurfacing of the church in Little Rome:

> With the Lord's grace, the embattled church [in China] again rose up. Churches everywhere were open. Priests returned to churches they had long been separated from to resume their familiar yet unfamiliar pastoral care. When religious activities first resumed, many Catholic men furtively watched from the sidelines [*tantou tan'nao*], while the Catholic women rushed into the churches without reservation to participate heartily in the renewed services, and also encouraged other Catholics to worship in public. (My translation)

Mr. Wang described women as the backbone of the Catholic Church in every respect, from their disproportional attendance at mass to their volunteer work in church-related activities. In Little Rome, two women served as lectors in 1996, and Father Liang actively recruited young married women. Women made up about three-quarters of the Little Rome choir. Mr. Wang had kept current with Pope John Paul II's pronouncement that the issue of women serving as priests was not to be pursued; his discussion of women's role in the Chinese church explicitly reflected this official Catholic position. Although he called for more involvement of women as lectors and catechists, there was no questioning of the Pope's stand against women priests.

The Overlap of the Ritual and Social Communities

Since Robertson-Smith and Durkheim, analysts have long accepted that rituals make a community—but how does this ritual community overlap with the village of Little Rome? Does one have to be Catholic to live in the village? Is everyone in Little Rome a member of the ritual community, with his or her name recorded in the church registry?

Victor Turner's highly influential model of the ritual community is based on his concept of "social drama analysis."[8] This perspective views society as a set of loosely integrated, semipatterned processes that subsume the "hidden contradictions and conflicts" of social life (Turner 1957: 1). Rituals manifest this structural failure to maintain unity and stability and are the means by which "groups [become] adjusted to internal changes and [adapt] to their external environment" (Turner 1967: 20). Turner's ritual analysis starts from Van Gennep's three-stage discussion of *rites of passage*: separation, liminality, and reincorporation. In the period of liminality, the normal structural bonds that characterize social relationships are dissolved in *communitas* (antistructure), where ritual participants can be made receptive to the meanings of the symbols that represent a culturally ordered cosmology of society. With its temporary elevation of alternative relationships and expressions of ties, *communitas* is pregnant with new configurations and ideas— ideas that upon reincorporation can potentially resolve the tensions within social structures.

Because symbols serve as a vehicle for expressing and reinforcing ideas, they play a critical role in Turner's conception of the ritual process. According to Turner, the "symbol is the smallest unit of ritual which still retains the specific properties of ritual behavior; it is the ultimate unit of specific structure in a ritual context" (Turner 1967: 19). Turner distinguishes between dominant symbols that refer to axiomatic values of a group and instrumental symbols that enable ritual efficacy. Dominant symbols are concise representations of disparate ideas and actions, with a multiplicity of meanings, that can appeal to and be subjectively understood by a wide audience. As embedded in the sensory experience of ritual, symbols communicate an "arrangement of norms and values that guide and control persons as members of social groups and categories" (ibid.: 28), storing and transmitting the cultural information that integrates society.

Baptism is an initiation into a ritual community—the universal Catholic Church. This ritual community, as seen in Little Rome's celebration of Christmas in 1996, is deterritorialized, not bounded by the political boundaries of Little Rome. Catholics from neighboring counties and relatives from overseas joined together in the celebration. In their use and promotion of post–Vatican II Catholic orthodoxy, the Catholics of Little Rome claim to be part of the universal Catholic Church, a point made during each mass in the profession of faith, when people say together, "I believe in one, holy, catholic, and apostolic Church."

To understand how the ritual community is related to the social community of Little Rome, we must first look at the wider context of the relationships between Little Rome and its neighboring communities. David Faure's (1986) model of Chinese rural society in the New Territories of Hong Kong can be used to illustrate these relationships. Faure starts from Freedman's (1966) classic segmentary model of Chinese lineages as a corporate group holding property maintained through the ideology of ancestor worship. Chinese villages, according to Freedman, are communities created out of a single lineage or interlineage alliances (see also Fortes 1953). Freedman's application of segmentary theory developed from anthropological studies in Africa may have oversimplified the reality of rural life in southern China but has served as the catalyst for numerous studies of Chinese rural society (see, for example, Rubie Watson 1985 for a critique of social practices within the lineage; Harrell 1982 for other modes of village social organization). Faure's critique brings in a whole set of ritual practices neglected by Freedman that demonstrate that the corporate lineage is only one possible structural principle that holds together Chinese villages; the other major structural principle is popular religion. Temples and ancestral halls, therefore, can also be the focus for the territorial representation of communities, with rituals bridging unrelated families and reminding them of historical alliances. Communities thus identify themselves as distinct from other communities through joint performances in and donations to individual temples and ancestral halls.

In Little Rome, the church holds a structural position similar to that of temples, in that the shared practice of Catholic tradition separates the community from neighboring communities, such as the nearby village of Dalubei. In Dalubei, Spring Festival ancestor worship services reinforce the lineage bonds between its citizens; in Little Rome the Christmas celebration reinforces the shared identity of people who have no agnatic relationships. (Affinal relationships between villagers, however, are widespread—people say that everyone in Little Rome is somehow related to everyone else.)

However, using Faure's test of community membership—rights of settlement—does not delineate a clear-cut community in Little Rome because of the historical legacy of the Maoist period. Rights of settlement were strictly controlled by the PRC state and, through the household registration system, were used to enforce its policies in both city and countryside (Potter and Potter 1990). One nearby hamlet, marked off as a separate production team, is administratively a part of Little Rome. Its inhabitants are mostly non-Catholic and as a result do not take part in the festivals or general social life of Little Rome. In fact, this hamlet is geographically separate from the village; it is not connected by paved or unpaved roads to the heart of Little Rome (the church and the concentration of small stores). This exception is the result of redrawing local political boundaries in the postsocialist period. Even within the heart of Little Rome, there are a few non-Catholic households. They have recently moved into the village and are renting houses from Little Rome families that have moved to other areas in China or have emigrated abroad (for example, the house of Tina Li, whose family had moved to Germany, was being rented to a non-Catholic family). These isolated cases are the exceptions that prove the rule; to be considered a member of the Little Rome community, a person must be at least nominally Catholic.

As Mr. Wang implies above, many middle-aged men fit this category of "nominal Catholics." Even after fifteen uneventful years of above-ground Catholic practices, many men still do not attend mass.[9] The two men who together are responsible for the security of Little Rome's five production teams do not participate in the ritual life of the community, but members of their families do. There are also many young men who do not attend mass because of the possible political stigma associated with believing and participating in religion, although they may participate in large communitywide rituals such as All Souls' Day and Christmas. Like the young Mr. Lai who was baptized in the event described above, however, these men are slowly returning to full participation in the ritual life of the community. Even retired cadres with Communist Party membership attend mass. Women of all ages can be regular participants because, unless they hold administrative positions outside the family, their religious activity is perceived as politically irrelevant. Even some women administrators, like the production team leader who was baptized with Mr. Lai, are fully joining the ritual community.

Practicing Catholicism is central to Little Rome's community identity, but not in the straightforward way that Durkheim and others have illustrated, whereby community solidarity is fostered through a shared cosmology. The role of Catholic ritual in Little Rome more closely resembles Victor Turner's model of *communitas*, where ritual mediates social conflict and competition among members of the community. Life-cycle rituals like baptism, calendrical rituals like Christmas, and everyday rituals like mass bring people together as equal children before God. The members of the Little Rome church, from Father Liang to nominal Catholics, recognize that the church ideology promotes social harmony: they often told me, "We help each other because we're Catholics." But the sacred space created by ritual does not eradicate the influences of the secular. People who do not get along outside of church also do not get along during mass, even when they are praying together; two households that were bickering over property lines kept an uneasy peace when they were physically together in church. This mixture of the sacred and the secular is perhaps most clearly evident in the administrative structure of the Little Rome church. Key administrative leaders are also ritual leaders, and police still must be contracted to provide security at special occasions and unusually large gatherings like Christmas. Such leaders embody both the authority of the state and the authority of the church.

Instead, practicing Catholicism is central to Little Rome's community identity because it distinguishes the members as a group from other communities, like neighboring Dalubei. The church stands in a structural position identical to that of the temples in Faure's model of Chinese rural society. But the church's effectiveness in maintaining social cohesion stems primarily from the basic fact of its difference from other modes of popular religion in local society.

This is not to say that Catholic theology and morality, the belief system of the Catholic Church, is irrelevant, and that any temple of some arbitrary cosmology could substitute. A transplanted mosque could not perform the same social function for the people of Little Rome because Catholicism, not Islam, is the faith of their fathers. Being Catholic means something more to the people of Little Rome because of the particularistic charismatic authority that kept the community together throughout their historical experiences. Other transnational organizations that symbolize an ideology of modernity, such as a McDonald's restaurant, could not fulfill the same function, because its social meaning would not give hope and comfort to families who have lost a loved one or reinforce the love felt by a young couple getting married. On the local level, because Catholicism is not widespread in other communities, the Little Rome church is central to village identity because of its difference; it is not just another temple in the local religious system.

Faure's point is that the temples of the gods, and the rituals like the *jiao* (Daoist sacrificial ceremony) celebrated in and around them, symbolize territorial unity (Faure 1986: 70); temples, through the performance of rituals, add a highly charged level of meaning to social relations, granting legitimacy to unbalanced power relations in the maintenance of social harmony (Kertzer 1988; Rubie Watson 1985). They give identity to a specific group precisely because of its difference from other groups, as the Blessed Virgin of Morro da Conceição in Brazil is different from other icons of Mary throughout the Catholic world (Nagle 1997). This specificity makes Mary a potent symbol for the people of Morro da Conceição, a focal point for both unity and dissension in this community. The same symbols sometimes give wider communities a rallying point. As Our Lady of Guadalupe gives Mary specificity for Mexican Catholics (Eric Wolf 1958), Chinese Catholics as a wider community especially treasure the Holy Mother of China (*zhonghua shengmu*), and Marian devotion is an essential part of everyday ritual (such as in the communal chanting of the rosary). Her pilgrimage site just outside Shanghai is a focal point for Catholics at the national level.

The Localization of a Transnational Religious System

The history of the Chinese Catholic Church has been a history of the localization of a transnational religious system, a history well documented from the perspective of international relations (see Leung 1992). To further an understanding of how this transnational religious system has become localized in Little Rome, let us examine two key events that have shaped the structural form of the Little Rome church: the establishment of the PRC, and the restructuring of Catholicism that took place during the meetings of the Second Vatican Council (1962–65), called Vatican II. Vatican II was a massive liturgical reform project that reoriented the Catholic Church toward localization and greater social activism. The reformers of Vatican II revised the ritual of the mass to include greater participation of lay Catholics in its performance. They also made the mass more local (and as a result, more accessible) by changing the ritual language from Latin to local languages and dialects.

The Vatican II reforms have been unevenly implemented in the Catholic churches in China. Priests graduating from the regional seminaries are taught to conduct the Vatican II mass, but some churches (especially some of the above-ground churches) still use the Latin mass. With its resurfacing in 1983, the Little Rome church adopted the Vatican II mass, orienting itself with contemporary Catholic orthopraxy. However, ritual practices such as the chanting of prayers before and after mass heighten the unique nature of Catholicism as it is practiced in Little Rome, making the church local. Other practices such as the heightened importance of All Souls' Day (discussed later) reflect local concerns in the veneration of ancestors.

The administrative structure (or ecclesiastical structure, as theologians would say), however, has been fully localized with the intervention of the PRC state. There is a rupture in the structural link between local Chinese churches like Little Rome and the Vatican. The most contentious issue between the PRC and the Vatican is the appointment of bishops, a right that both parties contend is solely their own. As a result, from the national level, with the insertion of the Patriotic Association, the structure of the Chinese Church does not fully follow Catholic administrative practices elsewhere in the world.

However, from the local perspective of Little Rome, the church is structurally identical to parishes in other parts of the world. With Father Liang at the head of the Parish Council (the Parish Council is also a structural reform from Vatican II), the church is in its day-to-day conduct very much Catholic and local. It is Catholic in that the sole authority of the parish is invested in the priest, who reports to his bishop at the next level. The county Patriotic Association is not involved in the day-to-day practices, ritual or mundane, of the Catholics in Little Rome. Although technically all Catholics in Little Rome are members of the county Patriotic Association because they belong to the church, the county Patriotic Association is far removed from the practice of Catholicism for everyone but the few administrative leaders like Father Liang, the sisters, and the catechists.

In its ritual practices, the Little Rome church follows the biblical injunction of giving to Caesar what is Caesar's but giving to God what is God's. For example, when organizing large events such as Christmas Eve Mass, the Parish Council closely follows the county regulations for large gatherings, such as contracting with local police to maintain public safety. The decision to build a new church followed the recommendations of the county building safety office. Relevant administrative structures like the Parish Council and the standing committee of the county Patriotic Association, required by the guidelines outlined in central directives for recognized religious organizations, have been fully registered.

However, in practices essential to Catholic tradition the people of Little Rome follow Catholic orthopraxy. People in Little Rome also have continued the practice of infant and child baptism and catechism classes for children, despite the national regulation that children under the age of eighteen are not allowed to participate in religious activities. The county government is aware of the summer catechism schools for children and has approved their meetings; and regulations against infant and child baptism are not enforced. The people of Little Rome are not unique in this respect; the activities in the neighboring village's New Year's ancestor worship are also officially prohibited, as are the earth god shrines (*bai gong*) scattered throughout the area. At least on the local level, the state has made accommodations for ritual practices to be conducted in a thoroughly Catholic manner. The localization of transnational Catholicism is thus closely linked to events and processes that take place on a global level (such as Vatican II) and at the national level.

CHAPTER 6

Getting to the Church on Time

In Little Rome, as in many other villages in China, the marriage ritual builds and reinforces community ties. As in other communities with a dominant pattern of patrilocal residence, marriage inducts new members into the community—namely, women from other villages. It reinforces community ties through communal participation in the marriage ritual. In this chapter, I discuss how the marriage process I observed in the Little Rome of the 1990s was a reflection of the times; the choices involved in determining the form of the celebration of two young people joining in matrimony lie at the intersection of myriad social processes, such as the increasing commodification of culture, transnational capital, and the contextualization of traditional ritual practices in postsocialist China. As a result, ritual events are meaningful only through an understanding of the social and economic contexts of newlyweds, their friends, and their communities. Weddings in rural Jiaoling county are intrinsically shaped by such transnational processes as global capitalism and modern nation-state development. Getting married in Little Rome involves interpretive moments, performances that combine the authority of the church with the authority of modernity for the newlyweds.

Lai Wuyan and Deng Huilan Marry

Just before the 1997 Spring Festival, Mr. Lai Wuyan and Ms. Deng Huilan were married in Little Rome's church. A couple of weeks earlier Huilan had come down to the village from her natal home in nearby Jiaocheng to be baptized. Before this, Huilan had attended catechism classes with Mr. Wang. Their planning a church wedding (*ling hunpei*), which these days usually entails the baptism of either the bride or groom, was not a surprise, since Wuyan's grandparents were especially active in the church, and one of his uncles was the secretary of the county Patriotic Catholic Church Standing

Committee and a catechist in the church. Many outsiders, especially women, who marry Little Rome residents are expected to become Catholic.

I first met Wuyan in the summer of 1995, when he was home from Shenzhen visiting friends and family during summer vacation. Like many of his peers, after graduating from middle school in 1992 he left Jiaoling to find a better-paying job in the rapidly developing areas closer to Hong Kong. In fact, his romance with Huilan developed in Shenzhen, where she also worked. Although their childhood homes were less than ten kilometers apart, they had not known each other until they met in Shenzhen. When they decided to get married, they asked an older female relative of Huilan's to act as a match-maker (*meiren*) to formalize the process for their two families. Like Huilan, this relative, now an active Catholic, had married into Little Rome many years before. Like other young adults who had left home for work in more prosperous parts of Guangdong, Wuyan and Huilan planned to get married around Spring Festival in Wuyan's hometown (*laojia*), when they and their friends would have holidays from work and could spend time at home.

GETTING MARRIED IN THE CHURCH

On the day of the church wedding, Wuyan received some last-minute cate-chism instruction before being tested by Fr. Liang and was baptized late in the afternoon. Like many young adults who grew up before the church was reestablished in the 1980s, he had not been baptized as a child. Unlike the baptism of his fiancée, however, Wuyan's baptism surprised many of his rel-atives, since he was an aspiring cadre working as a security officer in the Postal Service in Shenzhen. In the late Deng era, despite government policies concerning the freedom of religious belief, cadres are still actively discour-aged from publicly participating in religious activities.[1] Wuyan's baptism was attended by his fiancée and grandparents but almost no other commu-nity members—it was not a highly publicized event.

Before the church service, the couple presented their marriage license (*jiehun zheng*) to Father Liang. They had applied for it earlier through the township government; from the perspective of the state, the granting of the license is in effect the wedding—the official recognition of their status as a married couple. Father Liang later told me that he could not perform the wedding ceremony unless they had the marriage license in hand. The bride and one of her girlfriends then went to the church conference room in the rectory to get ready, while the groom went home to change his clothes.

With the help of her friend, a female cousin of the groom, the bride changed into a full-length white wedding gown (red is the color of traditional Chinese wedding outfits) and waited for the rest of the Lai wedding party to arrive. She wore a white veil pinned to the back of her head. The first to arrive were two elementary school–aged flower girls, dressed in matching red-and-white school uniforms (sweat pants and jacket). Sister Wang, who had earlier decorated the church with flowers for the occasion, came into the room to make sure the bride had everything she needed and brought more flowers for the couple to carry. The church bell rang to mark the start of mass, and the congregation slowly gathered to chant the usual prayers that precede mass. The groom's grandparents then arrived in the rectory, followed by the groom's mother (the father was deceased) and the bride's mother, and finally the groom himself, dressed in a dark Western-style suit (*xizhuang*). The wedding party waited for the chanted prayers to end, and then to the sound of firecrackers they marched to the main entrance of the church, led by the groom's grandfather.

As they reached the main entrance, the organist started Mendelssohn's wedding march accompanied by the singing of the choir and the congregation (there were over five hundred people attending that evening, more than usual for a Saturday vigil mass), and the wedding party proceeded up to the front of the church. The Lai wedding party took seats in the front pews, and the bride, groom, and their flower girls remained standing at the front of the church. Father Liang then started mass with the sign of the cross, conducting the Saturday vigil mass as usual, but with the added elements that constitute the wedding liturgy in Catholic churches throughout the world. After the opening prayer, which included a prayer for the couple, Father Liang led the congregation through the penitential rite.

The mass then continued with the Liturgy of the Word (shortened, first reading and responsorial psalm only), read by an aunt of the groom who regularly served as a lector in the rotation of lay readers. The readings were not specifically chosen by the bride and groom, as as they frequently are in other Catholic congregations in the world; rather, they followed the sequence specified for a Saturday vigil mass used by Catholic churches throughout the world. Father Liang then read the gospel and delivered a homily explaining the meaning of the wedding ceremony to the couple and the congregation. The main point of his homily was that the sacrament of marriage is not just a presentation of the couple to family and friends, but is also a presentation of the couple to God through the Holy Church (*sheng jiaohui*).

After the homily, Father Liang and the two altar boys descended from the altar to stand with the couple and preside over the marriage ceremony. The

Figure 13   Mr. Lai and Ms. Deng getting married in the church in 1997. They are flanked by their godparents.

couple first affirmed their intention to marry by responding "I do" (*yuanyi*) together to the declaration read by Father Liang. The priest then asked the couple to shake hands. Father Liang held the microphone in turn for Wuyan and Huilan as they declared their wedding vows to each other. After their vows, Fr. Liang blessed the rings and handed one to Wuyan. He took the ring and placed it on his bride's finger, declaring, "Deng Huilan, I give you this ring as an expression [*biaoshi*] of my love and respect, in the name of the Father, and of the Son, and of the Holy Spirit." Huilan followed suit, placing a ring on her groom's finger and declaring its significance.

The mass continued in typical sequence with the Prayers of the Faithful, some of which were specifically directed to the couple.[2] Fr. Liang recited the Liturgy of the Eucharist, again adding some prayers directed to the couple. During the Exchange of Peace, Father Liang, who usually remains at the altar, came down to shake hands with the bride and groom and the groom's family. Communion followed as usual; it was first offered to the new couple and then to the rest of the congregation. Mass was then closed by Father Liang, and the congregation chanted the usual prayer sequence that ends mass in Little Rome. There was no procession of the wedding party out of the church; rather, as the bride and groom exited, members of the congregation offered their congratulations.

GETTING MARRIED AT HOME

On the Tuesday following the church wedding, the Lai family held another wedding ceremony at their home. This home in the village had been built by Wuyan himself in 1996 and was occupied by his widowed mother. Unlike the church wedding, which was open to the entire village community, this event was by invitation only. When I had received the invitation for the wedding a couple of weeks before, this was the event listed on the invitation. The events in the marriage celebration at home more closely resembled non-Catholic wedding feasts that I had seen elsewhere and "traditional" weddings described in the literature on Hakka weddings.

Like most weddings in the Hakka region of Meizhou, the day started early. At 7:30, I made my way with a group from Little Rome to the bride's natal home (*niangjia*) in Jiaoling City, the nearby county seat. When we arrived, the bride had not yet finished dressing and putting on makeup. The group included a driver, the groom, the best man (*banlang*), myself and my motor-cycle driver (my neighbor, who was a cousin of the groom), and the match-maker. Our group from Little Rome sat around and watched some karaoke videos while the bride, a female cousin from Little Rome, and her two brides-maids (*banniang*) made final preparations. This time, instead of a white wed-ding dress, the bride was dressed in a red business suit (the color red follow-ing more traditional practices, though the suit itself was Western-style). On her lapel was a large red ribbon of the kind used to distinguish honored guests (*jia bin*) at ceremonies, which labeled her as the bride (*xinniang*). The groom was wearing the same suit he had worn to the church wedding, but that morning he also wore a large red ribbon marking him as the groom (*xinlang*).

Instead of the traditional sedan chair (*jiao*), the bride, her two brides-maids, the groom, and the older woman crammed into a black Toyota sedan, lavishly decorated to show off its function as the limousine for the bride. On the hood of the car was a large red "double happiness" character (*shuangxi*) clearly marking it as marriage sedan. As if that and the streamers and flow-ers across the top of the car and along the sides were not enough, there was also a miniature figurine (about eight inches tall) of a bride in a white dress with veil and groom in a tuxedo on the hood. Brides are expected to cry upon leaving their natal home, but Deng did not; she may have been distracted by the rush to get her out of the house and fit everyone in the car. As she was sent off by her parents, there were also no firecrackers to mark her leaving her natal home—for safety reasons, the county government had outlawed fireworks in the county seat of Jiaocheng since January 1 of that year.

But firecrackers were still allowed in the rural areas, and when the bridal party arrived in Little Rome, a roll of firecrackers was set off. The marriage sedan parked in front of the church (a common parking area for cars of visitors), so the bridal party had to march through the center of the village to reach the groom's house. The matchmaker led the procession, followed by the couple and then the bridesmaids. In an alley that led to the groom's home, the bride opened up a red handkerchief filled with hard candy. The couple had to scramble out of the way as a horde of Little Rome children, who had gathered closely in anticipation of this, dived at their feet for the candy.

The bride was directed into the house and stood in a line in the living room with the groom, the groom's grandmother, his mother, and the matchmaker, facing a crucifix, which was flanked by large pictures of Mary and Jesus (there are no ancestor tablets in the homes of Little Rome). The groom's grandfather stood in front of this line. They made the sign of the cross and then waited until the firecrackers died down. When it was quiet, the grandmother led the group in prayers: first the Lord's Prayer, followed by a Hail Mary, and then a Glory Be to the Father. They then closed with another sign of the cross. At this point, an uncle of the groom's directed the couple to bow (*bai*, worship) together, first toward God (i.e., facing the crucifix), then toward the grandparents, and then toward the groom's mother; last, the couple was instructed to bow toward each other. After each bow, the bride was given a *hong bao* (money placed in a ceremonial red envelope) by the grandparents and the groom's mother. After this, the couple and bridesmaids retired to the bridal bedroom.

The bridal bedroom was filled with furniture, part of the bride's dowry (*jiazhuang*) that had been set up earlier. The walls were decorated with the ubiquitous red-foil "double happiness" character. The bride sat on the edge of the new bed, which was stacked with new quilts. At the foot of the bed was a large dresser, and next to the head of the bed was a night table with two electric candles lit. Fruits and sweets were set out on a serving platter for guests, and other smaller gifts (music boxes, etc.) were crowded on the platter as well. An elegant new coffee table held a tea service, with which a female cousin served tea to the group that had gathered in the bridal bedroom.

After the groom's mother repinned the groom's *xinlang* ribbon (it continued to fall off all morning), the bride and groom picked up a cup of tea together and with four hands offered it to the groom's uncle, who had earlier announced the sequence of bowing. While handing over the tea, the bride called the uncle by his proper kin term, and the uncle gave the bride a

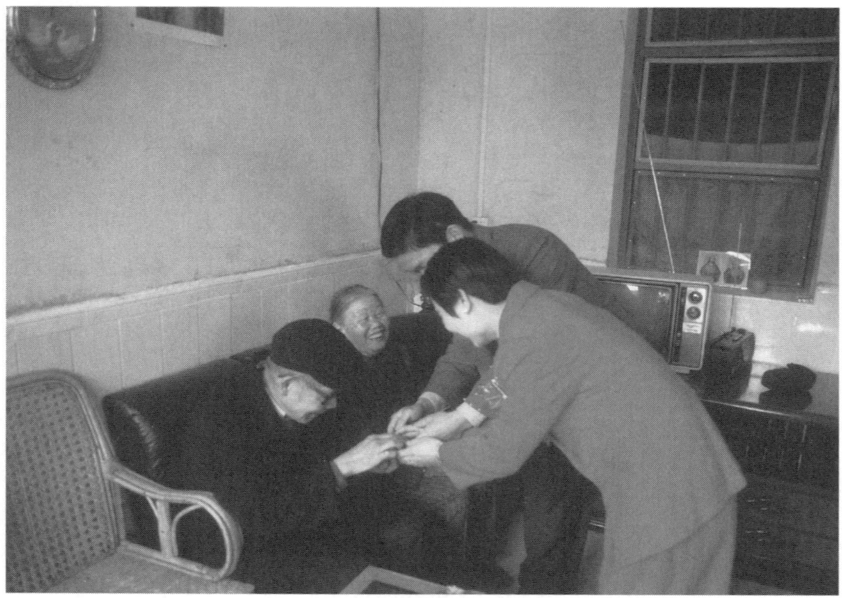

Figure 14   Mr. Lai and Ms. Deng presenting "four-hands" tea to Mr. Lai's grandparents during the lunchtime wedding feast held at the groom's family home.

hong bao.[3] The couple in this manner next served an aunt (though the groom did not hold the teacup, since he was busy again repinning his ribbon), who also gave the bride a *hong bao*. They then repeated this with a younger female aunt of the groom, but she jokingly rejected the tea, objecting that the bride had used the wrong kinship term. Many others would tease her in similar fashion, but this time the bride was in fact wrong—because of their closeness in age she had called the aunt "older sister." To make up for this mistake, the aunt made the groom stand behind the bride and wrap his arms around her to serve the tea, and then she played out the laughs until the bride and groom began to banter back at her. She finally accepted the tea and handed the bride a *hong bao*. This tea-serving ritual was repeated until all the relatives crowded in the bridal bedroom had been served and the couple had a large stack of *hong bao*, which the groom slipped into the drawer of the night table.

At this point, one of the groom's young relatives, the four-year-old grandson of the uncle who had directed the couple when they walked in, was taken

Figure 15   "On the way to a wedding." Written on the back of a photograph by
the Maryknoll priest who took the picture of this Little Rome dowry party in 1933.
Courtesy of Maryknoll Missioners.

into the bridal bedroom to sit on the bed. This tradition, as it was explained
to me, was to wish the couple luck in bearing a son. Then someone told the
couple that the groom's grandfather did not have any tea. One of his cousins
fetched the grandmother, and the groom went to find his bride so they could
serve tea to the couple together. After a delay, while the bride made more tea
in a different tea service, the bride and groom served tea to the grandparents.
As more guests arrived, they continued to serve them, at which point they
made me sit and accept tea.

Meanwhile, other Lai relatives (both men and women) were in the
kitchen and back courtyard preparing the lunch feast. The head cook, another
uncle of the groom, was often called upon by relatives to supervise preparations, since he was a cook in an elegant restaurant (*jiulou*) and was preparing to open his own small restaurant (*fandian*) on the main highway. More
guests continued to arrive, and the couple sat in the living room to greet
them as they came in. A large party then arrived, the female relatives of the
bride; the only male relatives with them were a few children no older than
eight. They were served tea not by the couple but by the young aunt of the
groom.

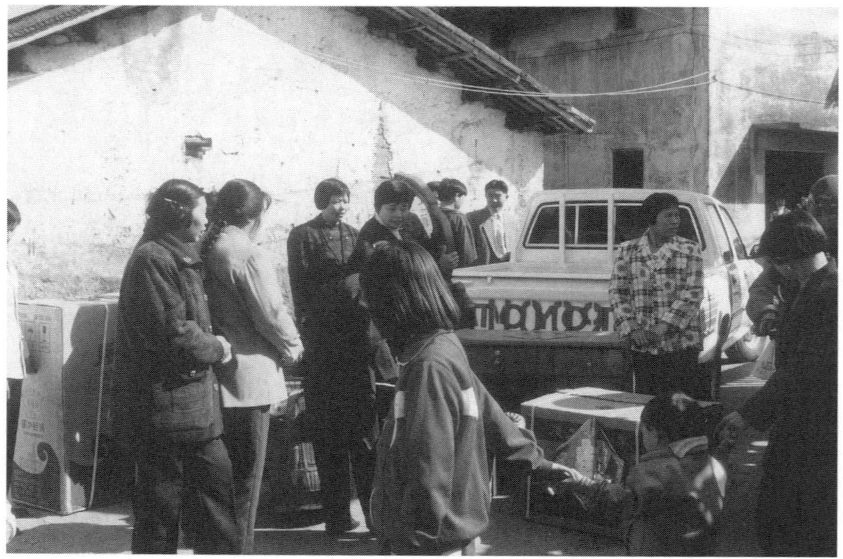

Figure 16   Dowry being unloaded from a pickup truck by Ms. Deng's natal family and friends during the wedding feast held at Mr. Lai's home in Little Rome.

At this point, the couple prepared for the arrival of the remainder of the dowry. The first item to arrive was a new motorscooter (125 cc), the preferred mode of transportation for the young well-to-do (especially women) in the Meizhou area. A group of male cousins and aunts of the groom, and the whole party of the bride's relatives, went with the groom to meet the pick-up truck carrying the remainder of the dowry. The back of the truck was filled with goods, including a washing machine (the box was decorated with the "double happiness" character), television, microwave oven, furniture, suitcases, area rugs, kitchen utensils, and assorted other items (shampoo, brushes, etc.). Since the truck was parked in front of the church, the dowry was on full display for everyone in the village to see, and people commented on its lavishness. Some of the female relatives, especially the bride's mother, made a point of arranging items so that they could be seen by villagers as she carried two ceremonial baskets filled with dowry items to the house. Neighbors later told me that the dowry was substantial because the bride's family was well-off; they had a retail business in the county seat.

The bridal bedroom was then crammed with as many items as could fit inside. Outside the dresser were stacks of linens and clothing. Two chickens, one cock and one hen, were in a bamboo cage next to the dresser—people told me that they represented the bride and groom, symbolizing the wish that they would multiply like chickens. Other items, like the large washing machine and television, were placed in another bedroom. More guests continued to arrive, and people gathered in groups throughout the house while they waited for lunch.

Around 11:30, the banquet started. Nine round banquet tables were set up throughout the house and in the house of neighboring relatives.Many of the younger guests could not be seated (including me), and two tables of ten were set up after everyone else had eaten—one table for the groom and the other young adults, and one table for the relatives who had served as cooks and helpers. The bride sat at a table with her relatives, and other guests were grouped together largely by family or friendship. There were two tables of neighbors; each neighbor family sent one representative to serve as "designated eater." The banquet food consisted of typical Hakka dishes that Mr. Lai (the cook) had also prepared for his older brother's housewarming party. The dishes included *meicai kourou* (braised pork with preserved vegetables), one of three dishes known throughout China as a Hakka dish; *gulu paigu* (sweet and sour pork ribs), an experiment of Mr. Lai's combining Western and Chinese ingredients; and *rou yuan*, a type of beef and pork ball that is widespread in Hakka regions. After the guests started eating, the bride and groom together served drinks—strong *bai jiu* (a rice whiskey), *niang jiu* (a mild homemade Hakka rice wine), and Pepsi—to each table of guests. The groom introduced the bride to neighbors and relatives, and the bride repeated the kin terms as she poured the drink. They made a toast with the entire table and then moved on until all the tables had been visited.

After the meal and some tea, some guests (mostly neighbors and more distant relatives) drifted back home, while others gathered in the various rooms of the house to chat. Around 2:30, the representatives of the bride's family brought out a suitcase that was part of the dowry and placed it on a table in the doorway of the house. A little boy from the bride's family ceremonially gave the key to the suitcase to the groom's grandmother, who handed him a *hong bao*. Guests gathered around to watch the grandmother struggle to open the suitcase; after she opened it she announced everything that was inside (mostly clothing), and then sprinkled about 1,000 RMB inside the suitcase. The groom's uncle then closed the suitcase and continued to direct the activities, distributing a stack of *hong baos* to the relatives, friends and neighbors who had helped with the wedding feast. The groom picked up the suitcase and put it back in the bridal bedroom, and then the bride's natal party prepared to leave. The groom's family had also prepared two baskets of gifts for the bride's family. The baskets were filled with linens, cookies, fruits, candies, and other gifts, but most important were what people referred to as the symbolic gifts (*youyiyi*): small amounts of rice, nuts, and pork. Such gifts, I was told, symbolized the union of the two families, as stated more explicitly in the banner (*duilian*) atop the home's main entrance. The mother of the bride carried these two baskets (and one of the chickens) on a shouldered pole to the vehicle that was driving them back home. After they left, the remaining guests scattered to different homes for a nap, and the bride and groom returned to the bridal bedroom. In the bridal bedroom, I accidentally walked in on the bride as she was crying, though she stopped the minute she saw me. Although she had not cried as she left her natal home, her emotions overcame her at a more private moment.

GETTING MARRIED IN THE RESTAURANT

After a few hours of rest in the late afternoon, the bridal party made its way up to a restaurant (*jiulou*) in Jiaoling City. A placard announcing the Lai-Deng wedding banquet was in place at the lobby of the restaurant, but the group went upstairs to the banquet room to make sure everything else was prepared. Nine tables, each seating eight, had been meticulously set with two different bottles of liquor, two bottles of soda, two packs of cigarettes, and two packages of tissues (cloth napkins had been placed in the glasses). About thirty minutes before the guests were supposed to arrive, the bride and groom, the two bridesmaids, and the best man went downstairs to greet the arriving guests, while others who had come with the bridal party went into a separate room to drink tea and chat.

The parking lot in front of the restaurant gradually filled with motor-cycles as the wedding guests started to arrive. For about forty-five minutes, the bride and groom and their attendants stood outside, greeting each guest individually. As the guests shook hands with the groom or the bride, they surreptitiously slipped a *hong bao* into his or her hands; all the *hong baos* ended up in the groom's large pockets, because the bride had nowhere to put them. As each male guest came in, the best man offered him a cigarette and lit it for him if he accepted. The guests then went upstairs and were served tea by the waitresses. After nearly all the guests had arrived, everyone slowly filtered into the banquet hall. Seats were not assigned, although one table in the front of the room was reserved for the bride and groom. Guests sat with friends, and some tables ended up all male or all female. The guests were mostly young people who were classmates and neighborhood friends of

Figure 17   Mr. Lai and Ms. Deng's evening wedding banquet at a restaurant in the nearby county seat.

the couple. Older guests were former teachers and colleagues of both families. Almost none of the guests, except for one table of young Lai relatives, had attended either the church ceremony the previous Saturday or the noontime wedding banquet.

In one corner of the large room, a television played musical selections from video discs; although the area was set up for karaoke, early in the banquet no one picked up the microphone to sing. As dishes came in wave after wave, the atmosphere filled with the boisterous calls of young men drinking liquor and the equally loud conversations of young women, some also drinking liquor but most drinking less potent wine or sodas. The evening became more raucous as the bride and groom left their table to make toasts with each table of guests. Accompanied by one of the bridesmaids and the best man, both armed with liquor for the bride and groom to make toasts, the couple visited each table and made jokes with the guests as the guests toasted them, wishing them future happiness.

As the liquor bottles gradually emptied (and at some more rowdy tables had to be resupplied), it became harder and harder for the bride and groom to make it through the toasts. Guests began demanding that the bride and groom do something or drink more before raising their glasses for a quick bottoms up. At one table, one of the men put a piece of meat on a toothpick and held it between the couple, who had to eat it. He slipped it away a few times so that the couple ended up in a kiss, before the table finally made the toast and let them move on. At another table, they were forced into contortions in order to drink out of each other's glasses. At yet another table, the groom was forced to carry the bride on his back around the table before the toast. The fun even extended to the best man and the bridesmaid, who were forced to substitute for the bride and groom and drink a toast with the table. A veteran of these wedding banquets, I sniffed the bottle from which the bridesmaid was serving the bride and groom and detected that the liquor they were drinking was watered down. Seeing me, the groom grabbed my arm and told me to keep it quiet, or else the night would be even harder for him and his bride than it already was.[4]

As guests reached their limit of food and spirits, tables slowly emptied into smaller side rooms equipped with karaoke equipment. In these smaller groups, people started to sing. After tea had been served and cigarettes passed around, guests gradually started to leave. By the time I left, some diehards were still singing, but the parking lot had emptied of many motorcycles.

Six Rites, White Dresses, and Restaurant Banquets

The wedding rituals of Lai Wuyan and Deng Huilan did not resemble the traditional "six rites" (*liu li*) I had read about in idealized descriptions of Hakka weddings. As described by the 1994 Jiaoling County gazetteer, the six rites are: engagement (*ding qin*), receiving the betrothal gifts (silk) (*na cai*), welcoming the bride (*ying qin*), worshipping the ancestors (*bai tang*), clowning around the nuptial suite (*nao dongfang*), and the third-day visit (*zuo sanchao*). Other writers have different categories, though all include some combination of ritual practices that fit into six categories.[5] Also, analyses of Hakka marriages almost universally begin with the traditional adage that marriage is based on the "commands of the parents and the arrangements of the matchmaker" (*funu zhi ming, meishuo zhi yan*) (see Liu 1995; Huang, Huang, and Zou 1993; *Jiaoling xianzhi* 1992).

According to these idealized descriptions of traditional Hakka weddings, the marriage ritual begins with the practices leading up to the engagement (Zhang Quanqing 1997; Xue 1997; Lin 1996). One family engages a match-maker (*meiren*) to find a suitable spouse for its son or daughter. After an appropriate mate has been identified, the families of the prospective bride and groom begin negotiations. First the groom's family gives a gift to the bride's family.[6] The completion of negotiations is marked by the bride's family's acceptance of betrothal gifts from the groom's, and may include a din-ner party. The descriptions do not specify when the brideprice (*shenjiayin*) is transferred to the bride's family, but it takes place sometime before the trans-fer of the bride. Finally, the bride is transferred from her natal home to her new home in a bridal sedan chair (*jiao*); tradition calls for the bride to wear a red dress (*qipao*) and to cry when she leaves her natal home (*ku jia*). The dowry (*jiazhuang*) accompanies the bride to her new home. Wedding ban-quets held at restaurants are not mentioned specifically, although the ban-quet held at the groom's home is highlighted in many accounts.

The Hakka weddings, both Catholic and non-Catholic, that I observed in the 1990s did not resemble the idealized tradition of the six rites. Although this discrepancy can be explained in part by my reliance on anthropological methodology rather than text-based analysis, a stronger case can be made for an emerging Chinese modernity. The only structural difference between the Lai-Deng wedding and other non-Catholic Hakka weddings that I observed was the inclusion of a church wedding. The "feasting-twice" phenomenon was common in the 1990s, limited only by the financial resources of the fam-ilies. Traces of the six rites were present in the Lai-Deng wedding and at other weddings that I attended; but in the late 1990s, the importance of the six rites as part of the marriage ritual process had become less pronounced. The new style of marriage practice—*xin hunyin xisu*, a phrase from the county gazetteer that distinguishes current practices from the old-style six-ritual weddings—has resulted from changes in the social and economic con-texts of young couples in rural Guangdong. Yan (1996) describes a similar phenomenon in rural northern China, where because of shifts in the eco-nomic environment the exchange of brideprice, dowry, and other marriage gifts must now be seen as a direct endowment of the young couple by the older generations rather than as an exchange between affines. Huilan and Wuyan's wedding was a "*negotiated* outcome," a negotiation between the couple and their families, between generations, and between a mythical tra-dition and an imagined modernity (see Argyrou 1996: 80). In Little Rome, the evolving postsocialist Chinese state also has a role in this negotiation process.[7]

Lai and Deng met on their own in Shenzhen while away from their families, without the intervention of a matchmaker. Many other young couples meet while working in Shenzhen or Guangzhou, resulting in a wider geographic separation of in-law families. For example, my neighbor Mrs. Deng spends most of her time in Hainan province taking care of her daughter's young son. Her second daughter met her husband while working in Guangzhou (his hometown), and they now live in their own home in Hainan, where his work took him.

The majority of recently married young adults also found their spouses on their own. In two marriages I attended, the bride and groom were teachers in the same school and met as colleagues. Another couple met as university students and now teach in the same university. As mentioned earlier, Chris Deng's girlfriend, Tina, had been the girl next door—until her family emigrated to Germany, greatly complicating their future plans. Some couples still meet through introductions. Tina's older brother came home from Germany and was formally introduced to his girlfriend by a family friend interested in helping him find a spouse. Some young people, when they start thinking about getting married, ask someone to intercede for them. In any case, when the marriage ceremonies take place, an older woman is found to act as the matchmaker, as in the Lai-Deng case described above.

In China, marriage has become a key arena for cultural contestations between tradition and modernity. Young American couples may find getting married stressful because of the involvement of family members, but Chinese couples also have to contend with a state that wants to be involved. In rural Jiaoling county, the Chinese state has organized grassroots "New-Style Marriage Councils" (*hunyin xinfeng lishihui*) that spread the word about the 1980 Marriage Law and promote "civilized" (*wenming*) marriage practices that do not involve impoverishing gift exchanges and excessive consumption.[8] Through the marriage laws, the Chinese state has sought to eradicate the power of the "feudal family" by raising the minimum age required to marry, expanding the rights of both women and men to select their own spouses, and reducing extravagant gift exchanges. The state's issuing of a marriage license, which legitimizes whatever type of wedding ritual couples and their families practice, is the culmination of the state's involvement in marriage.[9]

The limited success of such legislation, at least in rural Jiaoling county, can be seen by the repeated efforts of the county government to promote "civilized" marriage practices. In the late 1990s, brideprice and dowry continued to be exchanged. In fact, as a result of post-Mao prosperity in this northern Guangdong region, gift exchanges have become more and more expensive. Weddings in postsocialist Little Rome have become much more commodified than those held during the socialist period. For example, a woman who was married in the midst of the Cultural Revolution in the early 1970s told me that her brideprice was 39.9 RMB.[10] A woman who was married in the mid-1980s told me that her brideprice was 999 RMB, and the acceptable amount in 1997 was 9,999 RMB (US$1,200). Dowries, similarly, reflect changes in consumption practices. Huilan's dowry was substantial; the motorscooter alone, with insurance and taxes, would have cost around 6,000 RMB. One woman in her thirties told me that when she was married in the 1980s a bicycle was appropriate for a good dowry, and that dowries have changed a lot since then. Considering the average income of farmers, large dowries pose a real expense that can only be afforded through nonagricultural income. As a result, most unmarried young adults seek employment in Shenzhen, Zhuhai, or Guangzhou, where wages are significantly higher. When Wuyan started working in Shenzhen in 1992, he earned 600 RMB a month. Wuyan's grandfather-in-law estimates that between getting married and building a new home Wuyan spent close to 50,000 RMB—both the wedding and the new house were vivid demonstrations of his success and ambition in Shenzhen.

In her discussion of Hui wedding consumption patterns in northern Xi'an, Gillette (1997) says that increased displays of consumption at marriage rituals are demonstrations of the economic empowerment of young adults, especially women, at the cost of the state's loss of control over the distribution of consumer goods. These changes, as manifested by the wearing of white wedding dresses (at least for the formal pictures), demonstrate a cosmopolitan outlook, and marriage ritual becomes a means of constructing a globally oriented identity. The shift of wedding banquets from homes to commercial restaurants also reflects this cosmopolitan identity, where demonstrations of social status are even more commercialized than is reflected by dowry items. The commercialization of the wedding banquet, which has become the central event in marriage ritual in Jiaoling county, definitively marks Lai and Deng's arrival on the world scene. In fact, all Chinese ritual events have become highly commodified through the increased consumption of goods purchased in the market.

However, these changes have not obliterated tradition. Tradition was echoed in the Lai-Deng wedding, but it was transformed to fit those contemporary young adults' social context. For example, although no matchmaker was involved in the search for a spouse, someone was selected to fill the ritual role of *meiren* for the transfer of the bride to her new home. Instead of a bridal sedan chairs an automobile carried the bride to ritual events. Huilan wore a white dress for the church ceremony and for pictures, but on the day of the wedding banquets she donned the traditional red, albeit a Western-style suit rather than a *qipao*. Young adults did not invade the groom's home and crowd around the nuptial chamber for the traditional harassment, but the newlyweds were made to endure a new type of loving harassment as they toasted with each table in the wedding hall. According to the state, the six rituals have been greatly simplified to reflect China's social development. According to the young adult participants, however, the six rituals have been modernized, to reflect their globally oriented outlook.

Making Memories, Joining Communities, and Establishing Networks

Like the Lai-Deng parties discussed above, weddings are memorable events; they are the quintessential Kodak moment. Photography studios throughout the nearby county seat specifically target newlyweds for their business. White wedding dresses and tuxedos for the nuptial photo session can also be rented from these establishments. During my fieldwork, neighbors knew me as the photographer/videographer, and friends of friends often sought me out to take pictures. Gillette (1997) documents these newlywed visits to the photography studio as the appropriate moment to wear Western-style white wedding dresses (pink and red are more suitable for the actual wedding banquets, because of the association of white with death in China). Yan (1996) notes that the photo session before the wedding sometimes requires a trip to the city and is the first chance some young couples in Heilongjiang have to spend the night together. Even at the height of the Maoist period, couples took pictures. Older neighbors who were married during the Maoist period often showed me pictures of their weddings; they also provided a sermon on how expensive and tough things were back then. They say couples today live the good life, going to restaurants for their wedding banquets. Mr. Deng, my next-door neighbor, told me that despite the severe shortages in foodstuffs, when he and his wife got married in the late 1960s they at least had a chicken for their wedding feast, which was held at his house. He continued, however, that everything has changed with their growing prosperity in the post-socialist period.

The marriage ritual is an important rite of passage in the lives of young adults everywhere in that it transforms their social status—the way that people classify them.[11] In other words, weddings both do something and say something, in a more efficacious way than normal social intercourse through their use of multiple sensory media and the heightened awareness of their participants (despite the participants' ingestion of copious amounts of alcohol). Father Liang, Lai Wuyan, Deng Huilan, and everyone else who attended the church wedding and two wedding banquets used their own cultural experience to generate symbols and movements that are understood (with subjective nuances) by the participants (see Barth 1987). In having a church wedding, a wedding banquet at home, and a wedding banquet in the restaurant, Wuyan, Huilan, and the Lai family held an event that people would remember.

Wuyan and Huilan were not making memories for themselves alone, but also for the community and their networks of kin and friends. These memories are the building blocks that make up the history of Little Rome. Ritual events are especially charged events in social memory (see Jing 1996). Events such as the marriage of Wuyan and Huilan, especially for the Lai family and their friends and neighbors who participated in the wedding banquet at home, become a boundary-making mechanism and a time-marker in the shared experiences of members of the Little Rome community. Gifts given to the new couple by friends and neighbors are part of the larger gift exchange taking place within Little Rome, forging and renewing relations between community members (Kipnis 1997). For those in the wider Little Rome community, the Lai-Deng marriage is still significant in social memory. Through their participation in the church wedding, they acknowledged the addition of a new member, the in-marrying Ms. Deng, to the Little Rome community. Everyday conversations in Little Rome now include the new couple and gossip about their life in Shenzhen.

Examining ritual through the perspective of social memory adds historical depth to the relationship between ritual and society. Other models of ritual and its functionalist role in society, such as Turner's (1967, 1974, 1977) model of *communitas* and ritual as social drama, lack this temporal dimension in delineating how ritual is important in the making and reinforcing of community. The events that constituted the Lai-Deng wedding could be retold in terms of *communitas*, to argue that such symbols as the wedding rings or exchange of gifts between families renew social ties, or that an outsider, through the liminality of being a bride, becomes an insider of the Little Rome community. This type of analysis, however, is static, losing the critical dimensions of time and social change—for what was highlighted in much of the performance of this marriage ritual, such as the restaurant banquet, was the success of Wuyan and Huilan themselves in postsocialist modern China. What is lost in this model of *communitas* is the processual, history-making aspect of both the marriage ritual and community life itself.

The wedding of Wuyan and Huilan in Little Rome in the late 1990s was very different from their parents' and grandparents' weddings. Two or three generations earlier, little daughter-in-law marriages (*tong yang xi*) were prevalent. In nearby Shangnan village, approximately 75 percent of marriages made before 1949 were little daughter-in-law marriages, so called because the bride was transferred to her future husband's home as a child (Lin 1996). Catholics also practiced little daughter-in-law marriage, and the marriages of many of the older couples in Little Rome were arranged in this manner. Uxorilocal marriage, a form of marriage in which the groom moves into his bride's household (*zhao xu* or *zhao lang*), which continues to the present, is also not what it used to be. Because of the cultural need for male heirs in traditional Chinese patrilineages, a married couple who had produced only daughters was forced into the undesirable position of having to bring a man—one of their daughters' husbands—into the family. The children from a uxorilocal marriage often took their mother's family surname, and some husbands even changed their own surname. Men in uxorilocal marriages were often poorly treated by members of their wives' lineage and denied legal rights of inheritance or involvement in family decisions. The Jiaoling County Gazetteer proudly announces that "uxorilocally married husbands now have a legal position. Uxorilocal marriage is gradually transforming the social traditions (*yi feng yi su*) of marriage patterns" (*Jiaoling xianzhi* 1992: 667). According to the law, at least, men in uxorilocal marriages are no longer marginal.

Community life has also changed greatly over three generations. Before 1949, American Maryknoll missionaries were important in all facets of community life (see Wiest 1988), and Little Rome villagers worked and studied all over the world, maintaining extensive transnational networks. These circumstances changed dramatically during the Maoist period, but with the Deng era reforms, transnational connections have again become important. Young adults like Wuyan and Huilan are again venturing out of the village, transforming Little Rome community life.

As a corrective to Turner's model, others have included the temporal dimension by adding historical analysis to ritual.[12] More than just a way of expressing contemporary political and socioeconomic contexts, ritual can be used to create new social situations. Ritual is itself a culmination of historical experiences informed by narrative strands and cultural influences. Myerhoff explains, for example, that the combination of traditional Jewish and secular American practices to create a new ritual, the Graduation Siyum, shows how rituals "allow people to maneuver, fight on their own terms, choose the times, places, conditions, and shape of their claims" (1978: 107). Instead of ritual demonstrating history, or ritual as a product of history, ritual makes history through its shaping of social memory (Jing 1996). This is the perspective from which I examine the importance of ritual in Little Rome's community life.

In the Little Rome community, a church wedding is a key boundary maintenance mechanism (à la Barth) that demonstrates membership in the community. First, a church wedding is a public display of being a Catholic (*jiaoyou*), which in recent history has been risky. Lai's grandfather (on his mother's side) told me that Lai's decision to be baptized was a prominent achievement (*tuchu*) because he was the first national cadre (*guojia ganbu*) to do so in Little Rome since the reopening of the church in 1983. Deng's baptism, as mentioned earlier, was both expected and less risky: women have formed the backbone of Catholic activities since the post-Mao era because, unlike men, they fear God more than they do political reprisal.

There was much disappointment associated with another marriage that took place a month earlier. The daughter of a prominent Catholic family, herself a practicing Catholic and described by villagers as especially obedient (*ting hua*), decided not to have a church wedding. She was a teacher in a high school and felt that her colleagues would deem it inappropriate for her, as an example for her students, to show her Catholicism too strongly. Most important, her husband was not Catholic, so as a marrying-out daughter of Little Rome there was less pressure from the community for a Catholic wedding. A male colleague of hers, from Little Rome, also told me that although he is Catholic, he does not regularly attend mass. His wife and mother, however, are most devout and rarely miss a daily mass. In this context, by having a church wedding the Lai-Deng couple clearly placed themselves in the Little Rome community, while those who get married outside the church mark themselves as outsiders.

In 1995 thirteen older couples in Little Rome who for "historical reasons" (*lishi yuanyin*) had not had church weddings, organized a group church wedding. According to villagers, the community turned out in strong numbers to witness this mass. These couples, some of whom had been married as long as thirty or forty years, rented a bus to take friends and neighbors to the county seat for a restaurant wedding banquet.

The importance of the home wedding banquet for affirming kin ties has long been stressed by the anthropological literature on Chinese weddings. However, the restaurant wedding banquet is a relatively new phenomenon in mainland China, resulting from the prosperity of post-Mao China. Whereas the church wedding was a community event, and the home banquet a kin-and-neighbor event, the restaurant wedding banquet was largely a recognition of the couple's network of friends. As it was explained to me, these are opportunities for friends to get together and have fun, stressing the *ganqing* (human feelings) that Kipnis (1997) and Yan (1996) have discussed in detail. Though other analysts view such banquets as instrumental to the goal of developing *guanxi* networks, in at least the Lai-Deng case this perspective is less illuminating. In fact, the participants themselves downplayed the *guanxi* aspect of the event, perhaps because their work in Shenzhen makes their hometown networks less instrumental than they otherwise might be. Whereas the home wedding banquet celebrated the wedding as a family event, a celebration of the patriline, the restaurant wedding banquet is a celebration of the couple's rite of passage in their broader social contexts. Restaurant wedding banquets are more costly than home banquets and are vivid demonstrations of the economic power of young adults in China today. These banquets are attended mostly by other young adults, and the atmosphere is festive and decidedly modern.

Long-Distance Relationships

After the wedding, Wuyan and Huilan stayed in Little Rome for the Spring Festival festivities. They returned to Shenzhen, traveling with the rest of China's citizens who had to report back to work after the Spring Festival holiday. Huilan opened up a small store, and we heard in the village that their married life was good. Almost a year later, Wuyan returned to Little Rome for All Souls' Day (November 2, the day that Little Rome villagers "sweep the graves" [*sao mu*], a Catholic version of *qingming*), and he told me that Huilan had found it too much trouble to keep up a store and had returned to Jiaoling to work at her parents' store. When I asked him if living apart made married life difficult, he replied: "Well, it's pretty common now; even you and your wife have to do it." He was right, pointing out that long-distance relationships are common for young adult couples throughout the world—

the price of modern love. At that moment, his uncle came by to talk to him about a project for which they wanted to raise money, restoring the old Lai home. Now that Lai was married and a success, as was demonstrated by the extravagance of his wedding, he had to continue making such discursive demonstrations of modernity by participating in local philanthropy.

Catholic Ancestors

Funerals are highly charged emotional events, and because of their affective power they are key events in the creation of a shared local history for kin and neighbors. Coupled with ancestor veneration (perhaps one of the defining characteristics of Chinese culture; see Hsu 1971), funerary ritual defines the sense of community for both Catholic and non-Catholic Hakka villagers. For the people of Little Rome, funeral ritual and ancestor remembrance highlight the distinctions between Catholics and non-Catholics. Funeral ritual also reinforces intercommunity relations, as people mobilize to participate in funerary activities. To understand its role in their lives, however, funeral ritual must be contextualized in the larger ritual process through which villagers delineate who they are through the legacy of their Catholic ancestors.

Burying a Husband and a Father in Little Rome

As my family and I were sitting down to eat dinner one evening a week before Spring Festival, we heard a loud crash and screaming next door. At first I thought it was a family squabble, but after dinner I discovered that Mr. Ye had fallen down and hit his head on the stone floor. He had sustained severe head injuries and after being examined in the hospital was sent home to his family to die. Mr. Ye had received last rites from Father Liang at the hospital, but he never regained consciousness to make final confession and receive communion. He passed away the day after the accident.

Mr. Ye was one of the first villagers I met in Little Rome in the summer of 1993. Mr. Peng, a retired teacher active in the Little Rome Parish Council and whose house I later rented, had taken me to meet his friends and neighbors, one of whom was Mr. Ye. When I moved into the village with my family in October 1996, the Ye family members were especially hospitable; they taught us about village life, let us use their well when the running water was not working in our house (which the first month was the rule rather than the exception), and gave us vegetables from their garden. Just before his death, Mr. Ye had shown my wife and me how to make *lap nyuk* (H.) (the Hakka term for *la rou* in Mandarin), dried pork similar in flavor to American bacon. Mr. Ye had also lent me a videotape of his father's funeral in 1995 and talked with me extensively about burying his own father. He knew that I was interested in funeral ritual, as did nearly everyone in Little Rome, because during my preliminary fieldwork visits I had participated in many funerals, videotaping and taking pictures. Because Mr. Ye was a recovering alcoholic and in rather poor health, Mrs. Ye was more active in overseeing the family's farming duties and providing for the well-being of Mr. Ye's mother, who also lived with them. Their two daughters and one son had all left Little Rome to work in Shenzhen, but their son, Changyuan, often returned home when his duties as a driver were light. Changyuan happened to be home when his father passed away. The week before the accident, Changyuan had sat next to me at the evening Lai-Deng wedding banquet described in the previous chapter.

After the hospital released him, Mr. Ye was placed in his bed on the first floor. Dr. Wang, the village doctor, set up an IV unit and an oxygen bag to help sustain Mr. Ye until his untreatable head injury caused the inevitable death. During the morning, the Little Rome villagers who often serve as funeral workers waited by the house until their services were needed. The two Ye daughters living in Shenzhen had been notified when the accident took place the night before and arrived in Little Rome that afternoon. The house was filled with friends and neighbors who came by to console Mrs. Ye, who, hardhit by her husband's condition, remained bedridden for the next few days. Except at the Ye house, daily life went on as usual around the village. At the Ye house, everyone just waited around; the children and the doctor frequently sat in Mr. Ye's room to keep him company and make him more comfortable. That evening, after turning in around 10:00 P.M., we heard the deafening sounds of firecrackers next door and knew that Mr. Ye had passed away. A little later that night, when I walked over to the Ye house, Mr. Cao, the principal funeral specialist in Little Rome, was beating a large gong, and women were wailing loudly (Johnson 1988).[1] The funeral workers who had waited outside the house all day quickly went to work setting up the body in the living room, which was converted into a mourning hall (*sang tang*). The two daughters and the son sat in front of Mr. Ye's body as relatives and neighbors dropped by to express their condolences. Later that night, Changyuan left the living room to talk with one of his uncles and a neighbor about the funeral arrangements. Female relatives and neighbors went upstairs to console Mrs. Ye.

At 6:45 the following morning, a roll of firecrackers thundered next door, accompanied by the steady banging of gongs. The sounds of women's laments could be heard through the noise of the instruments. The body, dressed in a new suit that had been prepared the night before, lay to one side of the mourning hall. The women were gathered in front of the body, while others, mostly men, worked around them preparing for the funeral. People went into the house with large pressure cookers and woks to prepare meals for the steadily arriving mourners and workers. Others set up tables to make cloth banners (*cek bu* [H.]) and calligraphy signs. The master of ceremonies (*lishi* [M.]) set up a table to keep track of donations, adding names and donation amounts to a large red piece of paper posted by the main door. Mr. Lai, a catechist from the church, decorated the mourning hall with Catholic items from the church, including some large candles and a purple banner with a large white cross. Other neighborhood women worked outside, cleaning the yard and chicken coop so that food preparation could be done in the barn across from the house. Another Mr. Lai (the head cook for the wedding described in the previous chapter) took charge of the food preparation. These activities all took place before 9:00 A.M., when a prayer group of Catholic neighbors came to the house.

When the prayer group arrived, firecrackers were lit and the funeral specialist, Mr. Cao, repeatedly banged the gong to announce their arrival. The mourners, who had been wailing as the prayer group entered the mourning hall, quickly became silent. There were about twenty people in the prayer group, mostly older women as well as a few older men and young mothers. The other catechist, Mr. Wang, led the prayer group through the chanting of prayers. The prayer session consisted of twelve prayers, one gospel reading, and two songs from a shared prayer book, as selected by Mr. Wang. All of the prayers were petitions to Jesus Christ, the Virgin Mary, and the saints for their intercession in the forgiveness of the sins of the deceased. Most of the older members of the prayer group knew the prayers by heart; others, especially the younger members, chanted from a book. The group leader started each prayer by chanting the first line, and then the group joined in; sometimes they alternated chanting the lines throughout the prayer. Although the leader could choose from any of the funeral prayers in the shared prayer book, each session included the Lord's Prayer. In the middle of each Lord's Prayer, one group member took out a small bottle of holy water, bowed toward the cross, and then sprinkled some holy water three times on the body. When the prayers were completed, the group members returned home, though some of the older women went upstairs to console Mrs. Ye.

After the prayer group left, arrangements continued again in earnest.

Figure 18   A Catholic lay leader sprinkles holy water during the chanting of the "Our Father" at a prayer group visitation before burial.

More cloth banners were pieced together, and some men brought over bamboo rods to serve as banner holders. More relatives and neighbors came over to pay their respects, adding their names to the donation board. As more immediate relatives arrived (e.g., siblings of the deceased), they were greeted by the banging of the large gong and firecrackers. As noon approached, helpers began setting up tables for the lunch banquet. People seated themselves in groups of relatives and friends; just one representative from each surrounding house attended. After the meal, helpers cleaned up the eating areas and returned to preparing food for later meals. Neighbors continued to help the Ye family by tending the livestock and doing other errands. Throughout the day, Mr. Ye's three children and a changing contingent of female relatives of all ages sat in front of the body crying and wailing.

Around 6:00 P.M., the Ye's again hosted a meal for relatives, friends of the family, and other neighbors. After dinner, the immediate family (except Mrs. Ye, who was still bedridden with grief) and the visiting relatives all went to the church for evening mass, held that night in memory of Mr. Ye. With the addition of the Ye relatives and friends, the number attending was a bit higher than for a daily evening mass. After mass, another prayer group left

Figure 19   Catholic prayer group, made up of Catholic volunteers, leaving the home of the deceased.

directly from the church for the Ye house. This group of around forty people was again led by the catechist, Mr. Wang. After the prayer session, the mourners remained gathered in the mourning hall around the body, and neighbors gradually went home.

On the second morning after Mr. Ye passed away, the music and fire-crackers again sounded at 6:30 A.M. Neighbors drifted around the Ye house, while all of the mourners sat in front of the body in the mourning hall. The walls of the mourning hall were covered with banners that had been made the day before. These banners were made by the affinal relatives of the deceased, who are called the "six relations" (*liu qin*).[2] By 8:00 A.M., the Ye house was crowded with relatives, friends, and helpers. The husband of the second Ye daughter (the first-born daughter was single) had arrived from Shenzhen early in the morning; his donation to the Ye family, as posted by the door, was by far the largest, 500 RMB. The master of ceremonies took out a tray stacked with white mourning clothes and placed it next to Mr. Ye's picture, which sat on a table in the center of the mourning hall. The son of the deceased then picked up the tray of mourning clothes, bowed in front of one of his paternal uncles, and handed him the tray. The uncle placed the tray back on the table, and the master of ceremonies began calling out names of families to take their mourning clothes. The mourning clothes were white robes that people wore on top of their regular clothing, tied with a string around the waist; men's and women's mourning clothes were identical. Once all the mourning clothes had been distributed, the funeral workers prepared to transfer the body to the coffin, which had been placed inside the mourning hall. The production team leader had sent children, who were on school holiday for Spring Festival, to carry the funeral banners, and helpers took the banners off the walls outside to distribute them to the children. Not all the children were from the same production team; several neighbors sent their children to help, and my son also carried one.

While the funeral workers prepared to transfer the body to the coffin, the cries of the mourners picked up in tempo and volume. They reached their peak when the funeral workers prepared to shut the lid. Friends and relatives had to hold back several mourners who lunged toward the coffin. Once the lid was nailed to the coffin, the funeral workers tied the coffin to poles, which they shouldered, and the musicians prepared to lead the procession to the church. Firecrackers were set off as the procession started toward the church. Women helpers, carrying the sawhorses that supported the coffin, water, and baskets of fruits, led the procession, followed by two men who set off large firecrackers along the route. The musicians trailed the firecracker lighters, followed by the children carrying the funeral banners; the coffin carried by the funeral workers; the principal mourner, Changyuan, carrying his father's picture; his sisters and grandmother; other relatives; and then friends and neighbors. This order of procession was the same at all the funerals, Catholic and non-Catholic, that I observed in the Hakka homeland. The procession went through the center of the village and then directly into the church, where other villagers were gathered for the funeral service.

The coffin was placed near the front of the church in an area before the altar that had been cleared of pews. Father Liang came out in black vestments, robes that he wore only for funerals; a church elder placed a tall crucifix at the foot of the coffin. Father Liang then conducted the funeral service; like other Catholic funeral services throughout the world, it did not include a Liturgy of the Eucharist. This ritual distinction was further underscored by his conducting of the service in the pew area, away from the altar. After opening prayers, Father Liang read a gospel passage and then delivered a short homily. He spoke briefly about Mr. Ye, but the emphasis was on Catholic beliefs about death and the afterlife, namely that through the intercession of Mary and God's grace deceased Catholics would go to heaven and await the bodily resurrection that resulted from Christ's dying for the sins of the world. During the service, one of Mr. Ye's daughters brought out a stack of black mourning bands (*xiao*) for the villagers to wear on the right arm. As happened in the prayer groups, during the Lord's Prayer an elder stepped forward to sprinkle the coffin with holy water. Father Liang circled the coffin with incense and then led the congregation through a series of prayers. He closed the service, and people then regrouped in the church courtyard.

In the courtyard, relatives, friends, and neighbors gathered for a group picture. This group picture was taken at all the funerals I attended, Catholic and non-Catholic, and villagers always brought them out when I asked about people who had died or about the funeral ritual. After the picture was taken, the procession reassembled to walk to the Catholic cemetery on a mountainside called Holy Mountain (*Sheng Shan*) a little less than three kilometers away. Many of the villagers who had attended the funeral service did not join the procession, but approximately twenty other Catholics (forming a prayer group) did accompany the coffin to the burial site.

The procession followed the road that led to the main highway and then walked along the side of the highway to the turnoff onto a dirt road that led to the Catholic cemetery. The group continued to a clearing where the coffin was set up on a stand. In other funerals that I observed, a Catholic elder (a man with a clear, loud voice) usually thanked the people who had accompanied the procession and then directed three bows toward the deceased. The principal mourners were then instructed to bow toward the people who had accompanied them, and a smaller party of friends, neighbors, and relatives continued to the actual gravesite. At the Ye funeral, however, the elder was not present, and after taking more group pictures, the funeral specialist, Mr. Cao, only had the family bow toward the people who had accompanied them—this sparked some discussion that they should also bow toward the deceased, but by then many people had already dispersed.

The cloth banners were dismantled (the cloth would be carried back to the Ye house), but the paper banners were taken up to the gravesite. In non-Catholic funerals, this part of the ritual is called the "offering on the road" (*bailuji*), but Catholics call it the "midway break" (*zhongjian xiuxi*). At non-Catholic Hakka funerals I observed, only funeral workers and men and women of the immediate family and of generations not older than the deceased continued to the burial site; in Catholic funerals, a much larger party, including representatives of generations older than the deceased, continued to the burial ground for a final prayer session. At Mr. Ye's funeral,

Figure 20   Catholic families pose for this essential picture after the funeral service at the church; neighboring non-Catholic families take the same picture on the way to the burial site.

some non-Catholic relatives from outside the village immediately took off their mourning clothes at this point and headed back home, while other Catholic relatives (Mr. Ye's mother, siblings, and children) and neighbors continued on. This more communal participation among Catholics of Little Rome in the physical burial of the deceased is very different from the burial practices of non-Catholic Hakka, and like the shared burial area of Holy Mountain reflects the wider communal (instead of purely kinship) basis for funerary ritual in Little Rome.

Mr. Ye was buried next to his father, who had died the year before. Holy Mountain is part of a ridgeline that runs north-south, and most graves are oriented along the east-west axis; Catholics strongly assert that they do not invoke geomancy (*fengshui*) in the orientation of the burial site, but nearly all gravesites are oriented along the east-west axis, which is considered in traditional Hakka custom to be a more propitious alignment. The party made a slow climb up to the burial site. At times elderly people and the funeral workers carrying the coffin had great difficulty negotiating the steep slope and winding path through the trees. Upon arriving at the burial site, the coffin was promptly placed in the hole that had been prepared the day before, and the grave was partially filled in to secure the coffin. The female helpers placed candles and a basket of fruit in front of the coffin. At this point, the prayer group recited a final set of prayers; these were identical in format to the prayers previously conducted in the mourning hall. Throughout the prayers, the principal mourners knelt in front of the coffin, and the chief mourner, Changyuan, held his father's picture. After prayers were completed, each member of the prayer group and some mourners picked up a handful of dirt to throw on top of the coffin and then proceeded back down the mountain to go home. The funeral workers finished piling the dirt around the coffin until a mound was built up, the paper banners were placed on top of the mound, and the remaining funeral workers headed down the mountain to return home at around 10:30.

THE FUNERAL BANQUET

The funeral banquet was held around noon, with twelve tables, each seating eight, set up throughout the house. At the Ye house the donation board and other white signs from the funeral had all been taken down and replaced with a big sign in red thanking friends and neighbors for their support on this very sad and difficult occasion. On the ground floor, the funeral specialist, the funeral workers, and the photographer were all seated in one room (Mr. Ye's former bedroom) at two tables. Neighborhood women sat at three tables in the room that had been the mourning hall, and their children sat at one table. In the kitchen, more distant relatives and closer friends (plus myself and my family) occupied two tables. Upstairs, the family and close relatives sat at three tables, with Changyuan and seven of his close friends (all single young men) together at one table.

The atmosphere was more festive than before, although not as boisterous as a wedding banquet. The drinking at this funeral was more subdued than at other funeral banquets, perhaps out of respect for Mr. Ye's alcoholism, according to one neighbor. Even the usually rowdy table of funeral workers and the table of Changyuan's friends were relatively restrained. At this banquet Mrs. Ye emerged from her bedroom for the first time since her husband's accident; she had not attended the funeral service at the church or the burial. She still appeared distraught, and her usual loud and exuberant demeanor was noticeably absent; she barely spoke, and when she did her speech was very stilted.

In the middle of the meal, Changyuan and his two sisters, carrying bottles of wine and soda, went to each table to thank their guests for coming. They began downstairs among the invited neighbors and then made their way upstairs to their relatives and Changyuan's friends. People ate until all the dishes had been presented, and then most of the guests gradually drifted away. Neighbors who had served as helpers in the banquet preparation started cleaning up, and by the time they were finished everyone but some relatives and Changyuan's friends had left.

AFTER THE BURIAL

On the third day after Mr. Ye's burial, I noticed Changyuan hanging a red cloth over the main door to the Ye house; a red cloth was also draped over the door of Mr. Ye's former bedroom. Non-Catholics call the events of the third day after the funeral "circling the grave" (*yuan fen*) or "going up to the grave" (*shang fen*), but the Catholics in the village referred to this as "seeing red" (*kan hong*).[3] After visiting the grave and reciting prayers, Changyuan and the immediate family invited some relatives and friends over for a small banquet. Before sitting down to eat, Changyuan lit firecrackers, and then some twenty-five relatives and friends (including my family) sat down to eat. The meal had a more upbeat tone, signifying the conclusion of mourning. People told me that at this time items that belonged to the deceased are distributed to family members. Relatives and friends also reinforce or cut off relations by attending or avoiding this meal. Those who do not attend are considered "cut off" (*gog dan* [H.], *duanjue guanxi* [M.]), and people exchange small gifts or bring firecrackers to this event.

The Catholics in this village do not practice "veneration on sevens" (*zuo qi*), which entails visits to the graves and offerings on the seventh day after the burial and on different multiples of seven according to the local custom. Instead, a prayer group goes to the grave of a deceased person on the tenth day and the thirtieth day to again recite the prayer sequence described earlier. These visits are conducted early in the morning and are not followed by a banquet or gift exchange. Firecrackers are not set off at the gravesite. On the one-month anniversary of his father's death, Changyuan and his family asked Father Liang to perform the day's mass in Mr. Ye's memory; as in Catholic communities throughout the world, the requesting family usually gives the priest a small donation, or gift; in Little Rome in 1997 the size of the gift was 50 to 100 RMB for a memorial mass.

SECONDARY BURIAL

Like their non-Catholic neighbors, the people of Little Rome practice secondary burial (*er ci zang*, literally "second-time burial"), a practice documented by other anthropologists in southern China (James Watson 1988). After three or four years, depending upon the soil conditions, families exhume the body, clean the remaining flesh from the bones, and place the

Figure 21   Secondary burial, 1996. Body being excavated by members of the Zhang family; Mr. Cao, the funeral specialist, is standing in the grave.

bones in a large urn inside the ancestors' tomb. If they can afford it, descendants of the deceased build a semicircular cement tomb to house their ancestor's remains; Catholics also have a community mausoleum to house remains. The Ye family planned to perform this second burial, but that event did not take place during my fieldwork. Instead, I will describe another family's conduct of a secondary burial to make this ethnographic description of the funeral process complete.

Early one weekday morning in the fall of 1997, the Zhang family exhumed the body of a kinsman who had died four years earlier. His sister, a nephew, two nieces, and two other older female relatives were there to clean the bones. The nephew of the deceased had also asked four friends to come along for support. After climbing up Holy Mountain, the group first placed candles at the graves of other relatives and said the Lord's Prayer, Hail Mary, and Glory Be to the Father at each grave. Just before the funeral specialist, Mr. Cao, started the exhumation process, they set off a roll of firecrackers. When Mr. Cao opened the casket, the women started lamenting loudly, gradually tapering off as Mr. Cao handed them bones to clean. As the bones were cleaned with paper by all the attending relatives, they were rearranged on paper that had been spread on the ground. Mr. Cao then placed the bones into a large earthenware urn (*gim ngang* [H.]), starting with the feet and ending with the skull. Mr. Cao then covered the urn with a lid (inside the cover was the name of the deceased and his generation as it would appear on his tombstone), and the jar was carried down to the mausoleum.

At the mausoleum, the family placed two candles in front of the urn and started the same sequence of prayers. During the Lord's Prayer, one of the women sprinkled holy water in the tomb. The tomb was then sealed with cement, and the nephew lit another roll of fireworks. He later told me that this tomb in the community mausoleum was temporary; they planned to build an individual tomb next to his grandfather's at the original burial site. The group then returned to Little Rome, where they had a small lunch banquet.

Catholic Ancestors

Shortly after Spring Festival, the three young adults from the Ye family returned to their work in Shenzhen. On October 31, Changyuan and his unmarried eldest sister returned home to participate in All Souls' Day, commemorating the death of their father (the middle daughter had a young child in kindergarten, so did not make the trip home). All Souls' Day for the Catholics serves as the ritual equivalent of the Festival of Pure Brightness (*qingming*—the ritual holiday in May when Chinese pay homage to the ancestors by visiting their tombs). Non-Catholic villagers in the area visit family graveyards on a day selected by lineage segments (usually around the Pure Brightness festival). At this time, they "sweep the graves" (*sao mu*); they clean up the gravesite and present offerings to the deceased who have become ancestors (Rubie Watson 1988). Lineage subgroups visit graves over several days, until the day when the most remote documented ancestor is reached. I went with the lineage members of a non-Catholic village near Little Rome and was stunned by the large number of people who had returned to the county for the Pure Brightness Festival. According to participants, over fifteen thousand people of the Shen lineage were participating from the different counties of Meizhou, as well as from Taiwan, Hong Kong, and Southeast Asia. The local police were out in force, trying in vain to control the traffic jams of large buses and vehicles of all types. In the past, I was told, different lineages often renewed long-standing quarrels when they met en route to their respective tombs, but the Shen lineage always had the upper hand since they were the largest in the county. Many county and township cadres were also present to greet the many overseas Chinese who returned to Jiaoling for this event and to give speeches at a meeting held in the shared ancestral hall next to the tombs, recently constructed with extensive support from overseas relatives.

Children carried bright flags and banners indicating their lineage segment and current residence. Different segments throughout Jiaoling county staged their offerings in their home villages and then paraded to the tombs of the three remote ancestors that they shared. The village was about ten kilometers away from the tomb area, so a large bus loaded with people and a truck loaded with the offerings followed the main procession that marched through the county seat. The segments took turns laying out their offerings to the ancestor, according to seniority in the genealogy. The offerings of the Shen group that I was with included a wide variety of fruit (pomelos, bananas, and others), roasted pigs, raw goats, chickens, and assorted prepared foods. The Shen segment also had its own lion dancer and drummers; young men took turns dancing in the lion's head. At the tomb of one of the three remote ancestors (three brothers), from whom they all supposedly trace descent, the lion dancers first venerated the ancestors, and then crowds of people with incense rushed up for their turn. After the crowds dispersed a little, the elder generations then took a turn bowing to the ancestors as they were called up by one of the lineage segment elders, and then the group quickly repacked the offerings into the ritual carriers that they had used to transport the offerings from their village. Before they could completely dismantle their offerings, the next segment was already setting up its offerings. Large trays of fireworks were set off, which added to the chaos of smoke, noise, and people running about. The segment then returned to the village and shared a large feast in the ancestral hall. The foodstuffs and meat from the offerings were divided up among the participants, and families took their portions home after the meal.

On All Souls' Day seven months after the Pure Brightness Festival, Little Rome's version of *qingming*, just over a thousand people turned out, as well as two policemen but no county cadres. This annual community event started in 1934, when American Maryknoll missionaries administered the area. Below is an excerpt of the American pastor's description of the event:

> After the mass on All Souls Day, there was a procession to the cemetery, the
> first of its kind in [Little Rome]. The Christians gathered in the church, and
> then formed in line behind the crucifix. The way to the cemetery, nearly a mile
> distant, was traversed in silence, broken only by the recitation of the rosary
> and the singing of hymns. At the cemetery, the Christians, nearly a thousand
> in number, gathered while the Memorial Services for the dead were held. Many

pagans too, attracted by the unusual sight, watched from a nearby hill. May their casual interest grow rapidly into faith. (Maryknoll Mission Diary, November 1934)

A week before the event, a special committee of the Little Rome Parish Council met to discuss the logistics for conducting All Souls' Day to meet the county safety regulations. People were assigned as safety guards to help prevent injuries from firecrackers or traffic. On All Souls' Day, safety guards posted signs that fireworks were not allowed owing to the danger of injury. Families prepared offerings of fruit and flowers for the graves, and candles, crucifixes, and bottles of holy water for prayers. The food for the family banquets following the event at Holy Mountain had already been prepared and was set aside for their return.

Families and individuals made their way to Holy Mountain and gathered in the main clearing that housed the community mausoleum. Father Liang, the sisters, and the catechists had arrived earlier to prepare for the service and greet guests who had returned to Little Rome from different parts of China to participate in the event. At 8:30, the service started. The service followed the basic order of mass, without the Liturgy of the Eucharist. After the readings, Father Liang gave a brief homily on the significance of Christ's death and resurrection for the future resurrection of all the Catholic ancestors who lay buried, waiting for the day of Jesus' return. During the service, many people walked around the fringes, chatting and greeting friends, while the most devout Catholics—those who regularly attended daily and Sunday masses—focused on the service. Some families went straight to their own plots to start the tomb maintenance. At the conclusion of the service, the rest of the families scattered to their own tombs and cleaned the overgrown weeds surrounding the graves. Once the landscaping work was completed, families arranged two candles and a crucifix at the front of the tomb, along with offerings of fruit and flowers, and began their prayers. The combination of prayers varied from family to family, but most (like the Ye family) prayed a simple sequence of the sign of the cross, the Lord's Prayer (at which point the holy water was sprinkled on the tomb in three shakes), the Hail Mary, and the Glory Be to the Father.

Families started their ancestor veneration at the tombs of their most immediate ancestors, and then in groups visited the tombs of other relatives. The Ye family, for example, started at their father's tomb, then went to their grandfather's, and then visited the tombs of other relatives. Since most of the residents of Little Rome are related either by blood or by marriage, groups

Figure 22   All Souls' Day, 1997. Father Liang leading a service at the Catholic graveyard known as Holy Mountain.

moving from tomb to tomb often crossed paths. A year earlier, in 1996, at the height of the sweeping of the graves and prayers, the fireworks exploding on the slope were deafening, and smoke clouded the lower, more crowded area around the community mausoleum. In 1997 when Mr. Ye's children returned from Shenzhen to commemorate the death of their father, Holy Mountain was quiet. The county government had earlier that year prohibited the use of firecrackers in the county seat, tightening its vigilance over their use in large public gatherings. During All Souls' Day in 1997, the Catholics in Little Rome strictly adhered to the new regulations. After their rounds of visits were completed, families returned home to finish preparing for the lunch banquet.

Orthopraxy Revisited: Catholicism with Chinese Characteristics

The Ye family's burial and commemoration of a husband and father illustrates how people in Little Rome resolve the structural tension of being both

Catholic and Hakka. Much has been written about the historical contact moment, when the universal Catholic Church through its diverse missionary groups has transformed, and been transformed by, the society where missionaries spread the faith (see, e.g., Stewart and Shaw 1994). There is also a vast literature on the indigenization of Catholic practices after Vatican II. The basic strategy of the missionary enterprise, which entails the localization of ritual practices that enact a universal Catholic orthodoxy, is spelled out in a voluminous collection of historical accounts, starting with the description in the Bible of the early spread of Christianity outward from Jerusalem in the period shortly after Jesus' life. For the Catholic Church in China, these accounts center on the resolution of conflicting ideas and practices, official and popular, in the Catholic Church and Chinese society.

The key to the indigenization of the Catholic Church in China lies in the universal Catholic Church's emphasis on orthodoxy and a core of ritual practices (the mass and the seven sacraments), coupled with flexibility in the form of life-cycle ritual practices. Of course, this flexibility has been a highly contested domain in the past, as the Kangxi emperor and the seventeenth-century Jesuits discovered (Minimaki 1985; Mungello 1994), and it continues to be contested today in the realm of Sino-Vatican relations (Leung 1992; Madsen 1989). For the people in Little Rome, however, there is no conflict inherent in being both Catholic and Hakka Chinese. The construction of a Hakka Catholic identity for the people of Little Rome can best be understood by using the idea of orthopraxy to contrast how Catholics and their non-Catholic neighbors bury their dead.

Following Watson, I define orthopraxy as correct ritual practice, the "proper performance of rites" (James Watson 1988: 4). Using the lens of funeral ritual, Watson argues that a shared understanding of orthopraxy is the base upon which a sense of Han Chinese identity is constructed. From his ethnographic study of funerary rituals in Cantonese villages in the Hong Kong New Territories, Watson concludes that Han Chinese funerary rites (the ritual practices that begin with the death of an individual and continue until the body's removal from the community) are structured by nine distinct practices: (1) the announcement of the death to the community, by, for example, the ritual wailing of women; (2) the wearing of mourning clothes and other symbols of mourning; (3) the ritualized preparation of the corpse for burial, such as the "purchasing of water" (*mai shui*) to cleanse the body; (4) the transfer of goods to the deceased, believed to be accomplished by the burning of paper objects or food offerings; (5) the preparation of a written memorial, such as the soul tablet; (6) the use of money in ritualized contexts;

(7) the performance of music to mark transitions in the rites; (8) the sealing of the corpse in the coffin; and (9) the transfer of the coffin out of the community, as in the funeral procession (ibid.: 88, 12–15). Because Watson distinguishes between funeral rites and what he calls rites of disposal (that is, the burial and secondary burial), his analysis of the structure of Han Chinese funerals ends there. The proper conduct of funerary ritual along these lines distinguishes Han Chinese practice from that of non-Han minority groups in China, and from that of foreigners. Watson gives further historical examples of how the Chinese elite and the Chinese state sought to regulate and standardize the practice of funerary ritual, while largely disregarding the realm of belief. In other words, while recognizing the importance of shared beliefs in informing and giving meaning to ritual action, Watson concludes that in Chinese society practice takes primacy over belief.

The Ye funeral described above corroborates Watson's argument of the primacy of shared practice over shared belief in Chinese society, even for Christian Chinese families (ibid.: 88). In the Ye funeral and in other Catholic funerals that I observed, the structure guided the conduct of the funeral to a surprisingly large extent. This would not be the expectation, given the large disparity in the belief systems of the Catholics of Little Rome and their non-Catholic neighbors. Myron Cohen describes the contrast in Chinese popular religion between beliefs that emphasize salvation (as distinct from the land of the living) and beliefs that emphasize the interrelatedness of the lands of the living and the dead. Though not identifying Christianity as a strand of Chinese popular religion, Cohen explains how the dominant belief system of ancestor veneration, geomancy, and the tripartite division of the soul shapes ritual practices, leaving little room for ritual actions devoted to the salvation of the deceased, as in Mahayana Buddhist or Christian belief systems (Myron Cohen 1988). The professed beliefs of Catholics in Little Rome, especially concerning the soul and the afterlife, are markedly different from those of their non-Christian neighbors.

The elements that make Little Rome's funerary ritual Catholic are precisely those concerning salvation for the deceased: extreme unction, the twice-daily prayer group visitations, the funeral service, and the final prayers at the burial ground. Similarly, non-Catholic funerals that I observed emphasized the Buddhist salvation of the soul and included additional elements that punctuated the performance of the nine events. Even with the emphasis on the salvation of the soul, the Ye funeral and other Catholic funerals still contained the nine events, although some were modified slightly to match Catholic beliefs. For example, non-Catholic neighbors start the day of burial with the burning of paper spirit houses (*ling wu*). When burned, these spirit houses (which included paper servants, money, and other possessions—paper representations of karaoke equipment, automobiles, even airplanes are considered proper) are deemed to be transferred to the deceased in the afterworld. While the spirit house is burned, women use farm utensils to scrape the ground in order to ward off other souls who might steal the items from their deceased relative. Mr. Lai, a catechist who accompanied me to two funerals where they did this, told me that events like the burning of the spirit houses are illegal superstition (*mixin*), unacceptable to people who live in Little Rome not because they are prohibited but because such superstitious beliefs run counter to the teachings of the Church. Although spirit houses and paper money were not burned at Catholic funeral services, food items were among the offerings used. Since they were placed where non-Catholics would burn incense or paper money, moreover, the burning of candles during funeral, burial, and grave rituals such as All Souls' Day can be seen as a practice acceptable to both Catholic orthodoxy and Chinese orthopraxy.

The similarity in Catholic and non-Catholic funerary ritual highlights the strength of orthopraxy as a guiding principle in Chinese society. In fact, because of the shared structure of the funerary ritual, the people in Little Rome can be at once Hakka and Catholic.

Although my observations of Catholic and non-Catholic Hakka funeral ritual matched Watson's structure of Chinese funerals, one additional event made the ritual complete: the funeral banquet. I would further add that for any event to be considered a Chinese ritual gathering, there needs to be some kind of commensal event. The Ye family, like other families organizing funerals, expended a lot of effort and money on the funeral banquet and other meals for the people who worked and visited them. Both Catholic and non-Catholic marriage ritual, as described in the previous chapter, also feature banquets, as do other life-cycle rituals such as the celebration of the birth of a child (*man yue*) and housewarming celebrations. The importance of food in seasonal rituals such All Souls' Day, Christmas, and Chinese New Year has also been thoroughly documented, as has the symbolic exchange of food on ritual occasions such as ancestor veneration at *qingming*. For the Catholics in Little Rome, the most sacred part of the mass, the Liturgy of the Eucharist, is a shared meal of the body of Christ. I do not know of any Chinese ritual event, except for private individual practices such as prayers and vow-taking at Buddhist temples, that does not involve commensality, either physical or symbolic.

The importance of commensality in Chinese ritual events highlights the role of ritual in building community in China: people who eat together also stay together. Eating a meal together gives individuals the opportunity to share sentiment, an opportunity to enact a relationship that is portrayed as noninstrumental. The importance of banqueting in building and maintaining social relations in China has been documented in detail. Both Yan (1996) and Kipnis (1997) describe how eating together is a chance to express and experience emotion (*ganqing*). For the hosts, like the Ye family, it is a chance to thank friends and relatives who shared their bereavement and to thank funeral workers for their services, with an emphasis on the human side of the labor relationship. Banqueting makes ritual events more memorable and more social and thus reinforces people's sense of community.

Producing Locality: Being a Part of Little Rome

In his analysis of the impact of globalization on local communities, Appadurai gives prominence to the role of ritual in the production of locality, asserting that ritual produces "*local subjects*, actors who properly belong to a situated community of kin, neighbors, friends, and enemies" (1996: 179). Anthropologists, Appadurai concludes, should reexamine the study of ritual as essential in producing locality, an idea that resonates with earlier conclusions about the relationship of ritual and social structure from ritual theorists like Van Gennep, Turner, Barth, and Bloch. Appadurai, however, does not spell out exactly how ritual allows people to produce locality.

The liminality of funerary ritual, to use Turner's terminology, creates space for social critique within antistructure, as depicted in the laments of Hakka women (see Johnson 1988). Johnson concludes that women, largely excluded from the male public realm, can use the opportunity created by the liminality of funeral ritual to voice criticism that otherwise remains unheard. However, the reality of social structure never completely disappears, as is implied in Turner's model. The persistence of more mundane concerns in the charged space of ritual allows people to use ritual events to create, reinforce, and remove intercommunity social relations that produce locality. Participation in these ritual events, moreover, creates moments in social memory that place individuals, wherever they happen to live most of the time, within a shared community history.

First, the visits by prayer groups are an important element in defining who is and who is not a member of the Little Rome community. The prayer group visits organized by older, retired Catholic men and women (though always led by men) are an act of recognition that the deceased or the deceased's family is a member of the Little Rome community. Prayer groups often left the political boundaries of Little Rome to participate in the Catholic funerals of people in nearby villages, people who are considered part of Little Rome even though they live outside the geographic boundaries of the village. Correspondingly, the absence of prayer groups in a funeral within the village is a statement that the deceased is not a part of Little Rome. With the weakening of the administrative structures—household registration system, ration coupons, and work points—that control household and individual mobility in the post-Mao period, some families have left Little Rome and others have moved in. As a result, a few non-Catholic families, not more than four, reside in the village but are not considered members of the village. There is even one hamlet of houses, comprising most of a production team, that is on the geographic outskirts of the village and whose inhabitants are also peripheral to the social landscape of Little Rome because they are not Catholic.

Moreover, the size of the prayer group participating in a funeral is seen as an indicator of how embedded the family is in the Little Rome community. Before the funeral, I was told by some Catholic elders that the prayer group for the Ye funeral would probably be small, since neither Mr. Ye nor his relatives were especially active Catholics. However, twenty to forty funeral attendees was typical of other Catholic funerals I had attended; a neighbor later told me that perhaps my own attachment to Mr. Ye had shamed more people into coming. After the death of an especially influential Catholic, a Mr. Wang who ran a local credit union, more than fifty people joined in the different prayer groups. In 1991 when Bishop Lan died, over one thousand people from all over the prefecture went to Little Rome to participate in the funeral and prayer groups.

Rubie Watson (1988) describes how Cantonese villagers similarly use grave rituals, through the geomantic (*fengshui*) empowerment of lineage segments as public demonstrations of wealth, status, and power. Although the power of geomancy is denied (in public, at least) by the Catholics of Little Rome, people in more private conversations with me wondered if there was something to geomancy after all. One visiting former Little Rome resident, now living in New York City, told a crowd of people gathered in the rectory that Americans (he mentioned Donald Trump) were starting to hire Chinese geomancy masters (*fengshui xiansheng*) to help design office buildings and office space. Later, while walking around Holy Mountain with me,

Mr. Lai, who had heard the testimonial, told me that some Catholics still wonder if geomancy influences the fortunes of the living; how else can someone explain the rise of fortunes of one family and the decline of another? He suggested that maybe geomantically favorable locations were a result of God's special grace to some people.

Such musings, however, are not part of public discourse in Little Rome, especially among people who are outside the faith.[4] In the gospel readings and homilies, differential worldly successes and failures are dismissed in favor of an ideology of success in a person's personal faith before God. Those who are better off are expected to be more active in works of charity; the church in Little Rome and its smaller sister church in the nearby county seat maintain a capital fund of 135,000 RMB (US$16,500), the interest from which is used in Catholic assistance to the poor and needy of the area. Worldly success and failure are believed by the people of Little Rome, like their non-Catholic neighbors, to stem largely from individual ability and connections.

Although four decades of scientific socialism have not totally displaced beliefs about geomancy, such traditional explanations are increasingly hard to come by, especially among the younger generations. For example, when I was returning from the secondary burial, a neighbor, Ms. Cao, asked me if I had been afraid to go to the excavation of a body. I expected to hear a Catholic version of death pollution, but instead, she said that I must be careful because excavating human remains is unsanitary (*bu weisheng*). She asked if I had handled the bones myself; if not, she wanted to give me food to bring home. Since traditional ideas about death pollution run counter to Catholic orthodoxy (James Watson 1988; Whyte 1988), such ideas are readily dismissed by Catholics in Little Rome. Their non-Catholic neighbors, similarly, do not associate funerary ritual practices with pollution and ghosts, but primarily with maintaining tradition and identity.

Second, the performance of funerary ritual demands that community members physically reaggregate. The three Ye children, all working in Shenzhen, only return to Little Rome for special events such as Spring Festival and All Souls' Day, but there was no question that they would return when their father got hurt and for the funeral. To not return for an event like a funeral is in essence to cut off relations with relatives and to signal one's exit from the community. Even after retiring, many who have moved to different regions of China or overseas still return to Little Rome for funerals; and a neighbor who had spent her childhood in Malaysia returned to Little Rome to get married. As described in the literature of the Chinese diaspora, this is expressed by the cultural idiom "fallen leaves return to their roots" (*luo ye hui gen*) (Wang 1991; Yen 1995). For those who have lived overseas, the Chinese state retains an immigration category for returning overseas Chinese like these, as well as a category (*tan qin*) for Chinese with other nationalities who require visas to visit their ancestral home.

The children of Mr. Ye, who live and work in Shenzhen, still refer to Little Rome as their home. In China, when people ask where you are from, the answer they expect is not your current domicile—regardless of the place of residence listed in the state's household registration system—but your hometown (*laojia; guxiang*). The hometown is a pervasive cultural trope in China, as place-based identity is in other societies (Ching and Creed 1997). At least in the littoral southern China region, the majority of young adults who participate in either labor or educational migration maintain extensive links with their natal homes through remittances (money that is badly needed in rural areas) and through extended visits. A person's hometown is not necessarily where one grew up but the place where one's ancestors are buried.

As a result, funerary, burial, and grave rituals are key events in identity formation in China. When improperly performed, damage is done not only to individuals but also to communities. Jing describes in detail the sense of community shame resulting from the loss of ancestral remains and improprieties in the reestablishment of ancestral tombs. In 1961, when the single-surname village in northwestern China where Jing conducted his fieldwork was relocated to make way for the construction of a dam, many villagers were given only a few hours to evacuate their homes. Tombs were quickly dug up, if they were retrieved at all, and during the move ancestral remains were mixed up, improperly handled, or partially lost. Many graves were rebuilt without any ancestral remains, a fact that remains unspoken, taboo in conversation. As poignantly described by Jing, the result is a deep-rooted sense of community shame and loss; he reports that the 1991 communal reconstruction of a Confucian temple (the villagers claim descent from Confucius) is partial redemption for the community's failure to care properly for their ancestors (Jing 1996: 69–86).

Like the ancestral tombs in the Gansu village described by Jing, the community graveyard of Holy Mountain is a key source of community identity for the Catholics of Little Rome. With the importance of ancestors in community, family, and individual identities, Catholics in Little Rome have created spaces in Catholic ritual for the ancestors. The importance of All Souls' Day takes a much more prominent role in the liturgical cycle of Chinese

Catholics than elsewhere, because it is essentially the celebration of the ancestors. The Catholics of Little Rome do not have documentation of their own genealogies, in stark contrast to their non-Catholic neighbors. Until the Vatican acknowledged ancestral rites in the 1970s—three hundred years after the rites controversy that resulted in the Qing dynasty's persecution of Catholics and the disbanding of the Jesuits worldwide—the keeping of genealogical records was considered a pagan practice.[5] With the absence of an ancestral hall (and domestic ancestral tablets in the home), the cemetery has become the community's ancestral shrine. The inscriptions on Catholic tombstones strongly resemble the entries placed on non-Catholic ancestral tablets. The Catholic cemetery is essentially a genealogy, a landscape that keeps the records of Little Rome's ancestors.

Third, the community performs funeral ritual together, with the help of family, friends, and neighbors. In Little Rome, where there are over thirty different surnames, everyone can claim relations with any other family as a result of intermarriage within the village. Unlike other, more typical Hakka villages, no dominant lineage serves as the principal element of village social structure. Instead, the local Catholic church is the primary organizing principle for social life. When people in Little Rome are mobilized for an event, whether burying a neighbor or building a road, they rely on friends and neighbors to help out. This is not to say that non-Catholics do not make good neighbors (or that all Catholics make good neighbors), although people in Little Rome made comments to that effect. For example, people in Little Rome told me that women often use the opportunity of mourning laments to criticize people, sometimes even cursing them (*zou ngad yin* [H.]). According to informants, one difference between Catholic and non-Catholic funeral ritual is that the lamenting Catholic women do not curse other people quite as much as the non-Catholics do.

County cadres also say that people in Little Rome are exceptionally neighborly; one cadre told me that people in Little Rome do not fight with each other as they do in other villages because their Catholic faith tells them to be good neighbors. The same county cadres also praised the simplicity (*jiandan*) of Catholic funeral ritual, in comparison with the elaborate Buddhist performances that some non-Catholics organize for their funerals. When they formally introduced me to the village in 1994 (though I had first seen the village in 1993), county cadres told me that Little Rome was a model modern community (*wenming cun*), noting that Catholic practices are in line with modernity because of their simplified funeral ritual; people just pray together and sing, without the elaborate performances or sacrifices demanded by feudal superstition. The cadres did not go into detail about the persistence of many traditional funerary and burial practices even in Little Rome. After describing the prevalence of traditional funerary and burial practices in the region, even among CCP members and national cadres, Zhang (1995) concludes that the persistence of traditional practices in local Chinese society results from the importance of remaining filial (*shouxiao*) toward the ancestors in defining morality (*daode*).

Making Ancestors Without Incense

The proper conduct of funerary ritual is critical in maintaining the authority of the church and social links between people in Little Rome. As a result, although Catholics in Little Rome and their non-Catholic neighbors have very different beliefs about death, their funerary practices are structurally identical. To fail in the proper conduct of funerary ritual, or in other grave rituals such as the veneration of ancestors, is to deny one's ancestors—and to be without ancestors in Chinese society is to be without an identity.

If there is such a strong similarity in ritual structure, how is this reflected in the social structure? If death and ancestor ritual is a celebration of the lineage for the non-Catholic neighbors of Little Rome, what is being celebrated by the Catholics? Through their practice of funerary and other grave rituals, the people in Little Rome celebrate their church, their community of faith. When they bury friends or relatives and remember them in special masses and on All Souls' Day, people in Little Rome affirm their identity both as individuals and as a community—their individuality through the specificity of deceased ancestors and their shared community as members of the Little Rome church.

CHAPTER 8

Do-It-Yourself Socialism

Although all of the previous chapters have focused on some aspect of Catholicism, not everything that happens in Little Rome is directly church-related. However, the Little Rome church provides the social framework, even for those activities not overtly associated with the church. In this chapter, I examine one such event—the building of a new paved road—to illustrate how even in the most mundane of activities a sense of authority and community emanates from the social center that is the church.

With the dismantling of the socialist apparatus that had regulated rural life in the Maoist period, the church has stepped in to ground community life in Little Rome. In pulling back from a command economy, the Chinese state has also pulled back from many infrastructural tasks such as road maintenance. Organizations like the church in Little Rome and lineages in other villages have stepped in to fill the void left by the state. People have had to find alternative sources of capital investment in their hometowns and have developed new lines of patronage outside the state apparatus.

Building Friendship Road

The house my family and I lived in in Little Rome was on the southeastern edge of the village, looking out over the gardens and rice fields between the heart of Little Rome and the hamlet of production team five. The path leading around the village to our house was unpaved, made from packed dirt. It was surrounded by irrigation ditches that fed water to the rice fields, and when it rained the walk home could be very muddy. One day in mid-February 1997, after the Chinese New Year celebrations were over, two of my neighbors, Mrs. Cao and the newly widowed Mrs. Ye, came over to chat with my wife and me. After a while, the conversation turned to the path, about how much better it would be if it were paved with cement. I was reminded of a previous conversation with Mrs. Cao in which I had told her how much I appreciated the community's welcoming of me and my family and that I wanted to find a way to thank everyone. Now I immediately understood that the women were investigating whether I was interested in helping to pave the road, and I quickly agreed that I could help out.

One evening about a week later, my neighbors Mr. Deng and Mr. Lai, and Mr. Ye—one of the two cadres responsible for public safety in the village (not a direct relation of Mrs. Ye)—came by to chat with me about building the road. Even though I was good friends with Mr. Deng and Mr. Lai, Mr. Ye did most of the talking, explaining what they were planning to do. He told me that Mr. Deng had volunteered to take charge of the project (*fuze*) and that Mr. Lai would be the construction chief (*shifu*). Mr. Ye told me that paving the road would cost about 4,000 RMB (US$480). I offered to contribute half of the amount, 2,000 RMB (US$240), and Mr. Ye said that the community would contribute the other half. Mr. Ye thanked me on behalf the community, and the men left.

The next day, I gave the 2,000 RMB to Mr. Deng, and we talked about his plans to make the road. The people who live in that part of Little Rome had long wanted to pave the road but had not been able to raise the money to do so. Moreover, no one had wanted to take responsibility for the project without having adequate resources to do the job. Working with the state to have the road paved was also not a simple matter. Many of the people who lived in the southeastern corner had built their homes after decollectivization in the early 1980s. During the Maoist period, the land in that corner of the village had been regulated for use as garden land, but with the establishment of the responsibility system, which allowed households to use their land allocation for any purpose as long as they met their rice production quota, these people wanted to get out of the more crowded village center and build larger homes. As a result, the area was one of mixed administrative responsibility. Some households were members of production team two, many others (like Mr. Deng) were in production team three, and a few households were in production team four. Without unity in command, there was little motivation for any of the production team leaders to push for resources from the administrative district and take responsibility for paving the road. But once I had agreed to provide half the money, Mr. Deng was willing and able to raise more money from his neighbors, track expenses, and mobilize neighbors to work on the project. This was a slow time in the farming cycle, about a month before the first planting of rice; as a result, many other projects were also under way in Little Rome, including widening a portion of the main road going out to the main highway.

TABLE 2

Final Tally of Donations to Road Construction

Donors	Amount (RMB)	Donors	Amount (RMB)
Mr. and Mrs. Lozada	2,000	Mr. Lai	150
Mr. Lai	100	Mr. Wang	10
Mr. Feng	200	Mr. Wang	100
Mr. Lai	200	Mr. Lai	100
Mr. Deng (project chief)	200	Mr. Lai	100
Mr. Lai	300	Mr. Wang	50
Mr. Wang	300	Mrs. Zhang	50
Mr. Lai (construction chief)	200	Mr. Lu	50
Mr. Ye	200	Mr. Xie	10
Mrs. Cao	200	Mr. Lai	100
Mr. Liao	100	Mr. Zhang	100
Mr. Lai	200	Father Liang	200
Mr. Wang	200	TOTAL	5,420

Mr. Deng kept a public running tally of donations by posting a sign on the side of a neighbor's house (see Table 2; names are listed in the order in which donations were received). Each household bordering the road was asked to donate at least 200 RMB, and those farther down the road who would use it were asked to give 100 RMB. All the Lais listed were from the same lineage; the old Lai home was located just behind the new Lai homes that bordered the road. In addition, Mr. Deng solicited money from some of his sisters, who had long ago married out of the village; these were the smaller donations of 50 RMB or less. As the project progressed and appeared a little short of money, Mr. Deng requested assistance from the church. Father Liang could not contribute a large amount to the road project because the church was already committed to the expansion of the main road and the construction of the new church. Nonetheless, he personally contributed 200 RMB to the project.

The work started early on February 28 with the preparation of the roadbed. This involved shoring up the irrigation ditches on the sides with rocks, constructing a small bridge over one of the ditches, and removing a layer of approximately eight inches from the road. In some areas, garden

Figure 23   Neighbors working together to build a road in 1997.

walls had to be torn down to accommodate the widening of the road. After staking out the area, Mr. Deng and Mr. Lai encountered their first conflict. Mrs. Cao complained to me that Mr. Deng and Mr. Lai did not plan to pave the road all the way up to the front of her house (she lived on the extreme southeastern corner of Little Rome). Mrs. Cao, a close friend of my wife's, was known to everyone as being influential in our family's decision-making process. When we first arrived, she showed my wife where to buy things in Little Rome and the nearby county seat, and my wife daily picked vegetables in her garden. It was no accident that Mrs. Cao and Mrs. Ye were the first to approach us about helping out with the road. Thus when the road was staked out, Mrs. Cao felt that because of her efforts in involving me in the project the road should be extended about ten meters to her front door. Because of our friendship, I had no choice but to support her request, and after some discussion, Deng and Lai agreed to do so if there was enough money. When the paving specialists started their work, they began at her house, exactly where she wanted the road to go.

Most of the people clearing the road were neighborhood women, one or two from each household. Besides Deng and Lai, Ye Changyuan and I worked on the project nearly every day. The husband and father-in-law of one road worker worked with us intermittently, as did a male teenager who had just graduated from middle school. Neither Mr. Deng nor Mr. Lai assigned anyone particular jobs; before starting work, we talked about what needed to be done and people just jumped into the work. They brought their own tools and wheelbarrows from home. The women worked with hoes, making large piles of dirt and rocks, while the men loaded the wheelbarrows and pulled them to a waste site on the eastern outskirts of the village. While one of the men was pulling the heavy load to the waste site, one of the women would come along to help push the heavy wheelbarrow up a small hill. The women were very reluctant to pull the wheelbarrow themselves. For about five days we did this road-clearing work, starting early in the morning around 7:30, quitting for lunch around 11:30, and starting again at around 2:30 and working until dinnertime at 6:00 (we did not work on Sunday).

One morning, Mr. Deng's son and Mr. Ye started work by tearing down Mrs. Cao's garden wall. After they had torn down half of the wall bordering the new road, Mrs. Cao emerged from the house screaming at them to stop. She claimed that she had not agreed to the tearing down of her garden wall and was in a rage about the part that had already been dismantled. Everyone gathered around her, saying that her wall needed to go so that the road could be made wide enough for cars and small trucks to make the ninety-degree turn by her house. But she refused to give in, and neighbors started to lose patience with her. She then started yelling at the two younger men, the younger Deng and Ye, screaming that when her son got back from Germany he would beat them up. It did not help matters when they started laughing, but after a while Mrs. Cao calmed down. Mr. Deng and Lai agreed to rebuild the part of the wall that had already been torn down, and the road was not widened where her garden wall remained. She rejoined the neighborhood workers, who still teased her about the outburst, but remained in a bad mood for the rest of that day.

When cadres from the administrative district (*guanliqu*) and county came to inspect the expansion of the main road, they were guided by Mr. Ye and Mr. Wang, who together supervise the five production teams of Little Rome. The well-dressed cadres were brought over to see our roadwork, and on one of my wheelbarrow trips to the waste site I was introduced to them. The Little Rome cadres made a big production of my helping with the labor, telling them I had contributed to the project not only financially but also physically. Despite communist rhetoric about the importance of physical labor for all social strata (an ideology made practice during the Maoist period), the cadres were surprised that an "intellectual" (*zhishifenzi*)—let alone an American one—was digging up rocks and dirt and hauling them away. Later that evening, I received a visit from the two Little Rome cadres, who asked me to help support the expansion of the main road. They explained that the main road into Little Rome needed to be widened because of the increased truck and car traffic. I had seen the announcements about raising money for this project: commercial enterprises in the village were required to contribute at least 100 RMB, and people with tractors and motorcycles were required to contribute at least 50 RMB. Additional donations were solicited from all the households around Little Rome. While we were working on the road, we had seen the two cadres ask Mr. Lai's father for a similar donation. My neighbors warned me that cadres from all over the county would be flocking to my house and that I should refuse to help them in their projects. They told me that I should tell them that I was an intellectual, a teacher, and not a rich business person (in postsocialist China, as in the United States, intellectuals may have a lot of social capital, but people in Little Rome know that truck drivers have more real capital). In fact, this is the story that Mrs. Cao, my family's self-proclaimed protector, told some cadres from another village who had heard that an American was living in Little Rome. In this case, however, we did not want to antagonize the other villagers in Little Rome who already associated our family with our neighbors' group, so we ended up contributing 500 RMB to the project.

Because all those working were neighbors, people were very casual with each other, making jokes and telling stories; we took breaks when the majority of people went to sit in the shade. Sometimes, individuals left to run a brief errand, as when Mrs. Cao went to feed her pigs or Mrs. Wang to water her garden. After taking many loads to the waste site on the eastern part of the village, we amused ourselves by having one person ride in the empty wheelbarrow back to the work area while the other person pulled it (one of the few times that women were willing to pull the wheelbarrow was with me standing in the back). Because most of the workers were women, there was a lot of smoking and joking among the men and women working together. Once my wife visited us while I was talking with one woman; as soon as she left, another younger mother berated me for continuing to flirt with someone while my wife was there! Since our supervisors Deng and Lai did not have an official position like production team leader, the work environment was very relaxed and informal.

On the morning of March 3, Mr. Deng, one of the neighborhood women, and I went to a nearby lumber mill to get wood that would frame the road. That afternoon we went to a metal shop at the main road and picked up the iron rods that would keep the cement in place. We bought cement from the local store that my family patronized for most of our dry goods and food items. The other neighbors finished preparing the road surface and blocked off the irrigation ditches on the sides of the road. With all the material purchased and the road prepared, the paving specialist and three workers showed up the following morning and started laying down the cement. Mr. Deng told me that the paving specialist was a friend of Mr. Lai's who lived on the other side of the main highway, and that the three paving workers had been found in the neighboring township of Sanzhen. Now the neighborhood workers began supporting the paving team by hauling in sand and rocks to the appropriate locations. Some neighborhood women brought water in for the workers. The cement was mixed on the road surface itself near where the workers were laying the cement. Except for the tractors that hauled the sand and rocks to Little Rome, all the work was done manually. The workers worked all day, and then took a break at 4:00 P.M.

Mr. Lai's wife prepared a snack of noodles for the paving specialists, which Mr. Lai invited me, the specialists, and Mr. Deng into his house to eat. When we were finished, the other neighborhood women working on the road then came in to eat. After this short break, we continued the paving work until it grew dark, and the specialists, Mr. Deng, and I had dinner at Mr. Lai's. At this meal, liquor (*baijiu*) was served, and the meal was more relaxed. The outsiders took this opportunity to pepper me with questions about America and about what I was doing in Little Rome. Despite my explanations, they concluded that I must be an overseas Chinese helping out people to whom I was somehow related.

The paving was completed on the following day, and people went back to their own farming chores while the cement set. Mr. Lai continued to work on reconstructing the walls that had been torn down and making sure that the sides of the irrigation ditches held fast.

Mr. Lai put up the new sign on our neighborhood road, now called "Friendship Road." They had wanted to name the road using my Chinese name, but I suggested that it should be named "Ah Gui Road" (Ah Gui was the name of Mrs. Ye's dog). Everyone was happy with "Friendship Road," but our ongoing joke was to continue to call it "Ah Gui Road."

After the completion of the road, Mr. Deng and Mr. Lai paid a formal visit to our home and presented our family with gifts to show the community's appreciation for my support (although Mr. Deng visited us almost daily, this time he was dressed in more formal clothing). The gifts included a bottle of liquor and four scrolls of calligraphy that were purchased in the nearby

TABLE 3

Friendship Road Expenditure Report

Date spent	Materials purchased	Amount (RMB)
Feb. 27	Red paper, glue	.70
Feb. 28	Heavy twine	1.30
Mar. 4	One carton of Meizhou cigarettes (for road-paving specialist workers)	16.80
Mar. 5	Contracted fee for specialist workers	400.00
Mar. 6	1,000 bricks to replace Mr. **'s wall	200.00
Mar. 7	Contracted fee for specialist overseer	90.00
	Iron rods	86.30
Mar. 8	Cement	2108.80
	Rocks (including delivery fee)	1044.00
Mar. 9	1,000 bricks to replace Mrs. **'s wall	200.00
Mar. 11	Meal served to specialist overseer and workers	90.00
	Miscellaneous wood	10.00
	Road sign (stone cut)	100.00
	10 cement blocks to replace Mr. **'s wall	66.00
	Sand	18.00
Mar. 14	Gifts for Mr. Lozada	96.00
	Payment to Mr. XX	20.00
	Payment for Mr. Lai's work	172.50
	Payment for Mr. Deng's work	150.00
	Payment for workers from neighborhood (7 RMB/day)	532.00
TOTAL EXPENDITURE		5,402.40

county seat. Such gifts were expected in projects that involved major donors, and unlike the other neighborhood women and men who did the road work, I was not paid the 7 RMB daily wage. The gifts were included in the project budget; the final expenditure report showing how the money was spent was posted next to the donation board on the wall of a neighbor's home (see Table 3). Because the budget was relatively small, a stone donor's tablet was not constructed at the foot of the road.

Two weeks later, we had our first real test of the road—a truck with build-

ing materials for one of my neighbors tried to make it through. The road was
wide enough for the vehicle, but because we had not widened the road at
Mrs. Cao's garden wall, the truck could not make the ninety-degree turn. By
the time the driver gave up, it was dark, and a crowd of neighbors with flash-
lights had to help the driver back up the road. This provoked another round
of discussion with Mrs. Cao about her wall, but she was adamant. Mr. Deng's
son suggested that I knock down the wall when we moved out of the village,
so Mrs. Cao couldn't catch us. This became another ongoing joke, but to this
day I think Mrs. Cao watched us carefully to make sure her wall stayed up.

Working Women

The dominance of neighborhood women on the road-building crew was not
surprising. Women also make up the overwhelming majority of agricultural
workers during rice planting and harvests. After conducting a survey in eight
Chinese villages, Croll and Huang reported that agriculture in postsocialist
China is seen by farmers as an "unprofitable, unattractive, and even redun-
dant economic activity" (1997: 128), and that labor migration, particularly by
men, to major industrial centers is a necessary income supplement for farming households. The lifting of many restrictions on mobility, both within
China and internationally, has resulted in a tremendous rate of permanent
and temporary migration, involving close to 120 million people (Croll and
Huang 1997). This has resulted in what has been referred to as the feminization of Chinese agriculture.

In Little Rome, there is also a Hakka cultural tradition of women working
in farming, marketing agricultural products, and doing other paid labor outside the home. Hakka women traditionally had greater parity with men than
women in other ethnic groups, and as a result, a more balanced gender ideology has become one symbol of modern Hakka ethnicity. The seminal historian of the Hakka, Professor Luo Xianglin, elevated Hakka women in the ethnic discourse when he categorized their cultural position as a "special
characteristic" (*te xing*) of Hakka culture, asserting that "Hakka women are
the most hard-working and independent women in China, and among their
sex command the most respect for their contributions to society and to the
Chinese nation" (Luo 1933: 241; my translation). Hakka apologists have continued this tradition, and the result is the almost required inclusion of a commentary on Hakka women in every Chinese treatise on Hakka society and
culture (CHCR 1987; Fang 1994; Huang, Huang, and Zou 1993; Kiang 1991).

A traditional explanation of the use of an official title for women on Hakka ancestral tablets illustrates how Hakka women symbolize the Hakka spirit:

> Once upon a time, the Mongols from the north were preparing to invade China proper, so the legend goes. But before the Hans were ready for a fight, the Mongols mysteriously retreated. The curious Han emperor wanted to know why. The scouts returned to tell him that the invaders saw several groups of Hakka women on their way to the mountains to pick firewood. They were so orderly, so sturdy-looking, and so many in number. Besides, each of them carried a long spear-like stick on their backs. The Mongols mistook them for woman soldiers. "If their women are so strong and so well-trained, their men must be even better." So the invaders beat a hasty retreat. The Han emperor was so pleased that from then on all Hakka women should be called "ruren" (scholar's wife), a title given to court officials. Thereafter, all Hakka women have been calling themselves "ruren." (Kiang 1991: 66)

Hakka women are further glorified because as a group they did not practice footbinding. Although they were derided by other Han Chinese groups in the past and given pejorative labels such as "big feet," in the more contemporary literature the absence of footbinding demonstrated the progressiveness of Hakka culture. Missionaries working among the Hakka extolled the virtues of Hakka women, praising their "normal feet and erect bearing" (Lutz and Lutz 1998: 176).

Some elements of Hakka culture such as "mountain songs" (*shan ge*) reinforce a more balanced gender ideology than is found in society in general (Li 1996). Mountain songs are a focal element in the objectification of Hakka culture by ethnic activists and in the 1990s are a highly commodified genre of singing. Highly stylized mountain songs are always performed during gatherings celebrating Hakka ethnicity, such as the biannual World Hakka Association meetings. Mountain songs usually involve two singers, a man and a woman, who take turns singing, each responding to the other. They are mostly love songs and traditionally have been associated with courtship. People in Little Rome told me that some missionaries objected to mountain songs because of the perception that they led to wanton sexual behavior (*bu daode*). Li reviews this tradition of mountain songs as evidence that there was less segregation between Hakka men and women in work and play than among other Han Chinese ethnicities (1996: 13–14).

The expanded social world of Hakka women, however, implies neither gender equality nor equal authority with men in local social life. In her study of a Hakka emigrant village in the Hong Kong New Territories, Bracey concludes that the "freedom" of Hakka women to work does not mean that their life is better than that of their Cantonese counterparts:

> It has meant that she has been allowed to perform much of the heavy labor, such as tilling the fields and carrying heavy loads of firewood, which other Chinese reserve for the men. There is a Cantonese proverb to the effect that a person who misbehaves in this life is punished by being reincarnated as a Hakka woman. (Bracey 1967: 4–5)

In his study of family economics, Myron Cohen describes in great detail how Hakka women create and manage family wealth (1976: 178–86). For the Hakka in a rural Taiwanese community, Cohen asserts that although there is no distinction in gender roles in the management and cultivation of the family farm and management of household funds, men still have the dominant position as the head of the household (*jiazhang*) (ibid.: 88, 91). Likewise in Hong Kong, Hakka women have a stronger tradition than Cantonese women in the nondomestic work force (Johnson 1976: 119–20).

Hakka women working outside the home thus have a greater public role than other Han Chinese women. Because of their ability to work outside the house, earn money, and develop extrafamilial relationships,[1] it may seem that Hakka women have higher social status in the community (Gough 1975). However, the same is not true for professional women (Hakka and non-Hakka) in Taiwan, where for women to succeed in both their professional and their family lives they are expected to remain "simple" (*danchun*), meaning "within the boundary of society's expectations" (see Bak 1994: 226).

Similarly, neighborhood women in Little Rome work within the boundaries of society's expectations. In the road-building project, it may not have been inconceivable for Mrs. Cao and Mrs. Ye to serve as project head and construction chief, but it was unlikely because of their gender. It is not surprising to see women working in the fields, raising pigs, or staffing a counter in a store, but it is unusual for the boss (*laoban*) to be a woman. Jobs that are physically suitable for either gender are still considered to be male jobs, such as driving the tractors that delivered the rock and sand and even pulling the wheelbarrow. Four of the five production team leaders in Little Rome were women, but their authority in postsocialist China is much more limited than it was during the Maoist period. Mrs. Cao summarized the situation for me by saying that in Little Rome people still "respect men and belittle women" (*zhong nan qing nu*). Working outside the home has not leveled the gendered playing field for Chinese women but rather has maintained the valuation of men over women (see Salaff and Sheridan 1984 on women factory workers in Hong Kong). In 1997 women were 39 percent of the labor force throughout China, but they accounted for 61 percent of the laid-off workers during the slowdown in the Asian economy (Rosenthal 1998).

However, working outside the home has given the neighborhood women the opportunity to develop relationships outside of the family. These extra-familial relationships reinforce the authority derived from kinship-related sources such as the uterine family (a woman's children and mother, a domain where women play the dominant role in family processes). As described by Wolf, the "women's community" exerts pressure on the decision-making processes through their collective power to make men lose face (see Margery Wolf 1972). In Little Rome, this women's community is institutionalized within the public space of the church. As described in Chapter 5, women dominate church activities through their frequent participation in mass, prayer groups, and other ritual events. Women are the heart of the church in Little Rome, and without their participation, the church staff could neither maintain nor expand the position of the church in the community. They are linked spatially through the close proximity of their houses; but more important, they are linked socially through the church.

Of those working on the road project, only one of the neighborhood women was not a fervent Catholic; the Lai lineage was also highly active in church leadership and activities. The social authority of the ritual community, fed largely by the activities of women, made it difficult for people to avoid contributing money to the building of the road, the expansion of the main road, and other public works projects.

Shifting Boundaries in the Postsocialist Period

In 1953, when land reform took place in Little Rome, the people of Little Rome farmed plots of land assigned to them by cadres, as they had before the establishment of the People's Republic. Two years later, however, the land was taken back by the state, agriculture became collectivized, and the production team system was established. Through the production team, the collective managed agricultural production as well as the lives of Little Rome inhabitants. At that time, Little Rome had three production teams (see Map 3): production team one came from the western part of Little Rome, team two from the southeastern part of the village, and team three from the southern part.

Map 3.   Little Rome in the 1950s

Daily life was strictly managed during the collective period. The production team leader managed the economic resources of the entire production team to meet a quota established by the collective. He or she was also responsible for the political education of team members and mobilized the team for participation in the various campaigns undertaken during the Maoist period. Each member of the team was assigned specific tasks and was remunerated through a system of work points (see also Potter and Potter 1990). Households were also bound to a specific residence, with large houses divided among several families. The state's political goal in establishing this kind of local penetration using the production team structure was to shift loyalties to the state, away from kinship and traditional patronage ties (Huang 1989).

The production team structure in Little Rome became even more tightly integrated with the state through the establishment of communes (*gongshe*) in 1958. When the commune system was implemented, Little Rome's three production teams were divided into eight. This was part of Mao's failed experiment in accelerated development known as the Great Leap Forward, and many of Little Rome's residents died of famine-related illnesses during this time (see Becker 1996). When asked about the Great Leap Forward, some villagers talked about how the old church building had served as a canteen for the entire village for a short time, and everyone talked about how little food there was to eat. The Great Leap Forward's commune system was abandoned in 1960, when land was returned to the production brigade (*dadui*, the level of administration that is now referred to as the administrative district), and small amounts of land were returned to individuals for gardening (0.03 *mu*). The following year, the management of production was again shifted to the production team. In 1965, on the eve of the Cultural Revolution, the number of production teams was reduced from eight to five, the number that exists today (see Table 4, Map 4).

With the establishment of the responsibility system upon Deng's ascension to power, land was again redistributed to each household; in 1980 each person received 0.53 *mu* (except children whose birth caused a family to exceed the family planning quota). Since then, there have been two county-level readjustments due to household demographic changes (in 1985 and 1989), but the changes were not substantial for people in Little Rome. With the return of the land to the household and the loosening of residential controls, many families started building new houses on land that had previously been assigned to them for gardens. Most of the houses in the southeastern corner were built during this expansion in the mid-1980s, including our house.

The once orderly geographic distribution of production teams in Little Rome became chaotic. Previously, the responsibility for maintaining or building new infrastructure could clearly be attributed to one production team; under the current system it is unclear which production team is responsible for certain public areas of the village. Furthermore, production team leaders in the postsocialist period do not have access to the resources or the control over individuals that they had during the Maoist period (Greenhalgh 1993). As rural cadres (*nongcun ganbu*) they lack the power and influence of national cadres (*guojia ganbu*) in the structure of postsocialist local government (see Huang 1989: 133–34). In 1996–97, the leader of production team three only once assembled team members to work on a project—the

TABLE 4
Population of Little Rome, 1980 and 1997

	Number of households	1980 population	1997 population
Production team 1	45	160	152
Production team 2	66	187	218
Production team 3	48	168	168
Production team 4	61	214	213
Production team 5	43	157	147
TOTAL	263	886	898

maintenance of an irrigation ditch. During the postsocialist period, responsibility for maintaining infrastructure has largely devolved to individuals and informal groups. Even when responsibility can clearly be established, such as the expansion of the main road in Little Rome, it is difficult to get resources from the administrative district. When coupled with the severe budgetary constraints of local governments in postsocialist China, the dismantling of the production team structure has resulted in the privatization of infrastructure development. To develop roads or build new schools, rural people have had to find new patrons.

The search for new patrons is not only sanctioned by the state; it is encouraged and fostered by local administrative structures, as I discussed in Chapter 2. Philanthropy from locals and overseas Chinese relieves the demand on the state for the maintenance and development of infrastructure. Newspapers and magazines frequently print stories about overseas Chinese who returned to their "native soil" to donate money for the construction of a school or road. When a native of Little Rome was hit by a truck where he worked in the Pearl River delta, neighbors collected donations to pay for his medical care. County cadres later posted an announcement in the village (on a blackboard across from the church) praising the modern socialist spirit that had spurred such "civilized" (*wenming*) compassion. A small article later appeared in the Meizhou Daily, praising the Little Rome community (and specifically citing the donation of an American anthropologist). Ideological promotion through the media in China does not have the high price tag of

Map 4.   Little Rome in 1965

similar "public service announcements" in the United States (witness the U.S. government's $195 million expenditure on antidrug advertisements in 1998), and is much cheaper for the local government than building a school or a road or paying for the operation. The use of ideological campaigns, in this case the state promotion of philanthropy, has long been part of the repertoire of the Chinese state. During the turmoil of the Maoist period, such ideological campaigns made up for the lack of state administrative structures in the central government of the People's Republic (see White 1989).

Villagers rely on traditional mechanisms of patron-client relations to encourage philanthropy. Both the more lasting stone monuments to donors

Figure 24   Elementary school board leaders meeting with overseas Chinese to discuss school conditions in 1997. The overseas Chinese in attendance had all contributed money to the school in the past.

for large capital projects (like the building of a church) and the more ephemeral red paper donation lists for smaller purposes (such as a funeral) elevate the social value of philanthropy. In his analysis of ancestral halls in the Hong Kong New Territories, James Watson (1993) explains that individuals donate large amounts of money to attain the immortality of a lasting capital investment in ancestral property. The naming of roads and buildings in the schools and universities of Hong Kong is another clear demonstration of the cultural valuation of attaining such immortality.

For second- or third-generation overseas Chinese, however, this cultural logic has largely lost its significance. For example, in Little Rome when the main road was repaved in the late 1980s, a large stone monument was erected to honor the donors. Like the donations for the new church, most came from local individuals. The church itself also heavily supported the project. The largest donor was an overseas Chinese family living in America.

When the retired surgeon discussed in Chapter 3 was touring the local elementary school, his adult daughter, Gabriela—also a physician from New York—jokingly told me that her father was there to "spend our inheritance." She wanted to see the classroom that was named after her brother.

For her, the value of such philanthropy is not immortality but the validation of her roots, her identity as a Chinese-American. One of the villagers, a retired English teacher, wrote this story about an earlier visit Gabriela had paid to Little Rome. I cannot express this episode better than he does himself, so I will include his story in full:

There lives an eighty-year-old woman, all skin and bone, named W.X., in Jiaoling county, Guangdong. She has two sons, one in New York, as a Doctor of Medicine and Fellow of American College of Surgeons, the other also in New York as a staff in a restaurant; she has a daughter who is my wife, and a stepdaughter who has been married to a peasant in Fujian.

It was in the second year after liberation that her second son left her and his homeland for Hong Kong to study. Ever since then she anxiously expected to see him day and night, but it was all in vain. Thirty years passed. On the night of April 4, 1979, her second son, who left America for his house to see his old mother, arrived home safely, which made her extremely glad.

Soon it was time for him to be back to America, as the passport required. You can imagine what it was like "being unable to see her second son any longer."

Ever since then, she would stand at the entrance to her house in the daytime, expecting to see her second son and her eldest son, who left her just before liberation for Taiwan and went to America some years ago. Sometimes she dreamed a sound dream of seeing her sons' families.

Much to her joy, on the midnight of October 15, 1980, her second son's wife got home to see her. But a few days later, her son's wife had to leave her for Beijing to call on her elder brothers whom she hadn't seen for more than thirty years.

From then on, she would ask me and other relatives to write to her sons, telling them to return home so that she could see them and theirs before going to heaven.

She was very much pleased that her second son really did return home on the midnight of December 26, 1984, with his son E. and daughter Gabriela, who are both studying at college. As soon as she saw them, she embraced first her second son, then her grandson, and finally her granddaughter, her eyes brimming with tears. Her desire of seeing her second son with his son and daughter came true in the end.

One night after the arrival of her son, there were many relatives and friends talking with her son in the hall when my mother-in-law called me to come up to her, telling me to ask in English for her granddaughter to sit beside her, because she doesn't speak or understand a single word of Chinese. I did so.

After a few seconds, my mother-in-law got up and took Gabriela by the hand and went into the room where she would sleep.

She lay in bed right away while Gabriela was sitting silent on the bedside with a lot of relatives in the room. About five minutes passed this way. Suddenly my mother-in-law told me to ask Gabriela to lie in bed on the same side. But it wasn't long before she even hinted with her hand that Gabriela would lie closer to her, which caused all the relatives to feel very much surprised.

First, she told me to ask Gabriela if she would want to take her to America. Gabriela readily agreed.

Then, my mother-in-law told me again to ask Gabriela whether she would be driven off if she asked their father to bring her back to China when only one month passed. Gabriela made a promise that she herself would never do it, and she would persuade her father not to do it, if he were to do it.

Finally, she asked Gabriela: "Can you promise to come back to China again to see me when you have finished college?" Gabriela did so. "How about every four years?" Gabriela also did. Shortly after she asked Gabriela: "How can you get so much money?" "In order to come back to China again to see my grandmother, I'll save money" answered Gabriela, bursting into tears.

Hearing these words, my mother-in-law nodded in satisfaction several times and smiled a nice smile. Some of the relatives also smiled and some relatives' eyes were filled with tears. I couldn't refrain from tears, too.

What a moving scene!

At nine o'clock, on the evening of June 24, 1985, her eldest son really got home alone to see her, which made her extremely happy. She longed for her eldest son's return day and night for a complete thirty years. You can surely feel what it was like "seeing her son again."

Hearing of my brother-in-law's arrival, I, with my second son, went to say hello to my mother-in-law and her son. "Now you ought to be satisfied, my dear mother-in-law, because in the end you saw your eldest son with your own eyes. How glad you are!" She made no answer, only smiling.

Philanthropy and the Gift

In the beginnings of anthropology, there was the gift. Long an anthropological staple, theorists have unpacked the meaning of the gift in many different ways. Some have said that a gift has meaning because of its *hau*, the residual spirit of the giver (Mauss 1967); others say that its meaning lies in the social obligation of reciprocity (Sahlins 1972); still others have said that what is important in gift exchange is what is not given (Weiner 1992).[2] The literature, however, has largely portrayed the exchange of material between individuals and groups as a balanced system, where equilibrium is somehow maintained and everyone comes out even. Little has been said about the donation, where reciprocity must be achieved in another realm because of the inequality between the donor and the recipient. The following discussion explores a framework for understanding philanthropy.

A distinction must be made between gift giving and philanthropy.[3] Philanthropy is distinct from the remittances sent home by itinerant workers. Although transnational in range and enormous in scope, remittances are intended for family use (in 1996, Chinese workers living abroad sent home remittances of US$840 million; Saywell 1997). In contrast to gift giving and remittances, philanthropy involves the donation of money for a specific community purpose (such as a construction project or the expansion of a university department), where the donor has access to resources not available to the recipient and the donation has been solicited by the recipient or the recipient's representatives. Despite the enormous impact of philanthropy in Chinese social life, as testified by the stone monuments and plaques honoring donors throughout postsocialist China, few studies have analyzed philanthropy as a social process.

Although philanthropic organizations have long been a part of the social landscape in Chinese history (see Wakeman 1998), their organizational structures were retooled to more closely resemble the Western models of philanthropy based on the success of missionary organizations during the Republican period (Duara 1997). The rise of philanthropy as a salient social process may have started in the late Ming, with the rise of a merchant class that sought to gain political access and legitimize their traditionally disdained social status (Joanna Handlin Smith 1987). Brook (1993) further maps out the historical commercialization of Chinese society onto a social contour of philanthropic organizations, both religious and secular, and the rise of a public sphere ("gentry society") outside the domain of the state. The highly influential Buddhist Compassion Relief Society in Taiwan in the late 1990s annually contributed over US$20 million for relief efforts in locales as diverse as China, Ethiopia, and Italy. Huang and Weller (1998) cite this philanthropic organization as a strong example of an indigenous civil organization that stands between the state and individuals. Noting that the membership of the Buddhist Compassion Relief Society is 80 percent Taiwanese women, Huang and Weller assert that one reason women engage in philanthropy is to extend their social sphere into a public realm dominated by men.

The differences between the social environment of Taiwan and mainland China, however, are enormous, and philanthropy in China must be seen from a different perspective. In an analysis of Chinese civil organizations, Pei (1998) concludes that the absence of a large private sector and of individually controlled economic resources rendered philanthropy relatively unimportant on the mainland until the early 1990s. He further suggests that in the absence of further political reforms there is little likelihood that nascent philanthropic organizations can result in the development of civil organizations like that described by Huang and Weller. Philanthropy in China, therefore, is not primarily directed toward cultivating political legitimacy and influence, at least for the donors. What then is the social logic that motivates donors to contribute large amounts of money for community activities?

For overseas relatives and friends of Little Rome's villagers, philanthropy appears to be a means of maintaining membership in the Little Rome community. The names of donors and the amount given, whether listed temporarily on a sheet of red paper or permanently inscribed on a stone monument, can be seen as a community membership list. The building of the road solidified relationships formed through proximity, through the church, and through kinship. For larger capital projects involving donations from overseas relations and friends, donations attest to the commitment that people like Gabriela and her father have to Little Rome. In the absence of daily face-to-face contact, such displays of commitment are vital for sustaining membership in the Little Rome community (see also Olwig and Hastrup 1997 for a similar explanation of remittances and kinship networks).

In Chapter 2, I described how local cadres encouraged philanthropy and investment from overseas kin and friends in their search for patrons to fill the space vacated by the state. This instrumental perspective, however, is muted in the more intimate relations of a community like Little Rome. Gabriela and her father invested time and money in their ancestral hometown out of a sense of service, of payback to the people of the community who helped to make them who they are. In Little Rome, many used Catholic metaphors to explain why they are doing so, as in the gospel story of Zaccheus used during the church opening ceremony discussed in Chapter 3.

In other words, what I have called the privatization of public works may be a misnomer from the perspective of the people who are building the roads themselves. To an outsider who sees the local county government divesting itself from village expenditures, the privatization picture seems accurate. But from the perspective of the people in Little Rome, do-it-yourself socialism is a way of building community. Building the road together, from resources that they themselves accumulated, reinforced friendships across the boundaries of production team assignments and agnatic kinship. It also cemented my own family's position in the community. Word spread to people outside Little Rome that the American not only donated money to the project but also worked himself, hauling rocks and sand. It was the labor that I invested, more than the money, that gave meaning to our being part of Little Rome. When neighbors advised me (and told others) not to participate in projects in other villages, they were also reminding me of community boundaries.

CHAPTER 9

Being Hakka in the Hakka Homeland

People in Little Rome are not just Catholic; they are also part of a worldwide diaspora. They are Hakka in the Hakka homeland, an identity that has become an increasingly important cultural authority as transnational processes penetrate the Chinese hinterland. In places outside the Hakka homeland, such as Hong Kong or Taiwan, being Hakka is a salient social marker when neighbors are Cantonese or Fujianese. Political candidates in Taiwan appeal to Hakka voters for their support (Martin 1996), and many economic exchanges between the Southeast Asian diaspora are shaped by ethnicity (Wang 1991). But what does it mean to be Hakka when almost all your neighbors are also Hakka? In Little Rome and other communities in the Hakka homeland, a Hakka identity grounded in illustrious ancestors and primordial histories has paradoxically become a marker of modernity. Diaspora identity has become an important part of local social processes as transnational processes have increasingly made this rural village global.

Who Are the Hakka?

Hakka ethnic identity developed out of specific historical events that made being Hakka a socially recognized form of self-identification and ascription by others. These events, such as the Hakka-Cantonese wars and the Taiping Rebellion (a Hakka-led rebellion inspired by soteriological elements of Christianity), were critical in the process of ethnogenesis for Hakka communities outside the Hakka homeland (see Spence 1996; Cohen 1968; Gladney 1991; Constable 1994). Because ethnogenesis arises out of contact with other groups (Keyes 1981), Hakka ethnicity developed outside the Hakka homeland, and like Catholicism it was brought back into the Hakka homeland during the postsocialist period through the proliferation of exchanges with overseas friends and kin who sought to reestablish links with their native place. Whereas those in the diaspora use the Hakka homeland as proof of their Chinese ethnicity, those who live in the Hakka homeland use Hakka ethnicity as a claim to modernity. To illustrate this, I will first describe what it means to be Hakka in the Hakka homeland in the post-Deng period.

Thousands of people attended the opening ceremony for the Sakyamuni Cultural Center (a Buddhist temple) in Jiaoling county on November 17, 1996. Funded largely with a US$2.5 million donation from an overseas Hakka family in Thailand, the Sakyamuni Cultural Center was part of the county's development of the Changtan reservoir area (about ten kilometers north of Little Rome) as a major tourist attraction. Highlighted on the county tourist maps that were first published in 1997, the Sakyamuni Cultural Center and Changtan reservoir area are frequently visited by county residents. Because of its fame as a Catholic community (and because it has attracted so many diaspora Chinese and foreign visitors), Little Rome was also marked on this map. During vacations and on special occasions, many Little Rome families made their way up to Changtan to visit the cultural center and another nearby Buddhist temple and to enjoy a boat ride on the reservoir. During the 1997 Spring Festival vacation, many villagers from Little Rome made sure to visit the newly constructed Hakka Museum in the cultural center. The Hakka Museum was a key part of the itinerary for the alumni of Jiaoling High School's fortieth reunion, organized by my landlord, Mr. Peng, a retired elementary school math teacher.

At the main entrance of the Hakka Museum is a definition of the Hakka that follows that of the Hakka historian Luo Xianglin: they are a subgroup of the dominant Han ethnic group of China that migrated southward from central China during five documented periods of mass migration (Luo 1992; Char 1969). Their ancestors were oppressed and unable to gain access to land; they arrived in the south as refugees or "guest people" (a literal translation of the term Hakka). As settlers on marginal lands, however, Hakka leaders maintained their true allegiance to Han Chinese dynasties and were prominent among loyalist partisans against the foreign Jurchen Jin (265–420 C.E.), Mongol Yuan (1271–1368), and Manchu Qing (1644–1912) dynasties. There are monuments to Qiu Fengjia, a Hakka leader of the Taiwanese independence movement against Japanese colonialism, scattered throughout Jiaoling county, and his ancestral home has been preserved by local cadres.

A locally produced guidebook provides more "official" detail about the Hakka and the "land of culture" (*wenhua zhi xiang*)—a slogan often used by cadres, business people, and other prominent residents to describe the Hakka homeland of Meizhou prefecture. According to the guidebook, the

Hakka ancestors who fled from the north were predominantly from elite, scholarly families who, despite the hardships of this mountainous and unforgiving territory, continued their extended tradition of education (CHCR 1987: 22). Prominent Hakka, whose biographies fill the many Chinese publications celebrating Hakka culture, are closely identified with certain schools. Jiaoling High School, the school most sought after by Little Rome residents for their children, was established by Qiu Fengjia.

For the Hakka in Jiaoling county, Qiu Fengjia and other historical and contemporary notables embody the "Hakka Spirit" (*kejia jingshen*). People in Little Rome and other parts of Jiaoling county interpret Hakka ethnicity through manifestations of the Hakka Spirit in the concrete achievements of their neighbors and famous local people. One neighbor who knew of my interest in the Hakka gave me a book by a local writer called *Stories from the Shiku River* (Xu 1996) that featured people from Little Rome. This book is primarily a collection of biographies of historical figures and success stories about Jiaoling county, from the Yuan dynasty to the present. It documents the philanthropy and activism of people from villages like Little Rome (mostly diaspora Hakka in the United States, Southeast Asia, and Taiwan) who rose to positions of financial, professional, and political status. It includes the New York physician mentioned in earlier chapters and Father Paul Zhang. The book closes with several essays on elements of Hakka culture (such as mountain songs) and more general descriptions of the Hakka Spirit. According to Xu, the Hakka Spirit developed from a combination of ancient Han culture and the experience of overcoming migratory challenges in the mass exodus from the central Chinese plain. The result is the culture of today's Hakka, who "generally are industrious, courageous, entrepreneurial, and absolutely patriotic and loyal to China and their native place; though scattered afar, they never forget their roots and profoundly remember their ancestors" (Xu 1996: 243; my translation). These success stories fuel the hopes of people in the homeland, who as holders of the Hakka Spirit by virtue of their ancestors' struggles, claim their place in global modernity.

This construction of Hakka identity as embodied in the Hakka Spirit has been studied in great detail by scholars, both Hakka and non-Hakka, and all have had to acknowledge, in support or critique, the seminal work of Hakka historian Luo Xianglin. Leong concludes that the popularity of Luo Xianglin's thesis on Hakka identity comes from "its unambiguous statement of a number of Hakka cardinal beliefs" (Leong 1997: 29). This interpretation is indeed the dominant understanding of Hakka identity in Little Rome and throughout the Hakka homeland of Meizhou prefecture. Other interpretations of Hakka origins have challenged Luo's thesis, however, demonstrating the importance of social context in discussions of Hakka ethnicity.

One work that has sparked debate inside and outside the Hakka homeland comes from Meixian, from my host and colleague Fang Xuejia of the Hakka Research Center, Jiaying University, Meizhou. His research and fieldwork have led him to believe that the Hakka are the product of the intermingling of migrant Han and local She (a nationality, *minzu*, recognized by the PRC as distinct from the Han) (Fang 1994). Fang documents archeological remains from the local Yue kingdom (from the late Zhou to the Han period, 206 B.C.E.–220 C.E.) and current popular religious practices to show that a large number of Hakka cultural characteristics are definitively absent in northern Han Chinese culture and must derive from a precontact indigenous culture. Chan Wing-hoi (1995) makes a similar argument by tracing the disappearance of ordination names associated with Yao (another nationality) and She ritual practices from Hakka genealogies from the Hong Kong New Territories. Their disappearance was part of the process of Hakka adaption to Han lineage culture.

By focusing on the migration history of the Hakka, Leong (1997) also concludes that the ancestors of the Hakka were largely local non-Han people and that Hakka ethnicity arose out of historical encounters between people who lived in the mountainous peripheries of southern Chinese market regions and locals in major market towns and cities. The original migrants from the north who settled into southern mountain peripheries assimilated local She technologies of cultivation. Leong thus concludes that the Hakka developed an ecological niche and were better suited to open frontier lands nearer major market towns during the expansion of the eighteenth and nineteenth centuries. Chen (1997) makes a similar argument by contrasting Hakka and non-Hakka genealogical history for those who migrated south, demonstrating that the development of Hakka identity and use of what became the Hakka dialect was a result of their settlement in She mountainous areas. Hakka ethnic awareness and group solidarity solidified as conflicts with locals developed from the social and economic inequalities faced by these itinerant workers, traders, and temporary settlers.

A more radical thesis on Hakka identity comes from Taiwan, where Hakka activists are key players in Taiwanese politics (Martin 1996). Kiang's (1991) emphasis on the differences between the Hakka ethnic minority and the dominant Han majority is based on evidence from genealogies, historical records, and genetic research that show Hakka ties to Central Asia. According to Kiang, the Hakka must be seen not as a subethnic group of the Han majority, but as a separate ethnic nationality with its own culture. According to Kiang, the Hakka as an ethnic group are closer in origin and culture to the Koreans and Japanese, with whom they share a primordial ancestry. Hakka ancestors are genetically not Han; they are assimilated Xiong-nu who challenged Han domination in the third century B.C.E..[1] The Hakka supposedly partially assimilated to Han culture and suppressed their true identity in order to avoid persecution (Kiang 1991: 15). Unlike other Han subethnic groups who maintain claims to specific Chinese regions, the Hakka propensity for migration and "their eternal search for a homeland" underscores their Central Asian nomadic origins, retained in spirit if not in practice with a shift to a sedentary lifestyle.

Although scholars of Hakka culture and society contest the origin of the Hakka as described above, they all agree that Hakka ethnicity arose as a historical phenomenon. Historical events such as the Hakka-Cantonese wars (see Myron Cohen 1968) and the Taiping Rebellion in the mid-nineteenth century galvanized the cultural solidarity of Hakka dialect speakers into a self-identified ethnic group. The polarized explanations of the origin of the Hakka themselves come out of the historical context of scholarship. Luo's seminal account was written in reaction to social prejudice faced by Hakka people from Cantonese and other Han Chinese subethnic groups. During the early twentieth century, Hakka scholars reacted strongly to the categorization of the Hakka as aboriginal and to other disparaging treatments of the Hakka. Such discriminatory treatments in local county gazetteers inflamed the already tenuous ethnic relations in the Pearl River delta and other areas outside the Hakka homeland, in much the same way that the 1989 Muslim Hui protested the publication of books that denigrated Islam (see Gladney 1991). Accounts of the northern origins of the Hakka by Lou and other historians were meant to situate the Hakka firmly within the Han social sphere (see Erbaugh 1996: 209). Similarly, the significance of Kiang's account of the Inner Asian origins of the Hakka can only be understood in light of the Taiwanese Hakka ethnic movement. This perspective, radically different from the traditional understanding of Hakka origins, is part of the process of establishing "the new Hakka" (Martin 1996). This strand of Hakka ethnic mobilization is inextricably linked to the political context and social history of Taiwan, and as Martin concludes, cannot be separated from people's positions on the future of Taiwan.

Recent writings on the Hakka have traced their ethnic history to the present only on the periphery of the Hakka diaspora and have shown how local contemporary events have shaped what it means to be Hakka in a multicultural setting (Martin 1996; Constable 1996; Johnson 1996; Oxfeld 1996; Carstens 1996). But what does it mean to be Hakka in the Hakka heartland of Meizhou prefecture in the post-Mao period?

Few scholars have written about the contemporary situation of the Hakka on the mainland.[2] In an examination of the wider national discourse (and the absence of one) on Hakka ethnicity, Erbaugh (1996, 1992) traces the origins of many CCP leaders to Hakka areas; he links various aspects of the CCP revolution, such as the targeting of landless and poor groups like the Hakka, the Hakka history of rebellion and conflict, and the prevalence of early CCP Soviet bases in Hakka areas, to conclude that the CCP revolution can be seen as a Hakka enterprise. The Hakka role in the CCP revolution was subdued, however, to sustain the CCP's nationalist agenda: the creation of a strong, unified, and modern Chinese state. During the Maoist period, regionalism (*difang zhuyi*) in the form of ethnic identities grounded in specific localities was specifically targeted by the CCP as it sought to strengthen the new community of the People's Republic of China. Hakka ethnicity in the Hakka homeland "came out of the closet" only during the post-Mao era when the poorer and more remote areas like Meizhou prefecture solicited overseas funding for various projects.[3]

Since coming out of the closet during the Deng era, local Hakka in the Hakka homeland have accelerated their promotion of projects that address Hakka identity, such as the construction of the Jiaoling county Hakka Museum. Although the Hakka dialect remains a distinctive marker of Hakka ethnicity, what it means to be Hakka is driven neither by linguistic characteristics nor by distinct religious practices, but by kinship. Because Hakka ethnicity in the post-Deng era is grounded in kinship and locality in the Hakka homeland, it can be instrumental in soliciting overseas investment and philanthropy by local cadres in Meizhou. Many overseas patrons—and especially their descendants—do not speak Mandarin, let alone Hakka. The central donor for the Sakyamuni Cultural Center gave her speech in English. Others living in the more prosperous areas of the Pearl River delta are more comfortable speaking in Cantonese than in Hakka when they return to the Hakka homeland for ritual events like *qingming*. Hakka ethnicity is a cultural interpretation of descent that is not necessarily bound by objective markers of ethnicity such as language (see Keyes 1981).

Promoting Hakka Ethnicity in the Homeland and in the Diaspora

Local cadres and entrepreneurs in the Hakka homeland are engaged in diverse efforts to promote Hakka ethnicity. County and prefectural officials emphasize the unique positioning of Meizhou as the Hakka homeland in projects such as the building and promotion of tourist destinations such as the Sakyamuni Cultural Center and the Hakka Museum. As the train from Shenzhen crosses into the Meizhou area, a brief introduction to Meizhou and the history of the Hakka is announced over the loudspeaker. Local products, such as Hakka rice wine (*kejia niangjiu*), are celebrated on billboards lining roads to the airport and railroad station and in advertisements. People in the Hakka homeland are well aware of the increased interest in Hakka ethnicity in Hong Kong, Taiwan, and overseas Chinese communities and have incorporated into their ethnic awareness a sense of being modern.

A HAKKA UNIVERSITY

Research in Hakka history and culture has been rekindled by interest from overseas Hakka activists and academics and has led to the expansion of educational institutions in the Hakka homeland, such as Jiaying University.[4] Jiaying University was established in 1985 with the approval of the provincial government and the support of overseas Chinese, especially a successful Hakka businessman in Hong Kong. Up to 1997, donations by overseas Chinese totaled 60 million RMB (US$7.3 million). Since its founding, Jiaying University has continually expanded and increased its offerings. In 1988, nearby Jiaying Teachers' College was integrated into Jiaying University. The university was a junior college (*zhuan ke*), where full-time students receive the equivalent of an associate's degree after two or three years of study; the majority become teachers in the elementary, junior high, and high schools of the seven counties of Meizhou prefecture.

In 1998, Jiaying University had thirteen academic departments, 230 faculty members, 4,500 full-time students, and 3,000 correspondence students.[5] The department with the largest budget and the most students is Foreign Languages, whose primary focus is to train English teachers for local elementary and high schools (in 1997, approximately one-fifth of the department's students majored in international trade). In 1998, Jiaying University received permission from the provincial government to upgrade its facilities and personnel to become a four-year university (*ben ke*) whose graduates will receive the equivalent of a bachelor's degree. That same year, Jiaying

University also received its first group of foreign students (from the United States and Malaysia) for summer language study and an introduction to Hakka culture.

As Jiaying University upgrades its curriculum, the university president and leadership of Jiaying are focusing on Hakka culture in their outreach to overseas Chinese, as the university brochure explains:

> Jiaying University seeks to promote its educational structure, to upgrade its level of teaching, scientific research, and management, and to improve classroom teaching in order to make Jiaying University a high-quality and influential regional university of academic excellence that especially promotes Hakka culture. (My translation)

The Hakka Research Center has been an integral part of Jiaying's efforts to promote Hakka culture. In 1997 the Hakka Research Center maintained an active local research program, an academic program, and outreach to foreign scholars and overseas Chinese. In addition to the *Journal of Hakka Research*, Jiaying's Hakka Research Center publishes the Traditional Hakka Culture Series, which by 1998 had released seven of ten planned books. The books of the Traditional Hakka Culture Series are the outcome of a collaborative research program directed by John Lagerwey of the École Française Extrème Orient. In this prolific and highly visible research program in the Hakka world, local scholars like Fang Xuejia and Yang Yanjie of the Fujian Academy of Social Sciences seek out local intellectuals (*zhishifenzi*) who are interested in conducting fieldwork in their home counties.

These locals are mostly retired teachers or, more rarely, cadres in the county cultural office (*wenhua ju*) who want to promote Hakka culture. Their published articles—though critiqued by some foreign academics as nonprofessional—contain extensive ethnographic detail about life in the Hakka homeland.[6] During my fieldwork, I worked with one such person from Jiaoling county, Lin Qingshui (a retired math teacher), whose Hakka research was a passionately pursued labor of love. The retired teachers who conducted this research were recognized for their expertise on local culture and viewed almost as local heroes. Mr. Lin wrote not only for the Traditional Hakka Culture Series but also for a magazine published by the county government primarily for overseas Hakka.

The Hakka Research Center connects with people beyond the Hakka homeland both through its publications and through its research staff who participate in academic and social conferences outside of Meizhou. The growth of "Hakkaology" (*kejia xue*) beyond the confines of the Hakka homeland led to the first meeting of the International Association of Hakka-ology in Hong Kong in 1992 (Erbaugh 1996: 228–30). The second meeting was convened in Meizhou in 1994. The third meeting of the International Association of Hakkaology, in Singapore in 1996, was held at the same time and place as the Thirteenth World Hakka Gathering. The Hakka Research Center was represented by Fang Xuejia and four other scholars from Jiaying University. A television film crew from Meizhou TV was also sent to Singapore to record the events for local broadcasting back in Meizhou.

Because the two meetings were combined, Hakka activists and academics mixed together in what became an immense celebration of Hakka culture (including performances of Hakka mountain songs and a banquet for four thousand people). At times, the panel discussions became explosive as the contrasting agendas of Hakka activists and academics came into conflict. After the conference, Hakka activists complained that one of the shortfalls of the Third International Hakkaology Conference was its use of either Mandarin or English for presentations (the majority of papers were presented in Mandarin) rather than Hakka. Preservation of the Hakka dialect is a major thrust of Hakka activists (especially those from Taiwan), and the use of Mandarin and English at a Hakka meeting was seen as a betrayal of Hakka identity. Some of the critiques blamed the Singapore government, where the government's promotion of Mandarin and English over Chinese dialects like Hakka is seen by many activists as the suppression of Hakka ethnicity.

Promoting Hakka ethnicity, like perspectives on the origin of the Hakka, is a social enterprise shaped by factors other than ethnicity, such as nationalism and status. Whether one is a Singaporean Hakka, a Taiwanese Hakka, or a mainland Hakka informs one's academic and activist discourse on Hakka identity. Diaspora ethnic movements come together out of diversity, resulting in a tendency for segmentation along different fault lines (such as nationality or religion). Constable (1996) makes a similar conclusion about Hakka ethnicity: that a shared (real or imagined) history of their ancestors serves as a focal point for maintaining ethnic solidarity. Although Hakka identity arose out of differences from other groups in Hong Kong, Taiwan, and Calcutta, in the Hakka homeland where all neighbors are Hakka, ethnicity arose out of the resumption of transnational processes.

Erbaugh (1996) asserts that ethnic awareness grew in the homeland as state policy began promoting the cultivation of overseas ties. That policy change led to the development of ethnic awareness in Meizhou, but it was not hopes of overseas investment that motivated Little Rome residents to visit the county Hakka Museum or motivated Lin Qingshui to do fieldwork in his native county. People in Little Rome learned about their Hakka identity through indirect contact with other ethnic groups and from Hakka experiences overseas. In 1995, Father Liang gave me an unpublished manuscript that explained Hakka ethnicity in Taiwan (the manuscript was given to him by a visitor from Taiwan and interestingly was modeled on and cited Barth's 1969 model of ethnicity). Television programs that show Hakka celebrations outside China are featured on the local Meizhou TV and archived in Jiaying University's video library. To be Hakka in the Hakka homeland, then, is to be modern, with membership in a global social group.

Moreover, because of the post-Mao mobility of labor and commodities, there is a strong awareness of other ethnic groups even in the Hakka homeland. Hakka young adults working in Shenzhen, Zhuhai, and other prosperous areas in the Pearl River delta regularly come into contact with Cantonese people (although none of those I interviewed mentioned ethnic discrimination). They are all fluent in Cantonese, having learned it even before they left Little Rome through television and music. Canto-pop dominates the music scene in the Hakka homeland, far eclipsing sales of famous Taiwanese Hakka mountain song singers among young adults. Without knowing Cantonese, young Hakka men and women would not be able to sing many of the songs on trendy karaoke video CDs. As these young adults settle down in Shenzhen and other Pearl River delta areas, they face the same problem of maintaining Hakka language skills for their children that Hakka in Hong Kong face (Constable 1994). Hakka young adults are marrying non-Hakka people, and the cultural strength of Hakka for these people is being eclipsed by the economic strength of Cantonese and the political strength of Mandarin.

HAKKA IN CYBERSPACE

Through the efforts of academics at Jiaying University, Hakka activists at the International Conferences on Hakkaology, and the many cadres and entrepreneurs soliciting patronage and conducting business transnationally, the Hakka homeland is strongly linked to the Hakka diaspora outside China. Through the Internet and local overseas Hakka associations, the diaspora is also connected to the Hakka homeland. One such Hakka community in cyberspace illustrates how transnational processes shape what it means to be Hakka all over the world, including in the Hakka homeland.

The Hakka Global Network (HGN) is a "manually run Internet mailing list" (Chin 1996) for subscribers who are interested in Hakka culture. Started in 1995, HGN provides a forum for a lively transnational discourse on Hakka culture and Hakka social experiences. It also provides information about Hakka cultural events around the world, the activities of Hakka organizations, and where to obtain Hakka-related material. In May 1997 there were 191 subscribers from sixteen countries, and the membership list and Hakka Web pages continue to increase through networking and affiliated Web sites.

The primary purpose of HGN is to "provide a vehicle for reaching Hakkas around the world and establish a virtual community [that discusses] Hakka issues of interest to Hakkas as well as non-Hakkas."[7] The broader aim of the HGN is the preservation of Hakka culture as Hakka become more and more dispersed throughout the world. HGN members are critical of the homogenizing influences of global forces (especially communications technology), yet ironically are using the global reach of the Internet to promote cultural identity.

Who are the members of the HGN? Unsurprisingly, the majority of HGN members appear to be a highly educated, well-traveled group scattered around the world (see also Rai 1995). According to an Internet survey conducted by Hsieh (a Hakka HGN member living in Canada) and my own observations, most of the HGN members appear to be young male professionals (Hsieh 1996), although some women and nonprofessionals also participate. Some are highly knowledgeable about Hakka history and tradition and are actively involved in Hakka organizations. During a period of HGN message traffic analysis, these activists, who constitute only 14 percent of the membership, sent over 70 percent of the messages on HGN.[8] They also participate in regional Hakka associations and attend events such as the Third Meeting of the International Conference of Hakkaology (one such activist was on a panel with me in Singapore).

HGN members promote organizations and activities that preserve elements of Hakka culture, especially the public use of the Hakka language and traditional Hakka customs (such as theater and music)—the cultural elements that Handler (1988) refers to as the *patrimoine* (the objectified heritage of an ethnic group). Like the Quebecois folklorists in Handler's study, HGN members are not preserving mythical, pristine Hakka folkways; rather they are actively inventing new Hakka traditions in a manner intelligible to the people of today. The discussion surrounding a theater group's revival of "tai-hi" (described by an HGN member as a Hakka version of Peking Opera) pointedly demonstrates this point. Although "tai hi" is being promoted as a traditional marker of Hakka identity, it is a relatively recent invention, according to one HGN member. Tai-hi is explained in a message to HGN members as having been developed in Taiwan about one hundred years ago (and is not thought to be brought over by Hakka immigrants from Guangdong); it was popular in temple festivals and a regular feature of theater from the 1940s to the 1960s.

HGN activity is not confined to the Internet, but spills over into the "real world." The most popular topic on HGN (discussed by 18 percent of the members) is access to Hakka resources outside the Internet, including radio and television shows, newspaper stories, music, and books. These announcements, although usually advertising resources available only to regional audiences (e.g., Taiwan or Singapore television viewers, California radio listeners) were of great interest to members outside the region and stimulated many exchanges. Announcements about Hakka organizations and Hakka-based activity to HGN members are further illustrations of how the Internet connects local social events to other locations. For example, when one HGN member asked for information about how to join a U.S.-based Taiwanese Hakka organization, another HGN member responded, describing the U.S. organization (headquartered in Dallas) and its twelve local chapters throughout the country. He also described the conventions and other activities that they have held. Hakka activities around the world, such as the Third International Hakkaology Conference and the Thirteenth World Hakka Grand Gathering in Singapore, became "local" activities for HGN members as news, plans, and other information were exchanged between members.

The localization of the HGN becomes more transparent in face-to-face meetings and tours organized by HGN members. Many HGN members reported meeting other members in Hong Kong, Taiwan, the United States, and Meizhou. Before embarking on a trip, some members asked others for travel and restaurant advice (one series of messages concerned Hakka restaurants around the world). These personal encounters, as reported by HGN members, reinforced already meaningful social ties established through computer-mediated communication (Parks and Floyd 1996).

HGN members achieve locality through sustained discourse over the Internet and through face-to-face meetings, while people in Little Rome see each other daily, at work and at play. How different are these two forms of locality? With the scattering of younger villagers to different parts of China and overseas, and with the renewed participation of overseas Chinese in village life, Little Rome's locality is becoming deterritorialized, as it is for the HGN. The heavy consumption of electronic media and other commodities that expand the repertoire of imagined possibilities makes it harder for people in this community today to sustain locality. For example, one of the few young, single men in Little Rome literally has to work hard to maintain his romance (i.e., to pay his telephone bill) with a woman who emigrated from the village to Germany. In other words, the deterritorialization of Little Rome is very much a part of everyday social life. Through the social processes described in the previous chapters, residents maintain locality through a variety of mechanisms—a locality that must be seen not as a physical property (an accident of geography or the design of the nation-state), but as a social process, ongoing and in flux.

Virtual communities like HGN reveal the weaknesses in previous conceptions of community (see Haas 1992 on "epistemic communities"). Through his model of corporate groups, M. G. Smith tries to expand the range of communities beyond that defined by governments: the city of Santa Monica, the Roman Catholic Church, an African lineage, and a university can all be seen as social groupings that play a role in the political organization of different societies (Smith 1974: 94). For Smith, a corporate group has: (1) continuity; (2) determinate membership; (3) an internal organization; (4) a unitary set of external relations; (5) an exclusive body of common affairs; and (6) internal administrative procedures (also see Moore 1989, which discusses Smith). As depicted above, HGN has continuity, a determinate membership, internal organization, a body of common affairs, and internal administrative procedures.[9] What HGN does not have is a unitary set of external relations—a single channel or set of procedures for dealing with outsiders. However, given the penetration of village space by transnational processes, neither does Little Rome have a unitary set of external relations.

In fact, the transnational flux of people and ideas is precisely the challenge that nation-states now face through their participation in global capitalism (Sassen 1996). State bureaucracies, like the overseas Chinese county offices discussed earlier, try to maintain sovereignty through the administration of overseas Chinese support in the county. However, many of their efforts are "after the fact" attempts to grant state legitimacy to philanthropy or investment secured through kinship, religious, or other social networks.

Thus the HGN and Little Rome lie on two extremes of the spectrum of locality as a social process: one is a deterritorialized community that strives to establish common ground, while the other shares common ground that is becoming deterritorialized. Both communities, nonetheless, create locality by developing shared histories and social exchange, by trying to maintain a neighborhood where everybody knows your name. But daily face-to-face contact is not a prerequisite for maintaining community intimacy. The intimacy HGN members achieve through dialogue over the Internet, is reinforced by personal visits and joint participation in Hakka activities. While residents of Little Rome share many experiences that form the basis of locality through everyday contact, they also rely on charged moments in kinship and ritual and their diasporic identity as Hakka in defining their community.

Internet access is available in Meizhou and is gradually gaining popularity among more well-to-do city residents. For residents of Little Rome, however, the Internet is something they know about only through television, something that people in places like Hong Kong and Shanghai can use. In 1998, however, there were a number of computer stores in the local county seat, and information about establishing an Internet account is explained in the county telephone directory. Although cyber-commmunication is still largely a part of the imagination, just as cellular phones and beepers were not long ago, the Internet is part of the repertoire that villagers will use to shape their future.

Ethnicity and the Creation of Locality

Outside the Hakka homeland, in multiethnic environments, the Hakka readily identify themselves by their ethnic group (Constable 1996). Moreover, ethnicity is the bond that ties the Hakka in the Hakka homeland to other Hakka individuals and communities throughout the world. In the Hakka homeland, ethnicity has become an important social factor in the transnational processes that have relinked mainland Hakka with the Hakka diaspora. How does ethnicity shape the interplay between local and diaspora social processes? Fieldwork evidence from the Hakka homeland suggests that ethnic processes at different spatial levels display characteristics of segmentary social processes (Herzfeld 1985; Evans-Pritchard 1940). In other words, as Charles Keyes concluded in the early 1980s, ethnicity is essentially a manifestation of kinship structures writ large that provides structure to social processes both within and between ethnic groups.

Hakka ancestors, given their prominence in the Hakka ritual domain, provide the "enduring power of ethnic appeal as structurating sentiments and as instant mobilizer of crowds for collective political action" (Tambiah 1992: 29). Like kinship, ethnicity can also be used instrumentally to attain status or material goals, the strategy of many local Hakka cadres (Abner Cohen 1969; Barth 1969). This balance of primordialist and instrumentalist interpretations of ethnicity has already been well explored in the anthropological literature on ethnicity (Keyes 1981; Gladney 1991; Eriksen 1993; Constable 1994). The next step in transcending the constraints of primordialist and instrumentalist interpretations of ethnicity, according to Tambiah, is to focus on the "communicational and semiotic processes through which individuals within an ethnic group are mobilized for action" (1992: 31).

This is precisely what Constable traces in her analysis of diaspora Hakka ethnicity, in which history serves as the "genealogy" through which Hakka Christians in a Hong Kong New Territories village construct ethnic identity (Constable 1994). For the villagers in Little Rome deep within the Hakka homeland, where as a group they have not had immediate encounters with other ethnic groups, ethnicity unfolds in a segmentary process. This process links people in Little Rome to the wider diaspora through intermediary groups—those attached through a definable kinship link, those living in Little Rome, other communities in the same county, continuing outward into an increasingly deterritorialized community. People in Little Rome use Hakka history as a genealogy writ large, positioning themselves in a line of descent from ancestors who moved from the Chinese central plain, but they do so in order to identify with particular historical and contemporary notables, who themselves are associated with a specific village or achievement.

People in Little Rome did not worry about Hakka ethnicity in the abstract—it was a given, a result of having forefathers who were Hakka, speaking Hakka dialect, eating particular foods, working hard, and living in the mountains. Specific events were explained as "Hakka tradition," though many of them (such as ancestor worship, sweeping the graves, and making deep-fried snacks from glutinous rice before Spring Festival) are also part of Han Chinese culture throughout the mainland and the Chinese diaspora. People did assert a particular style of Hakka architecture (round earth houses called *tu lou*, and "walled dragon houses" called *weilongwu*) that are more common to the Hakka, and they made sure to point out that the two renminbi Chinese stamp bore a picture of Hakka roundhouses. Being Hakka was a topic of conversation when stimulated by particular events, such as the broadcast of a Hakka celebration taking place in the diaspora (like the Thirteenth World Hakka Gathering in Singapore) or a news article about prominent Hakka elsewhere in the world. More particularly, people in Little Rome identified with the diaspora through people they knew. One leading Hakka scholar, John Lagerwey, visited me in Little Rome and met many of my friends and neighbors there. A couple of months after his visit, some villagers had gathered to drink tea and read newspapers and magazines in the church, when one neighbor showed me an article about a Hakka conference held in Zhejiang province that included John's picture, stimulating a discussion of why people throughout China and the entire world are interested in Hakka research.

People in Little Rome see and portray themselves as Hakka, experiencing diaspora ethnicity first through relatives living abroad and their native place associations (Goodman 1995) centered on the county and then through a wider ethnic group. Likewise, they experience their ethnicity when "being Hakka" is mobilized for projects such as the Sakyamuni Cultural Center or the building of the church. In his analysis of Cretan identity, Herzfeld focuses on subjective perspectives to "understand how individuals negotiate the tensions between the congruent but potentially conflicting levels of social identity that are implied by the segmentary model" (1985: xiv), as in the agonistic discourse over meaning between locals and the bureaucratic state. I have instead focused on the process of localization, for without the penetration of transnational processes, social mobilization along ethnic Hakka lines would be very weak, as Erbaugh concludes given the downplaying of Hakka ethnicity among cadres during the Maoist period.

With the penetration of transnational processes, various aspects of ritual and nonritual life become enactments of locality, a carving out of community space in a deterritorialized world. The previous chapters have focused on particular ritual and nonritual events to show how social practices reinforce and define locality when acknowledged members of the community are dispersed around the world. In identifying as Hakka, whether through the Hakka dialect, collective ancestor worship (on All Souls' Day or *qingming*), or research into local Hakka traditions, people identify themselves as members of a wider Hakka community. Hakka ethnicity, however, is more than simply an instrumental tool for attracting capital; it is the framework for understanding and living out modernity. In her examination of Hui modernity in China, Gillette (1997) found that Hui people saw modernity as being open (*kaifang*) and receptive to transnational forces, ideas, and trends. As people in Little Rome work hard to establish modernity in their part of the Hakka homeland, they are empowered by the visible demonstration of Hakka success stories, large and small, to seek out a goal already lived out by their Hakka relatives and friends in the diaspora, in places like Hong Kong and New York.

Diaspora Ethnicity and Transnational Religion

People in Little Rome are both Hakka and Catholic. According to themselves and others, they are members of both a diaspora ethnicity and a transnational religion. In social and ritual events such as weddings, funerals, and building a road, the confluence of disparate transnational processes coalesces into a coherent subjective understanding of what it means to be a part of the Little Rome community, to be Hakka, Catholic, and modern.

In one Christian Hakka community in the Hong Kong New Territories, for example, the local church reinforced and promoted Hakka identity: "Christianity did not serve as a way to escape Hakka ethnic identity, but as a way to preserve and celebrate it" (Constable 1994: 161). Because of their historical marginality, many Hakka outside the Hakka areas turned to Christian missionaries for support, education, and protection from hostile neighbors (Wiest 1977; Constable 1994). By becoming Christian, these historical converts doubled their marginality—they were Hakka in a largely Cantonese area, as well as followers of a foreign religion. Because of the Taiping Rebellion and their close association with foreign missionaries, Hakka Christians were further held in suspicion by the Chinese state. Nonetheless, with access to church resources and a strong sense of community fostered by the church, this community was able to thrive economically and maintain markers of Hakka identity. Building on their historical links with the Basel Evangelical Missionary Society, Hakka Christian communities have developed strong networks throughout the worldwide Chinese diaspora (Lutz and Lutz 1998).

Historically, Christian missionaries were important in the ethnogenesis of the Hakka. Accounts written by Basel missionaries Eitel and Lechler were used by Hakka scholars to bolster the legitimacy of Hakka identity (see Constable 1994; Lutz and Lutz 1998). These late-nineteenth-century missionary descriptions continue to be cited by contemporary Hakka specialists, even those not remotely concerned with Christianity (e.g., Fang 1994; Li 1996). These ethnographic descriptions of traditional Hakka life, written by missionaries to Hakka areas, are valuable recordings of past Hakka cultural traditions that have become objectified in places like the Sakyamuni Cultural Center for the promotion of ethnic identity in the Hakka homeland. These missionary accounts, of course, were written primarily to "perceive in a clearer way 'how the customs, the sense of life, the social order can meet with the manners and customs which have been brought to us through the divine revelation' " (Levesque 1969). Nonetheless, this corpus of material, combined with the efforts of local scholars such as those in the Jiaying University field project, continue to link Hakka ethnicity with Christian missionaries at a time when they are unable to come to the Hakka homeland for missionary work.

This brings up the question of ethnicity and religion—is there something in Hakka ethnicity that encourages conversion to Christianity? Religion is cited by theorists of ethnicity as a key boundary-marking mechanism; and for other Chinese ethnic groups such as the Muslim Hui described by Gladney, ethnic and religious lines often overlap. In the Hakka case, where Christian missionaries were key historical factors in Hakka ethnogenesis, there is no clear, defining evidence that links Hakka ethnicity to Christianity, in its Protestant or its Catholic form. Both Lutz and Constable, whose Hakka research is linked to Christian communities, conclude that although there are no definitive characteristics of Hakka culture that promote belief in Christianity, there are certain social circumstances—social discrimination, poverty, and emigration—that contribute to Hakka conversions to Christianity. Converts in turn brought their new faith to friends and relatives in their native place, resulting in what missionaries perceive to be disproportionate numbers of Hakka Christians and Catholics.

This more fluid analysis of the relationship between ethnicity and religion is not new to the anthropological literature. For example, Ortner (1978) concluded that rigid analytical categories such as ethnicity and religion do not reveal the importance of these social processes in shaping people's lives; she instead points to the interconnections between analytical categories. It is in this vein that the significance of Hakka ethnicity and Catholicism becomes clear in the lives of the people in Little Rome.

Catholicism links Little Rome to a network of other Catholic communities within and beyond the Hakka homeland. On one level they are linked by the administrative apparatus of the diocese, whereby a bishop in the prefectural capital of Meizhou assigns a priest from Wuhua county to Little Rome and a sister from Little Rome to a church in Fengshun county. On another level Little Rome maintains social connections to Catholic communities in other counties, such as in the celebration of Christmas when people from many different counties converge on Little Rome. On the transnational level, Catholicism also links Little Rome to Catholic communities throughout the world, as in the mobilization of outside resources for the building of the new church.

What drives ethnic and religious processes in Little Rome is the localization process. People and events from outside the physical confines of the community are made intelligible to people in Little Rome by their relation to the people and social memory of Little Rome. At times, these translocal flows follow Catholic lines. At other times, translocal flows are mobilized by the appeal of native place, of sharing Hakka ancestors. To be Hakka in the Hakka homeland is neither extraordinary nor compelling as a means of mobilizing people for local projects; but set against a history of Hakka ancestors and the global diaspora, being Hakka becomes an important marker of identity.

CHAPTER 10

Localization and Charisma in a
Transnational Village

President Clinton came to my neighbor Mr. Deng's living room in Little Rome, albeit over satellite television. Three generations of Deng men watched President Jiang Zemin's visit to the United States, periodically asking me questions about the United States. We watched President Jiang don an American colonial-period tricorn hat in Williamsburg and saw Prof. Ezra Vogel welcome President Jiang Zemin in Sanders Theater at Harvard University. My neighbors took great pride in the fact that their inquisitive neighbor was from Harvard and wanted me to make sure that when President Clinton came to China he would visit Little Rome and have tea with the neighbors.

About eight months later, Chris (the youngest of the three generations of Deng men) and I were browsing the Internet together. Earlier, I had often talked about the Internet with Chris, his father, and grandfather, especially after watching CCTV news stories about computers and telecommunications. They themselves had never used the Internet (though Chris had studied computers in his technical college), but they knew that I used e-mail and had seen digital pictures sent by my family from the United States. Throughout my fieldwork stay in Little Rome, I used their telephone to check e-mail by dialing out to Hong Kong, but we waited until I had local access to browse the Web. Chris asked me if I could find a picture of Monica Lewinsky. The newspapers had mentioned the White House scandal, but they had not printed a picture—Chris was curious what she looked like. We finally found a picture on the *South China Morning Post* Web page, and he exclaimed to me, "Wah, she's not that pretty—as president, he could have found a prettier one."

With the penetration of global communication networks like satellite television and the Internet, and with the massive movement of people to and from rural communities like Little Rome, it is tempting to see a transnational dialogue taking place between residents of Little Rome and people throughout the world. The reality of life in Little Rome, however, is that a wide social distance still separates it from Washington. Little Rome may be a transnational community, but it is not a global village. James Watson (1997) makes a clear distinction between globalism and transnationalism. Globalism is "an essentially impossible condition that is said to prevail when people the world over share a homogenous, mutually intelligible culture" (1997: 7). In contrast, globalization is a transnational process by which ideas, people, and commodities cross national boundaries. Little Rome is also not an international community, like the United Nations, representative of people in different nations throughout the world—Little Rome is particularistic, focused on a specific geographical and symbolic space. The areas on which I have focused—participation in a world religious tradition, the privatization of local sectors of the socialist economy, the global movement of people, and the mobilization of diaspora ethnicity—make Little Rome a transnational village, where people, ideas, and commodities intersect to form a coherent community through the localization process.

Arjun Appadurai has correctly written that "locality is an inherently fragile achievement" (1996: 179). People throughout the world work hard at maintaining communities, to stay local in a global world. Because these efforts at localization strongly inform people's social reality, the strategies that they employ to maintain communities should be at the heart of anthropological analysis. Localization, as implied by the term, is not a state of being, but an interpretive action performed by people. People in Little Rome employ a number of strategies to keep their community together in a deterritorialized social space. One of the key strategies is centered on the Catholic graveyard, in commemorations of their Catholic ancestors on All Souls' Day and, on a smaller community scale, in funerary ritual. While distinguishing Little Rome from other villages in Jiaoling county, the celebration of Catholic ancestors also embeds Little Rome in a wider network of Catholic communities throughout the world.

Other transnational processes have also shaped the localization process in Little Rome. With the mobilizing of Hakka ethnicity in the diaspora, people in the Hakka homeland have seen their communities, and their space, become objects of renewed interest. While the state and private enterprises mobilize to harness diaspora ethnicity, people throughout the Hakka homeland are discovering new ways to define themselves. Local cadres may prefer the political safety of emphasizing transnational ethnic links, but they have discovered as I did that diaspora ethnicity and transnational religion intersect. As most clearly illustrated in Nicole Constable's study of a Hong Kong village, Christianity and Hakka ethnicity are inextricably linked. In celebrating major projects like the building of the new Little Rome church and the Sakyamuni Cultural Center, which houses the county Hakka Museum, local cadres underscored aspects of ethnicity but could not ignore religious ties. From the state's perspective, the localization of transnational processes means their inclusion in the Chinese state's secular theodicy, through their incorporation into the bureaucratic reach of a state that transcends the specifics of time and place (Herzfeld 1992).

A focus on the localization process is well suited to anthropological methodology. Akhil Gupta and James Ferguson (1997) have illustrated the epistemological problems introduced by transnational processes in a discipline that privileges fieldwork as the source for knowledge. However, such challenges need not result in methodological angst; as I have illustrated throughout this work, the global can be seen in the most local of places. The blurring of boundaries—boundaries that Appadurai concludes have always been fluid—rather than being a problem *for* fieldwork can be the problem *of* fieldwork. In other words, what is necessary is not a shift in methods but a shift in perspective to looking at the connections between the local and the global. Transnational processes need to be seen from the ground up, from the perspective of the people who are living and localizing worldwide phenomena like transnational religion. This perspective has been the main strength of anthropology, and through its interpretations grounded in specificity, anthropology, like Little Rome, can continue to be a vibrant part of the global world.

The Work of the Local Imagination

Arjun Appadurai's focus on the growing importance of the *"work of the imagination* as a constitutive feature of modern subjectivity" (1996: 3) provides a powerful model for understanding the impact of transnational processes for people at different economic and technological levels. According to Appadurai, the work of the imagination is not solely an attribute of modernity and global capitalism; with the increasing importance of transnational processes it has become more salient in the lives of everyday people: "The imagination has broken out of the special expressive space of art, myth, and ritual and has now become a part of the quotidian mental work of ordinary people in many societies. It has entered the logic of ordinary life from which it had largely been successfully sequestered . . . [and] is no longer a matter of specially endowed (charismatic) individuals, injecting the imagination where it does not belong" (1996: 5). The work of the imagination locates the powerful attraction of Western modernity in the social realities of the people, who transform their everyday practices to attain the commodities and lifestyles promoted by the agents of global capitalism. It situates everyday people in the arena where ideas and practices of modernity are negotiated, recognizing the agency of people like the villagers in Little Rome.

Though transnational processes can be seen as an imposition of social practices and cultural forms by more-developed nations onto less-developed nations—what has been referred to by Joseph Nye (1990) as "soft power"—focusing on the work of the imagination underscores processes of persuasion instead of coercion in globalization. Whereas in previous models of cultural imperialism an economically powerful Western hegemony forced its cultural forms onto a passive third world, the work of the imagination shifts people's attention to less-developed areas like Little Rome. Appadurai and others have found that people in the third world exercise agency in giving local meaning to translocal cultural forms (see James Watson 1997; Jing 2000). People must be convinced, mostly in terms dictated by local social and cultural contexts, that globalization—be it the adoption of a transnational religion like Catholicism or participation in labor markets shaped by global capitalism—helps them achieve their own strategic goals in life. This is where the concept of charisma, as I have used it, is more than a heuristic device illustrating the localization of transnational processes in Little Rome; charisma helps us see that transnational processes are crucial in understanding how subjectivity itself is created in the third millennium.

In other words, understanding everyday social life today, whether in cosmopolitan centers or in local communities like Little Rome, requires understanding the role of transnational processes in the work of the imagination. Globalization itself can be seen primarily as an expansion of imagined possibilities for people with differential access to the tools that can transform the imagination into a reality.

Anthony Giddens describes the effects of modernity and globalization as resulting in a crisis in trust and authority. He argues that in the past, claims to authority were much clearer when particular local traditions were dominant in a particular society. Even when traditions were challenged, such as in the introduction of Buddhism to China, local communities had fewer choices as sources of authority. Giddens thus asserts that in contemporary societies a multiplicity of charismatic sources structure the work of the imagination: "Forms of traditional authority become only 'authorities' among others, part of an indefinite pluralism of expertise. . . . There are no authorities which span the diverse fields within which expertise is claimed—another way of repeating the point that everyone in modern systems is a lay person in virtually all aspects of society" (Giddens 1991: 195). This is essentially why charisma, in its multiple forms, must be examined in order to understand how the work of the imagination provides the fuel for everyday life. Human activities, whether in ritual or in the communal building of a road, translate and reinforce abstract charisma into concrete parts of local experience. Whether it be commodified charisma, as present in the high-priced dowry items on display at a wedding, or the attenuated charisma of the Catholic Church and PRC state, an argument must be convincing to be accepted into a person's individual cosmology. Charisma thus structures the work of the imagination, giving people in Little Rome reasons to get up every day, to work their fields, to save money to send their kids to school, to sojourn in distant places, and to go to church.

God Aboveground in China

Because Catholicism in postsocialist China is highly politicized, the ways in which practicing Catholicism defines community boundaries in Little Rome is not typical of other churches in China, let alone local churches in other parts of the world. Richard Madsen's study of Catholics in northern China (1998), where tensions between public and underground Catholics are high, highlights the specificity in which this description of Little Rome as a rural Chinese Catholic community must be regarded. Guangdong and the southern China littoral area are very different from other parts of China for the historical reasons discussed earlier, including the extensive migration of their population overseas and the state's reform policies, which have resulted in the greater liberalization of life in Guangdong. As a result, the picture Congressman Frank Wolf painted of the systematic persecution of Chinese Catholics is not the contemporary experience of people in Little Rome (see Chapter 1). The highly diverse situations of Catholics throughout China cannot be easily reduced to the dichotomy of an antagonistic church versus a persecuting state. Nor can Chinese Catholics be easily sorted into "real" Catholics loyal to the pope, following the dominant Catholic tradition, versus Catholics who collaborate with the state. In Little Rome the shared isolation and underground practices under fifty years of communism have resulted in the creation of a Catholic community with Chinese characteristics. In my view, speaking as an active lay Catholic, the people in Little Rome are authentic Catholics firmly grounded in the traditions and practices of the universal Catholic Church. Their links with foreign priests and nuns and other international Catholic organizations also confirm their Catholic standing.

In public discourse about who is truly Catholic in China, the conflicts between the public and underground churches center on the issue of authority. Using Dulles's model described earlier, one public bishop justified the legitimacy of the public church through charisma-derived authority, saying that authority stems directly from Christ in a church that is the body of Christ. In contrast, an underground bishop stressed an institutionally based authority from "communion with the Church" in the Vatican.[1] Madsen (1998) describes a reversed situation, where the public church in Tianjin is legitimized through institutional authority while the underground church is based on charismatic authority, all in the context of a strong state authority in Tianjin that produces an environment of "uncivility." These contrasting perspectives on the source of authority in public and underground churches result from the particular contexts of these communities and the level of discourse. Understanding the tensions between public and underground church communities requires historical and social contextualization. At the national level, Leung emphasizes that the tension between the PRC state and the Chinese Catholic Church results from a conflict over authority: the "particular nature of the Catholic with the Vatican, a tiny sovereign state" (1992: 3). This is not simply a contestation between the PRC state and the Catholic hierarchy over who exercises religious authority, but an issue of sovereignty in an era of transnationalism. Localization is thus the first step in unpacking the complexity of the Chinese Catholic Church.

The specificity of this local community then begs the question of what links the people in Little Rome to rural Irish Catholics in Donegal (Lawrence Taylor 1995) or urban Brazilian Catholics in Recife (Nagle 1997). Catholicism is politicized in China for different reasons than in Brazil or Ireland. Whereas activist priests armed with liberation theology may mobilize poor, disenfranchised urbanites in Recife, leading to sharp breaks within the Catholic Church, the Chinese church today is divided by the historical experiences of persecution and harassment during the Maoist period. Whereas religious and territorial space in rural Ireland is divided by parishes, charismatic priests, and sacred landmarks, Chinese Catholic communities in postsocialist China are surrounded by officially inspired atheism, popular Buddhist temples, earth-god shrines, and ancestral temples. What the residents of Little Rome do share with other Catholics worldwide is a religious tradition of hierarchy, rituals, and other social practices that transform a physical landscape into a local social space.

baigong	白宫	gongxi facai, lishi nalai	恭喜发财, 礼事拿来
baijiu	白酒	guanli qu	管理区
bailuji	拜路祭	guanxi	关系
baojuan	宝卷	guniang	姑娘
banlang/banniang	伴郎, 伴娘	guojia ganbu	国家干部
biaoshi	表示	guxiang	故乡
bu daode	不道德		
bu weisheng	不卫生	hong bao	红包
chun yun	春运	jia bin	嘉宾
chunjie	春节	jianban	煎坂
chunlian	春联	jiandan	简单
cunzhang	村长	jiao	教
dadui	大队	jiao	醮
daifu/daimu	代父, 代母	jiao	轿
danchun	单纯	jiao an	教案
danwei	单位	jiaotang	教堂
daode	道德	jiaowu weiyuanhui	教务委员会
daoli ke	道理课	Jiaying	嘉应
difang zhi	地方志	jiazhang	家长
duanjue guanxi	断绝关系	jiazhuang	嫁妆
dui lian	对联	jidujiao	基督教
		jiulou	酒楼
er ci zang	二次葬	juren	举人
fen jia	分家	kan hong/chuan hong	看红, 穿红
fengshui	风水		
fengshui xiansheng	风水先生	kejia	客家
fuze	负责	kejia jingshen	客家精神
gaige kaifang	改革开放	laoban	老板
ganqing	感情	laojia	老家
gongshe	公社	laorenjia	老人家
gongsuo	公所	lianyihui	联谊会

ling	灵	shifu	师傅
ling hunpei	灵婚配	shouxiao	守孝
ling wu	灵屋	shouhui jiaoyuquan	收回教育权
lishi yuanyin	历史原因	shuangxi	双喜
liu qin	六亲	shuyuan	书院
luo ye hui gen	落叶回根		
		tan qin	探亲
man yue	满月	tianzhu	天主
meiren	媒人	tianzhujiao	天主教
Meizhou	梅州	tianzhujiao aiguohui	天主教爱国会
minzu	民族	ting hua	听话
mixin	迷信	tong yang xi	童养媳
mu	亩		
		wan you zhen yuan	万有真原
niangjia	娘家	weisheng	卫生
niangjiu	酿酒	wenming	文明
nong mang	农忙	wenming cun	文明村
nongcun ganbu	农村干部		
		xia	下
qi	气	xiandaihua	现代化
qigong	气功	xiaoxue dongshi-	小学董事长
qingming	清明	zhang	
qipao	旗袍	xin hunyin xisu	新婚姻习俗
		xingzheng cun	行政村
renao	热闹	xinlang/xinniang	新郎, 新娘
		xiunu	修女
san hu:	三互	xizhuang	西装
hu bu lishu	互不隶属		
hu bu ganshe	互不干涉	youyiyi	有意义
huxiang zun-	互相尊重	yuan fen	圆坟
zhong		yuan xiao	元宵
sanjiao	三教	yuanyi	愿意
sang tang	丧堂		
sao mu	扫墓	zhao xu	招婿
shan ge	山歌	zhen	镇
shang	上	zhengxiehui	政协会
shang fen	上坟	zhishifenzi	知识分子
sheng	圣	zhong nan qing nu	重男清女
sheng ming	圣名	zhonghua shengmu	中华圣母
Sheng Shan	圣山	zhongxue wei ti,	中学为体, 西学
sheng you	圣油	xixue wei yong	为用
shengchan dui	生产队	zhujiao tuan	主教团
shengdanjie laoren	圣诞节老人	ziran cun	自然村
shen jia yin	身价银	Zongli yamen	总理衙门

CHAPTER 1

1. I use the term *postsocialist* to refer to the changes resulting from the 1978 introduction of market forces during the reforms initiated by Deng Xiaoping, interpreted in China as "socialism with Chinese characteristics." See Rofel 1999 for an exploration of postsocialism's impact on contemporary Chinese social relations and cultural forms.

2. "Deterritorialization" is the weakening of the link between social structures and cultural practices in specific geographic places. Deterritorialization results from the "time-space compression" induced by new technologies of communication and travel, and the resulting cultural adaptations to those new technologies (see Tomlinson 1999).

3. Luo Xianglin, writer of the seminal works on the Hakka, asserts that they are the descendants of northern Han Chinese who emigrated south following dynastic collapses, warfare, and other disasters (see Luo 1992; Constable 1994). Others contend that the Hakka are a sinified southern indigenous people (see Fang 1994).

4. See Wiest 1988 for a general history of the area when it was a Maryknoll mission area.

5. When first established, the village was in what was then Zhenping County.

6. China was the first mission site of this now international mission society.

7. It is of historical note that Maryknoll nuns, some educated as physicians in the 1930s and 1940s, were among the first women to leave the cloister of a convent or hospital and engage in full-time, peripatetic missionary work similar to that of their male counterparts (see Grondin 1956).

8. The legacy of St. Joseph's is symbolically made clear in Fudan Elementary, where the library is named after the last Chinese principal of the school, Fr. Zhang; the buildings of the minor seminary are still used as a middle school in Meixian and have not been returned to the Church despite the regulations of 1982 Document 19, which called for the return of confiscated property to recognized religious organizations.

9. These priests graduated from the Hong Kong Holy Spirit Seminary in 1952; they include the Wuhua-born cardinal of Hong Kong, Cardinal Wu.

10. For example, see the work of Godfrey Wilson and other anthropological ancestors working out of the Rhodes-Livingston Institute in the mid-twentieth century. Joan Vincent (1990) provides a contemporary, concise treatment of these topics.

11. Following Madsen and others, I use the term "public church" to signify the churches that are officially recognized by the PRC state, and the term "underground church" to signify the churches unrecognized by the PRC state (see Madsen 1998: 154, n. 25; on Sino-Vatican relations see Leung 1998, 1992).

12. This line of reasoning described by Tambiah emphasizes the political aspect of "distinction," in contrast to the economic grounding of Bourdieu's discussion of commodities, taste, and social capital.

13. Tambiah argues that charisma comes from extraworldly "transcendental claims to authoritative leadership, claims that are made by the leader and accepted by the followers" (1984: 325).

14. Using "communities" also avoids the colloquial problem with the term "neighborhoods" that Appadurai mentions.

15. See Clifford 1992 for an analysis of anthropologists as travelers.

16. My son did not attend the local school but was home-schooled, primarily by my wife. People in Little Rome were impressed that the U.S. government recognized home-schooling as an alternative education but thought that only "intellectuals" like my wife were qualified to do it.

CHAPTER 2

1. Taken from the interview transcript of a Maryknoll sister, China History Project, Maryknoll Mission Archives. Tianhou, or Mazu, is a female Daoist deity; Guanyin is the Chinese version of the bodhisattva Avalokitesvara.

2. James Pusey (1983) examined the impact of social Darwinism on the ideology espoused by reformist Chinese intellectuals in the late nineteenth and early twentieth century, demonstrating how the combination of Darwin's idea of evolution and Western demonstrations of power in China helped Chinese intellectuals challenge the authority of Chinese tradition. James Reardon-Anderson (1991) examined how chemistry education and research in China reflect wider changes in Chinese society and were part of a wider shift in Chinese cultural identity.

3. This approach is essentially what political scientists have done with the idea of "strategic culture"—ranked strategic preferences derived from paradigms common to decision makers—in trying to understand Chinese political strategy (see Johnston 1995).

4. The White Lotus movement refers to a series of soteriological rebellions against Chinese imperial dynasties (especially the Ming and Qing dynasties) by popular Buddhist-derived secret societies (see Overmyer 1976).

5. Kenneth Ch'en offers an interesting anecdote on Kumarajiva, an

eminent Kuchean monk-translator serving in the court of the Later Jin dynasty (late fourth- to early fifth-century C.E.): The emperor felt that Kumarajiva's extraordinary brilliance and understanding should be transmitted to offspring, so he assigned ten girls to live with Kumarajiva. Kumarajiva complied with the ruler's wishes but warned his audience to take only the lotus that grew out of the mud and to leave the mud alone (Ch'en 1964: 83). This illustration depicts the conflict between the Indian value of celibacy and the Chinese value of having many offspring.

6. The earliest Chinese writing found on oracle bones contains what are thought to be references to Xi Wang Mu. Other references in ancient classics include the *Han Shu*, the *Shan Hai Jing*, the *Mu Tian Zi Zhuan*, and the *Han Wu Di Neizhuan*. Yuan Ke concludes that Wang Mu Niang Niang is another name for Xi Wang Mu.

7. Laurentin compiled a list of Old Testament scriptures that have been interpreted to be prophecy of Mary; he lists ten scriptural references or allusions to Mary in the New Testament (Laurentin 1991: 8–49, 267–83).

8. Quoted from the *People's Daily* (Renmin Ribao), July 5, 1951, in A. Boniface "The Scapegoat: The Legion of Mary," *China Missionary Bulletin* 3(10) (1951): 826–31.

9. The May Fourth Movement, named for a student demonstration in Beijing on May 4, 1919, was a nationalistic intellectual revolution that sought to rebuild Chinese society and traditional culture to meet the challenge of Western imperialism. It shook the very foundations of Chinese thought.

10. In answer to the criticism of the parasitic nature of the Buddhist sangha, Tan-yao created Sangha households (families that submitted to the sangha an annual payment of grain kept for famine relief and as income for ritual activities) and Buddha households (criminals or slaves who performed manual labor under the direct administration of the sangha) (Hurvitz 1956).

11. See Lagerwey 1998. Lagerwey makes a clear distinction between *fenxiang* (incense division) network and a wandering god network, a distinction that has definitive social implications.

CHAPTER 3

1. The first reading was from 1 Kings 8:54–61; the responsorial psalm was from Psalm 84, the gospel acclamation was Matthew 7:8, and the gospel was from Luke 19:1–10.

2. These included *meicai kourou* (braised pork with preserved vegetables), *rouyuan tang* (meatball soup), *jiangyou ji* (steamed soy chicken), *chao yaoguo jiding* (chicken with cashews), *niang doufu bo* (pork-stuffed bean curd cooked in a clay pot), and *chao migaoban* (stir-fried glutinous rice cakes).

3. The distinction between chapel, *gongsuo*, and church, *jiaotang*, ignores the original Tang chapel and the men's and women's chapels.

4. A number of village members and other Hakka live in Mauritius.

5. Document 144 is the Administrative Regulations for the Management of Foreigners Participating in Domestic Religious Activities; Document 145 is the Administrative Regulations for the Management of Places of Religious Worship.

6. This circumstance is unlike the model described by Ulf Hannerz (1992), in which locals play a passive role because they are more territorially bound than transnational organizations and cosmopolitans, resulting in asymmetries of power at the local level. What is missing from Hannerz's model is the state's role in mediating transnational processes. Saskia Sassen (1996) concludes that arenas for transnational processes exist only through the complicity of states.

7. For Hong Kong proper names, I use the romanization used in Hong Kong publications, instead of the Mandarin.

8. Note that the second verse starts, "Elect from every nation, yet one o'er all the earth," and ends with "And to one hope she presses, with every grace endured." These words suggest many Catholics' hopes for the relationship between the Hong Kong and Chinese Catholic Church.

9. 2 Timothy 4:6–8, 17–18; emphasis added.

10. When asked how his Catholic faith had influenced his decisions as governor of Hong Kong, Patten replied: "I have never done a job before in which I've been so aware of the difference between right and wrong. I've never done a job before where I've so often had to say to people, 'Look, we must do this or that, not because it's expedient to do it, but because it's right to do it.' And I think that is a reflection, I hope, of my moral beliefs, my religious beliefs." (Barry 1997a: 52).

11. Bishop Luo Wenzao was appointed bishop of Nanjing in 1674 but was not consecrated until 1685.

12. In 1996 only 3.7 percent of the Hong Kong population was Catholic. All statistics on the Hong Kong Catholic population are from Charbonnier 1997.

13. For example, an interview in the English-language Hong Kong Catholic newspaper with SAR Secretary of Justice Elsie Leung Oi-sie prominently noted that she was a graduate of Sacred Heart Canossian College (*Sunday Examiner*, August 24, 1997).

14. Hong Kong is a special case now. Despite the return of sovereignty to China, since 1997 controls have been tightened, and it is even more difficult for mainlanders to enter Hong Kong.

15. Gregory Ruf's (1998) examination of a Sichuan village focuses on this process of community formation. The village he studied was defined by collective economic ventures that were extensions of the Chinese Communist Party. Cross-cutting alliances between cadres, kin, and friends shaped what Ruf calls the "managerial corporatist regime" that kept the community together, with leaders who fostered a civil morality. Part of why Little Rome is different

from the village described by Ruf is that the Sichuan village was an "administrative village" (*xingzheng cun*) as opposed to a "natural village" (*ziran cun*), to use Chinese cadre terminology.

CHAPTER 4

1. The Nestorian Church, centered in Persia, separated from Byzantine Christianity after 431 C.E. over the issue of the theological separation of divine and human persons in the incarnate Christ.

2. Paul Cohen goes into greater detail about Ma Xiangbo's career as a reformer and about his younger brother Ma Jianzhong, also a former Jesuit, who joined and left the order before his older brother (Edward Malatesta, personal communication, 1993).

3. The county gazetteer says the school was established in 1928; Little Rome's Mr. Wang said it was 1926; and the Maryknoll archives say 1925. I believe the Maryknoll date is correct since Fr. Shi was reassigned elsewhere in 1926, but was still in Little Rome when the school opened. The gazetteer information is from Mr. Wang, and Mr. Wang says that the year is from his own memory, reconstructed in the 1980s.

4. During the late Qing, the prefecture was named Jiaying; the area is now called Meizhou.

5. The Maryknollers who had been assigned to Little Rome for pastoral duties were listed on the memorial tablet by their Chinese names.

6. Bishop Gong was made a cardinal, and in 1997 was the oldest man in the College of Cardinals. He is also the symbolic center of a foundation based in Connecticut (where he lives at this writing) that actively lobbies for stronger American intervention against China for its persecution of Chinese Catholics.

7. Actually, Fr. Zhang (the headmaster of St. Joseph's) was chosen by the remaining priests as vicar capitular in 1953, because of the severity of Bishop Lan's prison sentences. Although Paul Lan was never officially consecrated by the Vatican as bishop, here I use the term by which the Catholics of Little Rome remember him.

8. These active attempts at indigenizing church architecture further underscore the point that Wiest (1988) makes concerning the symbolic representation of French imperialism in the cathedral in Guangzhou; such a structure is the exception that proves the rule.

CHAPTER 5

1. Little Rome still has a system of production teams (*shengchan dui*), which are the main political and economic administrative structure in the village. In 1997, Little Rome had five production teams, each encompassing between forty-three and sixty-six households, for a total of 263 households (see Table 6). The village is part of an administrative district (*guanli qu*)

containing 935 households, which in turn is part of a township (*zhen*). However, with the establishment of the responsibility system, whereby each household is obliged to meet a target quota of rice production that is sold to the state at a fixed price, the production team structure does not have the impact on daily social life that it did during the Maoist period.

2. The *man yue* (full moon) celebration occurs twenty-eight days after an infant is born and is the first time an infant is taken out of the house for public viewing (see Rubie Watson 1985).

3. This percentage was derived from comparing average daily mass attendance with the total population of residents in Little Rome.

4. Most of the prayer books were published by a neighboring diocese in Jieyang prefecture; others were published in Shanghai.

5. The rosary is a devotional fixed sequence of prayers to the Virgin Mary that includes the Apostle's Creed, the Lord's Prayer, Hail Mary, Glory Be, and Hail Holy Queen.

6. The year after I finished my fieldwork, during the holiday period PLA troops were deployed at the Guangzhou railroad station to prevent possible rioting by people who had waited days for a delayed train to Henan.

7. At the time I conducted the fieldwork for this project (1993–97), Little Rome did not have a village head (*cunzhang*) who alone was responsible for the village.

8. Social dramas are the "units of aharmonic or disharmonic social process, arising in conflict situations" (Turner 1985: 180). Turner further expands this framework in his analysis of the anthropology of experience (Bruner and Turner 1986; Turner 1985).

9. Many of these men were baptized as infants, however, before the church was closed down.

CHAPTER 6

1. For example, in the spring of 1997, I was told that a class monitor had made an announcement to his peers in the Foreign Language Department of Jiaying University that "those who believe in religion should not even bother to apply for party membership." This remark came after several students expressed an interest in Christianity. Although there is no specific policy prohibiting cadres from participating in recognized religious activities, many local cadres told me that cadres are still expected not to be religious.

2. The profession of faith was omitted, as is typical in masses for weddings and baptisms throughout the world.

3. Ellen Oxfeld points out (and I observed) that this banter during the serving of "four hands tea" (*si shou cha*) was common in other Hakka weddings (Catholic and non-Catholic) (personal communication).

4. At another wedding during my fieldwork, the attendants were not as

cautious with the bride and groom. After the banquet, the groom vomited in the van on our way home and was probably out for the night.

5. Cf. Myron Cohen 1976; Freedman 1970. Freedman summarizes the six rites as the family inquiry, genealogical and horoscope review, matching of horoscopes, transfer of gifts, wedding date selection, and bride transfer.

6. There are numerous names for these gifts, including *jian mian qian* (meeting money) and *mian hua qian* (face money); these gifts are not considered brideprice (*shen jia yin* or *ganzhe*).

7. A similar shift in wedding practices has taken place in South Korea (see Kendall 1996). Kendall finds that changes in wedding practices result from and are part of the Korean confrontation with modernity that has changed the educational patterns, employment possibilities, and consumption patterns of young Koreans. For example, Kendall finds that the growing economic potential of young marriage-age Koreans has led to a weakening of parental domination in their children's lives. One result is that arranged marriages have been replaced by "arranged meetings": a meeting of potential partners in order for each to examine the other with an eye toward marriage.

8. Similarly, in Korea, changes in consumption patterns have resulted in a shift from village weddings that take place at home to a "new-style wedding" that takes place in a commercial wedding hall (see Kendall 1996). Kendall concludes that marriage discourse becomes a key arena of contestation between tradition and modernity, an arena that involves nationalist agendas as the Korean state participates through its regulation (and later deregulation) of marriage practices.

9. Ikels (1996) reviews the 1950 and 1980 Marriage Laws and their implications for marriage practices in urban Guangzhou.

10. The brideprice amounts are configured to include the number nine, since nine is homophonic with the character for forever, implying the permanence of the marriage and the happiness.

11. Tambiah delineates a performative approach to ritual: people engage in ritual activities in order to achieve something. They are not just something that happens to people. The marriage ritual is performative because it is illocutionary (Austin 1962), staged, and indexical; it contains the symbolic commentary of nonritual constructs such as social hierarchy (Tambiah 1981).

12. For example, Bloch intertwines historical analysis with his presentation of the Merina circumcision ritual in Madagascar to show that ritual can often serve as a "barometer of the political situation" (1986: 165).

CHAPTER 7

1. Mr. Cao's services in orchestrating funerary ritual (namely, burial and exhumation) were in demand by people in Little Rome and neighboring villages. Serving as a funeral worker is a good source of additional income, and

Mr. Cao's seniority meant that he received a larger "gift" than the younger workers.

2. The "six relations" (*liu qin*) provide the banners as symbols that reaffirm kinship ties. As it was explained to me, the six relations are affines (relatives by marriage, including married-out women in the Chinese case), not agnates (relatives of the father or male side of the family). For example, if the deceased was a grandfather, the six relations are: (1) the family of the deceased (sons only, and no banner required); (2) the wife's natal family; (3) the sons' wives families; (4) the married-away daughters' families; (5) the families of the sisters of the deceased; and (6) the family of the mother of the deceased's family. The writings on the banners are laments in honor of the deceased and are marked with the names of the presenting relatives.

3. James Watson describes the termination of mourning, *chuan hong*, in Watson 1982: 165.

4. Here, Herzfeld's model of cultural intimacy is appropriate for understanding differences in presentation between Catholics in Little Rome talking to fellow-Catholics and their talking to non-Catholics (Herzfeld 1997).

5. The widespread popular religious significance of genealogy is verified by Jing's (1996) description of its role in ritual practices. In Little Rome, one village elder was trying to reconstruct a genealogy, now that having one is not seen as contrary to Catholic orthodoxy; I typed it out for him in Chinese for distribution to his kin.

CHAPTER 8

1. For example, women are active in the grain associations described by Myron Cohen (1976).

2. A thorough review of the anthropological literature on the gift can be found in Yan 1996: 1–21.

3. For a thorough explication of the role of gift exchange in the extension and reinforcement of social networks (*guanxi*) in postsocialist China, see Yunxiang Yan (1996) and Mayfair Yang (1994).

CHAPTER 9

1. See Barfield (1989) for a discussion of the Xiong-nu.

2. Exceptions are the work of John Lagerwey and Ellen Oxfeld. Oxfeld has written an excellent ethnography on diaspora Hakka in Calcutta (Oxfeld 1996); her more recent extensive fieldwork in the neighboring county of Meixian will be documented in a number of forthcoming publications.

3. Because Erbaugh focused on the broader national and historical contexts and lacked the opportunity for fieldwork in the Hakka homeland, she does not go into detail about what it means to be Hakka for mainlanders and bemoans their silence in nationwide social discourse (Erbaugh 1996: 228, 196).

4. Jiaying (Kaying [H.]) is the old prerevolutionary name for the city and the prefecture. During the Qing dynasty, Jiaying was a political unit (*fu*) just below the provincial government, as Meizhou prefecture was in 1998.

5. In 1998 the thirteen departments were: Mathematics, Physics, Chemistry, Biology, Geography, Chinese, Foreign Languages, Politics and Law, Economics, Finance, Electronics, and Arts and Architecture.

6. The books of the Traditional Hakka Culture Series, along with two other similarly designed research projects led by Professor Wang Chiu-kuei of the Institute of Anthropology, Academia Sinica, and Professor David Holm, University of Melbourne, were the subject of a 1998 conference, "Ethnography in China Today," hosted by the Chinese University of Hong Kong.

7. From "Hakka Chinese Homepage," http://www.asiawind.com/pub/hakka/charter.htm

8. A random sampling of 319 messages between October 1995 and June 1996 and all messages between July 1996 and September 1996; see Table 1) was input into a freeform database and then individually coded by sender, date, and topic. Topics were counted if addressed by more than three members.

9. Ninety percent of HGN discourse fell into the categories prescribed by the group's charter.

CHAPTER 10

1. These examples are from Bishops Jin Luxian and Fan Xueyan, in Tang and Wiest 1993.

Anderson, Benedict. 1991. *Imagined Communities: Reflections on the Origin and Spread of Nationalism.* New York: Verso.

Appadurai, Arjun. 1996. *Modernity at Large: Cultural Dimensions of Globalism.* Minneapolis: University of Minnesota Press.

———. 1995. "The Production of Locality." In Richard Fardon, ed., *Counterworks: Managing the Diversity of Knowledge*, pp. 204–25. London: Routledge.

———. 1981. "The Past as a Scarce Resource." *Man* 16(2): 201–19.

Argyrou, Vassos. 1996. *Tradition and Modernity in the Mediterranean: The Wedding as Symbolic Struggle.* Cambridge: Cambridge University Press.

Austin, John L. 1962. *How to Do Things with Words.* Cambridge, Mass: Harvard University Press.

Bak, Sangmee, 1994. "Professional Women's Work, Family, and Kinship: A Case Study Conducted at a TV Station." Ph.D. dissertation, Department of Anthropology, Harvard University.

Baker, Don. 1997. "World Religions and National States: Competing Claims in East Asia." In Susan H. Rudolph and James Piscatori, eds., *Transnational Religion and Fading States*, pp. 144–72. Boulder, Colo.: Westview.

Barfield, Thomas J. 1989. *The Perilous Frontier: Nomadic Empires and China.* Boston: Basil Blackwell.

Barry, Peter. 1997a. "A Profile of Christopher Patten, Last Governor of Hong Kong." *Tripod* 17(98): 49–52.

———. 1997b. "The Church in China: New Life." *Tripod* 17(100): 73–79.

Barth, Fredrik. 1987. *Cosmologies in the Making: A Generative Approach to Cultural Variation in Inner New Guinea.* Cambridge: Cambridge University Press.

———. 1969. "Introduction." In F. Barth, ed., *Ethnic Groups and Boundaries: The Social Organization of Cultural Difference.* Boston: Little, Brown.

Basch, Linda, Nina Glick Schiller, and Cristina Szanton Blanc. 1994. *Nations Unbound: Transnational Projects, Postcolonial Predicaments, and Deterritorialized Nation-States.* Basel: Gordon and Breach.

The Basic Law of the Hong Kong Special Administrative Region of the People's Republic of China. 1991. Hong Kong: Joint Publishing Co.

Bastid, Marianne. 1988. *Educational Reform in Early–Twentieth Century China.* Ann Arbor, Mich.: Center for Chinese Studies, University of Michigan.

Basu, Amrita, ed. 1995. *The Challenge of Local Feminisms: Women's Movements in Global Perspective.* Boulder, Colo.: Westview.

Becker, Jasper. 1996. *Hungry Ghosts: Mao's Secret Famine.* New York: Free Press.

Bloch, Maurice 1992. *Prey into Hunter: The Politics of Religious Experience.* Cambridge: Cambridge University Press.

———. 1986. *From Blessing to Violence: History and Ideology in the Circumcision Ritual of the Merina of Madagascar.* Cambridge: Cambridge University Press.

———. 1977. "The Past and the Present in the Present." *Man* 12: 278–92.

———. 1975. "Introduction: Why Oratory?" In Maurice Bloch, ed., *Political Language and Oratory in Traditional Society*, pp. 1–28. Academic Press.

Bourdieu, Pierre. 1984. *Distinction: A Social Critique of the Judgement of Taste.* Cambridge, Mass.: Harvard University Press.

Bracey, Dorothy H. 1967. "The Effects of Emigration on a Hakka Village." Ph.D. dissertation, Department of Anthropology, Harvard University.

Brook, Timothy 1993. *Praying for Power: Buddhism and the Formation of Gentry Society in Late-Ming China.* Cambridge, Mass.: Harvard-Yenching Institute.

Brou, Alexander. 1928. "Le Premier Jubilé de L'Université L'Aurore." *Études* 197(21): 284–98.

Brown, Peter. 1981. *The Cult of the Saints.* Chicago: University of Chicago Press.

Bruner, Edward M., and Victor W. Turner. 1986. *The Anthropology of Experience.* Urbana: University of Illinois Press.

Cahill, Suzanne. 1984. "Beside the Turquoise Pond: The Shrine of the Queen Mother of the West in Medieval Chinese Poetry and Religious Practice." *Journal of Chinese Religions* 12 (Fall 1984): 19–32.

Campbell, Ena. 1982. "The Virgin of Guadalupe and the Female Self Image: A Mexican Case History." In James J. Preston, ed., *Mother Worship: Themes and Variations*, pp. 5–24. Chapel Hill: University of North Carolina Press.

Carstens, Sharon A. 1996. "Form and Content in Hakka Malaysian Culture." In Nicole Constable, ed., *Guest People: Hakka Identity in China and Abroad*, pp. 124–48. Seattle: University of Washington Press.

Chan, Wing-hoi. 1995. "Ordination Names in Hakka Genealogies: A Religious
Practice and Its Decline." In David Faure and Helen Siu, eds., *Down to
Earth: The Territorial Bond in South China*, pp. 65–82. Stanford, Calif.:
Stanford University Press.

Char, Tin-Yuke. 1969. *The Hakka Chinese: Their Origins and Folk Songs*. San
Francisco: Jade Mountain Press.

Charbonnier, Jean. 1997. *1997 Guide to the Catholic Church in China*.
Singapore: China Catholic Communication.

CHCR (Zhongguo chengshi diqu congshu, Chinese cities and regions). 1987.
Meixian diqu (Meixian prefecture). Zhongguo Guoji Guangfan Chubanshe
(China International Radio Press).

Ch'en, Kenneth. 1973. *The Chinese Transformation of Buddhism*. Princeton,
N.J.: Princeton University Press.

———. 1964. *Buddhism in China: A Historical Survey*. Princeton, N.J.: Princeton University Press.

Chen, Nancy N. 1995. "Urban Spaces and Experiences of *Qigong*." In Deborah
Davis, Richard Kraus, Barry Naughton, and Elizabeth J. Perry, eds., *Urban
Spaces in Contemporary China*, pp. 347–61. Cambridge: Cambridge
University Press.

Chen Zhiping. 1997. *Kejia yuanliu xinlun* (New theories of Hakka origins).
Nanning: Guangxi jiaoyu chubanshe.

Chin, Francis. 1996. "Hakka Chinese Away from Home." http://www.panix
.com/~franchin/Hakka/ (September 2, 1996).

Ching, Barbara, and Gerald W. Creed, eds. 1997. *Knowing Your Place: Rural
Identity and Cultural Hierarchy*. London: Routledge.

Ching, Julia. 1993. *Chinese Religions*. Maryknoll, N.Y.: Orbis Books.

Ching, Julia, and Hans Kung. 1989. *Christianity and Chinese Religions*. New
York: Doubleday.

Clifford, James. 1994. "Diasporas." *Cultural Anthropology* 9(3): 302–38.

———. 1992. "Traveling Cultures." In Lawrence Grossberg, Cary Nelson, and
Paula Treichler, eds., *Cultural Studies*, pp. 96–112. New York: Routledge.

Cohen, Abner. 1969. *Custom and Politics in Urban Africa*. Berkeley: University
of California Press.

Cohen, Myron. 1988. "Souls and Salvation: Conflicting Themes in Chinese
Popular Religion." In James L. Watson and Evelyn S. Rawski, eds., *Death
Ritual in Late Imperial and Modern China*, pp. 180–202. Berkeley:
University of California Press.

———. 1976. *House United, House Divided: The Chinese Family in Taiwan*.
New York: Columbia University Press.

————. 1968. "The Hakka or 'Guest People': Dialect as a Sociocultural Variable in Southeastern China." *Ethnohistory* 15(3): 237–92.

Cohen, Paul. 1997. *History in Three Keys: The Boxers as Event, Experience, and Myth*. New York: Columbia University Press.

————. 1974. "Littoral and Hinterland in Nineteenth Century China: The Christian Reformers." In John K. Fairbank, ed., *The Missionary Enterprise in China and America*, pp. 197–225. Cambridge, Mass.: Harvard University Press.

————. 1963. *China and Christianity: The Missionary Movement and the Growth of Chinese Antiforeignism, 1860–1870*. Cambridge, Mass.: Harvard University Press.

Constable, Nicole. 1996. "What Does It Mean to Be Hakka?" In Nicole Constable, ed., *Guest People: Hakka Identity in China and Abroad*, pp. 3–35. Seattle: University of Washington Press.

————. 1994. *Christian Souls and Chinese Spirits*. Berkeley: University of California Press.

Covell, Ralph R. 1986. *Confucius, the Buddha, and Christ*. Maryknoll, N.Y.: Orbis Books.

Croll, Elisabeth J., and Ping Huang. 1997. "Migration for and Against Agriculture in Eight Chinese Villages." *China Quarterly* 149: 129–46.

Csordas, Thomas J. 1997. *Language, Charisma, and Creativity: The Ritual Life of a Religious Movement*. Berkeley: University of California Press.

Dean, Kenneth. 1998. *Lord of the Three in One: The Spread of a Cult in Southeast China*. Princeton, N.J.: Princeton University Press.

De Bary, Wm. Theodore, and Irene Bloom. 1999. *Sources of Chinese Tradition*. Vol. 1. 2d ed. New York: Columbia University Press.

Downs, William J. 1962. *A Historical Record of the Kaying Diocese, 1845–1961*. Unpublished manuscript, China History Project collection, Maryknoll Mission Archives, Maryknoll, N.Y.

Duara, Prasenjit. 1997. "Transnationalism and the Predicament of Sovereignty: China 1900–1945." *American Historical Review* 102(4): 1030–51.

Dubs, Homer H. 1942. "An Ancient Chinese Mystery Cult." *Harvard Theological Review* 35(4): 221–40.

Dulles, Avery. 1980. "Earthen Vessels: Institution and Charism in the Church." In Thomas E. Clarke, ed., *Above Every Name: The Lordship of Christ and Social Systems*, pp. 155–87. Ramsey, N.J.: Paulist Press.

Eckholm, Erik. 1999. "China's Rulers on Guard as Spiritual Sect Pushes the Envelope." *New York Times*, May 3, 1999.

Eickelmann, Dale F. 1997. "Trans-State Islam and Security." In Susanne H.

Rudolph and James Piscatori, eds., *Transnational Religion and Fading States*, pp. 27–46. Boulder, Colo.: Westview.

Entenmann, Robert E. 1996. "Catholics and Society in Eighteenth-Century Sichuan." In Daniel H. Bays, ed., *Christianity in China: From the Eighteenth Century to the Present*, pp. 8–23. Stanford, Calif.: Stanford University Press.

Erbaugh, Mary S. 1996. "The Hakka Paradox in the People's Republic of China: Exile, Eminence, and Public Silence." In Nicole Constable, ed., *Guest People: Hakka Identity in China and Abroad*, pp. 196–231. Seattle: University of Washington Press.

———. 1992. "The Secret History of the Hakkas: The Chinese Revolution as a Hakka Enterprise." *China Quarterly* 132: 937–68.

Eriksen, Thomas Hylland. 1993. *Ethnicity and Nationalism: Anthropological Perspectives*. London: Pluto Press.

Escobar, Arturo. 1995. *Encountering Development: The Making and Unmaking of the Third World*. Princeton, N.J.: Princeton University Press.

Evans-Pritchard, E. E. 1940. *The Nuer*. Oxford: Oxford University Press.

Fairbank, John K. 1983. *The United States and China*. 4th ed. Cambridge, Mass.: Harvard University Press.

Fang Xuejia. 1994. *Kejia yuanliu tan'ao* (The mystery of the origin of the Hakka). Guangzhou: Guangdong gaodeng jiaoyu chubanshe.

Far Eastern Review. 1936a. Aurora University of Shanghai: Part I. *Far Eastern Review* 32(9): 389–97.

———. 1936b. "Aurora University of Shanghai: Part II." *Far Eastern Review* 32(10): 446–53.

Faure, David. 1986. *The Structure of Chinese Rural Society: Lineage and Village in the Eastern New Territories, Hong Kong*. Oxford: Oxford University Press.

Featherstone, Mike. 1990. "Global Culture: An Introduction." In *Global Culture: Nationalism, Globalization, and Modernity*, pp. 1–14. London: Sage.

Ferguson, James. 1990. *The Anti-Politics Machine*. New York: Cambridge University Press.

Feuchtwang, Stephan. 1978. "School-Temple and City God." In Arthur P. Wolf, ed., *Studies in Chinese Society*, pp. 103–30. Stanford, Calif.: Stanford University Press.

———. 1974. "Domestic and Communal Worship in Taiwan." In Arthur P. Wolf, ed., *Religion and Ritual in Chinese Society*, pp. 105–30. Stanford, Calif.: Stanford University Press.

Fortes, Meyer. 1953. "The Structure of Unilineal Descent Groups." *American Anthropologist* 55(1): 17–41.

Frank, Andre G. 1969. "The Development of Underdevelopment." *Latin America: Underdevelopment or Revolution*, pp. 3–17. New York: Monthly Review Press.

Freedman, Maurice. 1974. "On the Sociological Study of Chinese Religion." In Arthur P. Wolf, ed., *Religion and Ritual in Late Imperial China*, pp. 19–41. Stanford, Calif.: Stanford University Press.

———. 1970. "Ritual Aspects of Chinese Kinship and Marriage." In Maurice Freedman, ed., *Family and Kinship in Chinese Society*, pp. 163–89. Stanford, Calif.: Stanford University Press.

Geertz, Clifford. 1973. *The Interpretation of Cultures*. New York: Basic Books.

Gernet, Jacques. 1985. *China and the Christian Impact: A Conflict of Cultures*. Trans. Janet Lloyd. Cambridge: Cambridge University Press.

———. 1956. *Les Aspects Économiques du Bouddhisme*. Saigon: École Française D'Extrême-Orient.

Gewertz, Deborah, and Frederick Errington. 1996. "On Pepsico and Piety in a Papua New Guinea 'Modernity.'" *American Ethnologist* 23(3): 476–93.

Giddens, Anthony. 1991. *Modernity and Self-Identity: Self and Society in the Late Modern Age*. Stanford, Calif.: Stanford University Press.

———. 1990. *The Consequences of Modernity*. Stanford, Calif.: Stanford University Press.

Gillette, Maris. 1997. *Engaging Modernity: Consumption Practices Among Urban Muslims in Northwest China*. Ph.D. dissertation, Department of Anthropology, Harvard University.

Gladney, Dru C. 1991. *Muslim Chinese: Ethnic Nationalism in the People's Republic*. Cambridge, Mass.: Harvard University Press.

Goodman, Bryna. 1995. *Native Place, City, and Nation: Regional Networks and Identities in Shanghai, 1853–1937*. Berkeley: University of California Press.

Gough, Kathleen 1975. "The Origin of Family." In Rayna R. Reiter, ed., *Toward an Anthropology of Women*, pp. 51–76. New York: Monthly Review Press.

Greenhalgh, Susan. 1993. "The Peasantization of the One-Child Policy in Shaanxi." In Deborah Davis and Stevan Harrell, eds., *Chinese Families in the Post-Mao Era*, pp. 219–50. Berkeley: University of California Press.

Grondin, Therese. 1956. *Sisters Carry the Gospel*. New York: Maryknoll.

Gu Yulu. 1987. "Zhendan daxue de chuanjian he bianqian" (The history and evolution of Aurora University). In *Zongjiao wenti tansuo* (An exploration of religion). Shanghai: Shanghai shehui kexueyuan zongjiao yanjiusuo.

Gupta, Akhil, and James Ferguson. 1997. "Discipline and Practice: 'The Field' as Site, Method, and Location in Anthropology." In Akhil Gupta and James Ferguson, eds., *Anthropological Locations: Boundaries and Grounds of a Field Science*, pp. 1–46. Berkeley: University of California Press.

Haas, Peter. 1992. "Introduction: Epistemic Communities and International Policy Coordination." *International Organization* 46(1): 1–35.

Handler, Richard. 1988. *Nationalism and the Politics of Culture in Quebec.* Madison: University of Wisconsin Press.

Hannerz, Ulf. 1996. *Transnational Connections: Culture, People, Places.* London: Routledge.

———. 1992. *Cultural Complexity: Studies in the Social Organization of Meaning.* New York: Columbia University Press.

Hanson, Eric O. 1980. *Catholic Politics in China and Korea.* Maryknoll, N.Y.: Orbis Books.

Harrell, C. Stevan. 1982. *Ploughshare Village: Culture and Context in Taiwan.* Seattle: University of Washington Press.

———. 1974. "When a Ghost Becomes a God." In Arthur P. Wolf, ed., *Religion and Ritual in Chinese Society*, pp. 193–206. Stanford, Calif.: Stanford University Press.

Harrington, Patricia. 1988. "Mother of Death, Mother of Rebirth: The Mexican Virgin of Guadalupe." *Journal of the American Academy of Religion* 56: 25–50.

Hayhoe, Ruth. 1989. *China's Universities and the Open Door.* Armonk, N.Y.: M. E. Sharpe.

———. 1987. "Catholics and Socialists: French Educational Interaction with China." In Ruth Hayhoe and Marianne Bastid, *China's Education and the Industrialized World: Studies in Cultural Transfer*, pp. 97–119. Armonk, N.Y.: M. E. Sharpe.

———. 1983. "Towards the Forging of a Chinese University Ethos: Zhendan and Fudan, 1903–1919." *China Quarterly* 94: 323–41.

Herzfeld, Michael. 1997. *Cultural Intimacy: Social Poetics in the Nation-State.* New York: Routledge.

———. 1992. *The Social Production of Indifference: Exploring the Symbolic Roots of Western Bureaucracy.* New York: St. Martin's Press.

———. 1991. *A Place in History: Social and Monumental Time in a Cretan Town.* Princeton, N.J.: Princeton University Press.

———. 1985. *The Poetics of Manhood: Contest and Identity in a Cretan Mountain Village.* Princeton, N.J.: Princeton University Press.

Holland, Lorien. 1999. "Breaking the Wheel." *Far Eastern Economic Review*, August 5.

Hsieh, Shirley. 1996. "Fostering Cultural Identity Through Design: Using the Internet to Discover Hakka Cultural Traditions in Modern Society." M. A. thesis, University of Guelph.

Hsu, Francis L. K. 1971. *Under the Ancestors' Shadow: Kinship, Personality, and Social Mobility in China.* Stanford, Calif.: Stanford University Press.

Hu Shih. 1937. "The Indianization of China: A Case Study in Cultural Borrowing." In Harvard Tercentenary Conference of Arts and Sciences, ed., *Independence, Convergence, and Borrowing,* pp. 219–47. Cambridge, Mass.: Harvard University Press.

Huang, Chien-Yu Julia, and Robert P. Weller. 1998. "Merit and Mothering: Women and Social Welfare in Taiwanese Buddhism." *Journal of Asian Studies* 57(2): 379–96.

Huang, Shumin. 1989. *The Spiral Road: Change in a Chinese Village Through the Eyes of a Communist Party Leader.* Boulder, Colo.: Westview.

Huang Shunqi, Huang Majin, and Zou Zipeng, eds. 1993. *Kejia fengqing* (Hakka traditions). Beijing: Zhongguo shehui kexue chubanshe.

Hunter, Alan, and Kim-Kwong Chan. 1993. *Protestantism in Contemporary China.* Cambridge: Cambridge University Press.

Hurvitz, Leon, trans. 1956. *Wei Shou on Buddhism and Taoism.* Kyoto: Jimbunkagaku Kenkyusho, Kyoto University.

Huntington, Samuel P. 1991. "Religion and the Third Wave." *National Interest* (Summer): 29–42.

———. 1973. "Transnational Organizations in World Politics." *World Politics* 25: 333–68.

Hutchinson, William R. 1987. *Errand to the World: American Protestant Thought and Foreign Missions.* Chicago: University of Chicago Press.

Ikels, Charlotte. 1996. *The Return of the God of Wealth: The Transition to a Market Economy in Urban China.* Stanford, Calif.: Stanford University Press.

Jiaoling xianzhi (Jiaoling County Gazetteer). 1992. Xingning, Guangdong: Guangdong renmin chubanshe.

Jing, Jun. 1996. *The Temple of Memories: History, Power, and Morality in a Chinese Village.* Stanford, Calif.: Stanford University Press.

———. 2000. *Feeding China's Little Emperors: Food, Children, and Social Change.* Stanford, Calif.: Stanford University Press.

John Paul II. 1997. "Message of the Holy Father to the Church in China" (Dec. 3, 1996). *Tripod* 17(97): 31–36.

Johnson, Elizabeth L. 1996. "Hakka Villagers in a Hong Kong City: The

Original People of Tsuen Wan." In Nicole Constable, ed., *Guest People: Hakka Identity in China and Abroad*, pp. 80–97. Seattle: University of Washington Press.

———. 1988. "Grieving for the Dead, Grieving for the Living: Funeral Laments of Hakka Women." In James L. Watson and Evelyn S. Rawski, eds., *Death Ritual in Late Imperial and Modern China*, pp. 135–63. Berkeley: University of California Press.

———. 1976. "Households and Lineages in a Chinese Urban Village." Ph.D. dissertation, Department of Anthropology, Cornell University.

Johnston, Alastair Iain. 1995. *Cultural Realism: Strategic Culture and Grand Strategy in Chinese History*. Princeton, N.J.: Princeton University Press.

Jordan, David K. 1972. *Gods, Ghosts, and Ancestors: Folk Religion in a Taiwanese Village*. Berkeley: University of California Press.

Jordan, David, and Daniel Overmyer. 1986. *The Flying Phoenix: Aspects of Chinese Sectarianism in Taiwan*. Princeton, N.J.: Princeton University Press.

Kendall, Laurel. 1996. *Getting Married in Korea: Of Gender, Morality, and Modernity*. Berkeley: University of California Press.

Kertzer, David I. 1988. *Ritual, Politics, and Power*. New Haven, Conn.: Yale University Press.

Keyes, Charles F. 1981. "The Dialectics of Ethnic Change." In Charles F. Keyes, ed., *Ethnic Change*, pp. 4–30. Seattle: University of Washington Press.

Keyes, Charles F., Helen Hardacre, and Laurel Kendall, eds. 1994. *Asian Visions of Authority: Religion and the Modern States of East and Southeast Asia*. Honolulu: University of Hawaii Press.

Kiang, Clyde. 1991. *The Hakka Search for a Homeland*. Elgin, Penn.: Allegheny Press.

Kipnis, Andrew B. 1997. *Producing Guanxi: Sentiment, Self, and Subculture in a North China Village*. Durham, N.C.: Duke University Press.

Kurtz, Donald V. 1982. "The Virgin of Guadalupe and the Politics of Becoming Human." *Journal of Anthropological Research* 38(2): 194–210.

Kwok, Nai Wang. 1997. "Zai zhimindi tongzhixia xianggang jiaohui de jiaose yu shixian" (Christian churches in Hong Kong under colonial rule). *Tripod* 17(98): 4–15.

Lagerwey, John. 1998. "Dingguang gufuo: Oral and Written Sources in the Study of a Saint." *Cahiers d'Extrême Asia* 10: 77–129.

———. 1996. "Festivals and Cults Among the Hakka." *China Perspectives* 4: 28–34.

———. 1987. *Taoist Ritual in Chinese Society and History*. New York: Macmillan.

Lang, Graeme, and Lars Ragvald. 1993. *The Rise of a Refugee God: Hong Kong's Wong Tai Sin*. Hong Kong: Oxford University Press.

Lardy, Nicholas R. 1980. "Regional Growth and Income Distribution in China." In Robert F. Dernberger, ed., *China's Economic Development Experience in Comparative Perspective*, pp. 153–90. Cambridge, Mass.: Harvard University Press.

Launay, Andrien. 1917. "Histoire des Missions de Chine: Mission du Kouang-tong." Paris: Anciennes Maisons Douniol et Retaux.

Laurentin, René. 1991. *A Short Treatise on the Virgin Mary*. Washington, N.J.: Ami Press.

Lee, Kitman. 1997. "Hong Kong Catholic Chinese: Their Identity as Hong Kong Citizens and Christians." *Tripod* 17(97): 14–30.

Legrand, F. X. 1949. *The Intellectual Apostolate in China*. Hong Kong: Catholic Truth Society.

Leong, Sow-Theng. 1997. *Migration and Ethnicity in Chinese History: Hakkas, Pengmin, and Their Neighbors*. Stanford, Calif.: Stanford University Press.

Leung, Beatrice. 1998. "Sino-Vatican Negotiations: Old Problems in a New Context." *China Quarterly* 153: 128–40.

———. 1992. *Sino-Vatican Relations: Problems in Conflicting Authority, 1976–1986*. Cambridge: Cambridge University Press.

Levesque, Leonard. 1969. *Hakka Beliefs and Customs*. Taichung: Kuang Chi Press.

Levitt, Peggy. 1999. "Social Remittances: Migration-Driven, Local-Level Forms of Cultural Diffusion." *International Migration Review* 32(124): 926–49.

———. 1998. "Local-Level Global Religion: The Case of U.S.-Dominican Migration." *Journal for the Scientific Study of Religion* 37(1): 74–89.

Li Yongji. 1996. *Xingbie yu wenhua: kejia funu yanjiu de xin shiye* (Gender and culture: new visions in research on Hakka women). Guangzhou: Guangdong renmin chubanshe.

Li Zhengfu. 1960. *Tianzhujiao jiaoyushi* (The history of Catholic education in China). Taipei: Guangqi Chubanshe.

Lin Qingshui. 1996. "Yuedong Jiaoling xian Xinpu zhen Shangnan cun minsu diaocha" (The traditional customs of Shangnan village, Jiaoling county). In Fang Xuejia, ed., *Meizhou diqu de miaohui yu zongzu* (Temple festivals and lineages in Meizhou), pp. 58–99. Meizhou: Guoji kejia xuehui, Haiwai huaren yanjiushe, Faguo yuandong xueyuan.

Liu Shanqun. 1995. *Kejia lisu* (Hakka ritual customs). Fuzhou, Fujian: Fujian jiaoyu chubanshe.

Loewe, Michael. 1979. *Ways to Paradise: The Chinese Quest for Immortality*. London: George Allen and Unwin.

Loo, Becky P. Y. 1998. "A Re-examination of the Lardy-Donnithrone Debate in the Provincial Context of Guangdong, 1949–1992." *Journal of Contemporary China* 7(17): 61–87.

Lozada, Eriberto, Jr. 2000. "Globalized Childhood? Kentucky Fried Chicken in Beijing." In Jun Jing, ed., *Feeding China's Little Emperors and Empresses: Children's Food in China*, pp. 114–34. Stanford, Calif: Stanford University Press.

Luo Xianglin. 1992 [1933]. *Kejia yanjiu daolun* (A treatise on Hakka research). Shanghai: Shanghai wenyi chubanshe.

Lutz, Jessie G. 1996. "Chinese Christianity and China Missions: Works Published Since 1970." *International Bulletin of Missionary Research* 20(3): 98–106.

———. 1988a. *Chinese Politics and Christian Missions: The Anti-Christian Movements of 1920–1928*. Notre Dame, Ind.: Cross Cultural Publications.

———. 1988b. "Christian Education in China: A Retrospective." *Tripod* 48: 28–48.

———. 1971. *China and the Christian Colleges: 1850–1950*. Ithaca, N.Y.: Cornell University Press.

Lutz, Jessie G., and Rolland Ray Lutz. 1998. *Hakka Chinese Confront Protestant Christianity, 1850*. Armonk, N.Y.: M. E. Sharpe.

MacInnis, Donald E. 1989. *Religion in China Today: Policy and Practice*. Ossining, N.Y.: Orbis Books.

Madsen, Richard. 1998. *China's Catholics: Tragedy and Hope in an Emerging Civil Society*. Berkeley: University of California Press.

———. 1994. "The Catholic Church in China Today: A New Rites Controversy?" In D. E. Mungello, ed., *The Chinese Rites Controversy: Its History and Meaning*, pp. 267–77. Nettetal, Germany: Steyler Verlag.

———. 1989. "The Catholic Church in China: Cultural Contradictions, Institutional Survival, and Religious Renewal." In Perry Link, Richard Madsen, and Paul G. Pickowicz, eds., *Unofficial China: Popular Culture and Thought in the People's Republic*, pp. 103–20. Boulder, Colo.: Westview.

Malatesta, Edward J. 1994. "A Fatal Clash of Wills: The Condemnation of the Chinese Rites by the Papal Legate Carlo Tommaso Maillard de Tournon." In D. E. Mungello, ed., *The Chinese Rites Controversy: Its History and Meaning*, pp. 211–46. Nettetal, Germany: Steyler Verlag.

———, ed. 1985. *The True Meaning of the Lord of Heaven.* St. Louis, Mo.: Institute of Jesuit Sources.

Martin, Howard J. 1996. "The Hakka Ethnic Movement in Taiwan, 1986–1991." In Nicole Constable, ed., *Guest People: Hakka Identity in China and Abroad,* pp. 176–95. Seattle: University of Washington Press.

Matsunaga, Alicia. 1969. *The Buddhist Philosophy of Assimilation.* Tokyo: Sophia University Press.

Mauss, Marcel. 1967. *The Gift: Forms and Functions of Exchange in Archaic Societies.* New York: W. W. Norton.

Minimaki, George. 1985. *The Rites Controversy, from Its Beginnings to Modern Times.* Chicago: Loyola University Press.

Mintz, Sidney. 1985. *Sweetness and Power: The Place of Sugar in Modern History.* New York: Viking.

Mohanty, Chandra, et al. 1991. *Third World Women and the Politics of Feminism.* Bloomington: Indiana University Press.

Moore, Sally Falk. 1994. "The Ethnography of the Present and the Analysis of Process." In Robert Borofsky, ed., *Assessing Cultural Anthropology,* pp. 362–74. New York: McGraw-Hill.

———. 1989. "The Production of Cultural Pluralism as a Process." *Public Culture* 1(2): 26–48.

———. 1987. "Explaining the Present: Theoretical Dilemmas in Processual Ethnography." *American Ethnologist* 14(4): 727–36.

Morley, David, and Kevin Robins. 1995. *Spaces of Identity: Global Media, Electronic Landscapes, and Cultural Boundaries.* London: Routledge.

Morris, Brian. 1987. *Anthropological Studies of Religion.* Cambridge: Cambridge University Press.

Mungello, David E. 1994. *The Chinese Rites Controversy: Its History and Meaning.* Nettetal, Germany: Steyler Verlag.

Myerhoff, Barbara G. 1978. *Number Our Days.* New York: Dutton.

Nagle, Robin. 1997. *Claiming the Virgin: The Broken Promise of Liberation Theology.* New York: Routledge.

Naquin, Susan. 1985. "The Transmission of White Lotus Sectarianism in Late Imperial China." In David Johnson, Andrew J. Nathan, and Evelyn S. Rawski, eds., *Popular Culture in Late Imperial China,* pp. 255–91. Berkeley: University of California Press.

Narayan, Kirin. 1993. "How Native Is a 'Native' Anthropologist?" *American Anthropologist* 95(3): 671–86.

Nee, Victor. 1991. "Social Inequalities in Reforming State Socialism: Between

Redistribution and Markets in China." *American Sociological Review* 56(3): 267–82.

———. 1989. "A Theory of Market Transition: From Redistribution to Markets in State Socialism." *American Sociological Review* 54(5): 663–81.

Nye, Joseph S. 1990. "Soft Power." *Foreign Policy* 80: 153–72.

Nye, Joseph S., and Robert O. Keohane. 1972. *Transnational Relations and World Politics*. Cambridge, Mass.: Harvard University Press.

Oi, Jean C. 1992. "Fiscal Reform and the Economic Foundations of Local State Corporatism in China." *World Politics* 45(1): 99–126.

———. 1991. "The Fate of the Commune After the Collective." In D. Davis and E. F. Vogel, eds., *Chinese Society on the Eve of Tiananmen: The Impact of Reform*. Cambridge, Mass.: Harvard University Press.

Olwig, Karen Fog, and Kirsten Hastrup, eds. 1997. *Siting Culture: The Shifting Anthropological Object*. London: Routledge.

Ong, Aihwa. 1999. *Flexible Citizenship: The Cultural Logics of Transnationality*. Durham, N.C.: Duke University Press.

Ong, Aihwa, and Donald Nonini, eds. 1997. *The Cultural Politics of Modern Chinese Transnationalism*. London: Routledge.

Ortner, Sherry B. 1978. *Sherpas Through Their Rituals*. Cambridge: Cambridge University Press.

Overmyer, Daniel L. 1986. *Religions of China: The World as a Living System*. Prospect Heights, Ill.: Waveland Press.

———. 1976. *Folk Buddhist Religion: Dissenting Sects in Late Traditional China*. Cambridge, Mass.: Harvard University Press.

Oxfeld, Ellen. 1996. "Still 'Guest People': The Reproduction of Hakka Identity in Calcutta, India." In Nicole Constable, ed., *Guest People: Hakka Identity in China and Abroad*, pp. 149–75. Seattle: University of Washington Press.

———. 1993. *Blood, Sweat, and Mahjong: Family and Enterprise in an Overseas Chinese Community*. Ithaca, N.Y.: Cornell University Press.

Parks, Malcolm, and Kory Floyd. 1996. "Making Friends in Cyberspace." *Journal of Communication* 46(1): 80–97.

Paul, Diana Y. 1985. *Women in Buddhism: Images of the Feminine in the Mahāyāna Tradition*. 2d ed. Berkeley: University of California Press.

Pei, Minxin. 1998. "Chinese Civic Associations." *Modern China* 24(3): 285–318.

Perry, Nicholas, and Loreto Echeverría. 1988. *Under the Heel of Mary*. London: Routledge.

Pott, F. L. Hawks. 1936. "Christian Education in China." *China Quarterly* 1(3): 47–54.

Potter, Jack M., and Sulamith H. Potter. 1990. *China's Peasants: The Anthropology of a Revolution*. Cambridge: Cambridge University Press.

Pusey, James Reeve. 1983. *China and Charles Darwin*. Cambridge, Mass.: Harvard University Press.

Rai, Amit. 1995. "India On-Line: Electronic Bulletin Boards and the Construction of a Diasporic Hindu Identity." *Diaspora* 4(1): 31–58.

Rawski, Evelyn S. 1988. "A Historian's Approach to Death Ritual." In James L. Watson and Evelyn S. Rawski, eds., *Death Ritual in Late Imperial and Modern China*, pp. 20–34. Berkeley: University of California Press.

Reardon-Anderson, James. 1991. *The Study of Change: Chemistry in China, 1840–1949*. Cambridge: Cambridge University Press.

Rofel, Lisa. 1999. *Other Modernities: Gendered Yearnings in China After Socialism*. Berkeley: University of California Press.

Rosenthal, Elizabeth. 1998. "In China, 35+ and Female = Unemployed." *New York Times*, October 13.

Rudolph, Susanne H., and James Piscatori, eds. 1997. *Transnational Religion and Fading States*. Boulder, Colo.: Westview.

Ruf, Gregory A. 1998. *Cadres and Kin: Making a Socialist Village in West China, 1921–1991*. Stanford, Calif.: Stanford University Press.

Sahlins, Marshall D. 1972. *Stone Age Economics*. Chicago: Aldine-Atherton.

Salaff, Janet W., and Mary Sheridan, eds. 1984. *Lives: Chinese Working Women*. Bloomington: Indiana University Press.

Sassen, Saskia. 1997. *Globalization and Its Discontents*. New York: New Press.

———. 1996. *Losing Control? Sovereignty in an Age of Globalization*. New York: Columbia University Press.

Saywell, Trish 1997. "Workers' Offensive." *Far Eastern Economic Review* 160(22): 50–52.

Segawa, Masahisa. 1986. *Hakka to Pundi, Hon-kon shinkai nosonbu ni okeru esunisiti no ichisokunien* (Hakka and Punti: an aspect of ethnicity in the new territories of Hong Kong). *Minzokugaku kenkyu* 51(2): 111–40.

Sered, Susan. 1991. "Rachel, Mary, and Fatima." *Cultural Anthropology* 6(2): 131–46.

Shahar, Meir, and Robert P. Weller. 1996. *Unruly Gods: Divinity and Society in China*. Honolulu: University of Hawaii Press.

Shi, Weng 1985. "Jiaoling tianzhujiao gaishu" (A brief introduction to Catholicism in Jiaoling). *Jiaoling xiuzhi tongxun* 10(2): 15–18.

Shils, Edward. 1975. *Center and Periphery: Essays in Macrosociology*. Chicago: University of Chicago Press.

Shirk, Susan L. 1993. *The Political Logic of Economic Reform in China.* Berkeley: University of California Press.

Shue, Vivienne. 1998. "State Power and the Philanthropic Impulse in China Today." In Warren F. Ilchman, Stanley N. Katz, and Edward L. Queen II, eds., *Philanthropy in the World's Traditions*, pp. 332–54. Bloomington: Indiana University Press.

———. 1988. *The Reach of the State: Sketches of the Chinese Body Politic.* Stanford, Calif.: Stanford University Press.

Smart, Alan. 1993. "Gifts, Bribes, and Guanxi: A Reconsideration of Bourdieu's Social Capital." *Cultural Anthropology* 8(3): 388–408.

Smith, Joanna F. Handlin. 1987. "Benevolent Societies: The Reshaping of Charity During the Late Ming and Early Ch'ing." *Journal of Asian Studies* 46(2): 309–37.

Smith, M. G. 1974. *Corporations and Society: The Social Anthropology of Collective Action.* Chicago: Aldine.

Spence, Jonathan D. 1996. *God's Chinese Son: The Taiping Heavenly Kingdom of Hong Xiuquan.* New York: W. W. Norton.

———. 1984. *The Memory Palace of Matteo Ricci.* New York: Penguin Books.

———. 1982. *The Gate of Heavenly Peace.* New York: Penguin Books.

———. 1980. *To Change China: Western Advisers in China, 1620–1960.* New York: Penguin Books.

Steedly, Mary. 1993. *Hanging Without a Rope: Narrative Experience in Colonial and Postcolonial Karoland.* Princeton, N.J.: Princeton University Press.

Stewart, Charles, and Rosalind Shaw. 1994. *Syncretism/Anti-Syncretism: The Politics of Religious Synthesis.* New York: Routledge.

Stockard, Janice E. 1989. *Daughters of the Canton Delta: Marriage Patterns and Economic Strategies in South China, 1860–1930.* Stanford, Calif.: Stanford University Press.

Strathern, Marilyn. 1995. *Shifting Contexts: Transformations in Anthropological Knowledge.* New York: Routledge.

Sweeten, Alan Richard. 1996. "Catholic Converts in Jiangxi Province: Conflict and Accommodation, 1860–1900." In Daniel H. Bays, ed., *Christianity in China: From the Eighteenth Century to the Present*, pp. 24–40. Stanford, Calif.: Stanford University Press.

Sze, Stephen Man Hung. 1996. "The Social Awareness and Intended Role of Catholic Intellectuals in Face of 1997." In Beatrice Leung, ed., *Church and State Relations in 21st Century Asia*, pp. 150–62. Hong Kong: Centre of Asian Studies, University of Hong Kong.

Tambiah, Stanley J. 1992. *The Nation State in Crisis and the Rise of Ethnonationalism. Punitham Tiruchelvam Memorial Lecture.* Colombo: Bauddhalotia Mawatha.

———. 1989. "Ethnic Conflict in the World Today." *American Ethnologist* 16(2): 335–49.

———. 1984. *The Buddhist Saints of the Forest and the Cult of Amulets.* New York: Cambridge University Press.

———. 1981. *A Performative Approach to Ritual.* London: British Academy.

Tang, Edmond, and Jean-Paul Wiest, eds. 1993. *The Catholic Church in Modern China.* Maryknoll, N.Y.: Orbis Books.

Taylor, Lawrence J. 1995. *Occasions of Faith: An Anthropology of Irish Catholics.* Philadelphia: University of Pennsylvania Press.

Taylor, William B. 1987. "The Virgin of Guadalupe in New Spain: An Inquiry into the Social History of Marian Devotion." *American Ethnologist* 14(1): 9–33.

Thompson, Roger R. 1996. "Twilight of the Gods in the Chinese Countryside: Christians, Confucians, and the Modernizing State, 1861–1911." In Daniel H. Bays, ed., *Christianity in China: From the Eighteenth Century to the Present,* pp. 53–72. Stanford, Calif.: Stanford University Press.

Ticozzi, Sergio. 1997. "Old and New Challenges for the Hong Kong Catholic Church." *Tripod* 17(97): 5–13.

Tomlinson, John. 1999. *Globalization and Culture.* Chicago: University of Chicago Press.

Tsukamoto, Zenryu. 1957. "The Sramana Superintendent T'an-yao and His Time." Trans. Galen Sargent. *Monumenta Serica* 16: 363–96.

Turner, Victor W. 1985. "The Anthropology of Experience." In Edith Turner, ed., *On the Edge of the Bush: Anthropology as Experience,* pp. 177–204. Tucson: University of Arizona Press.

———. 1977. "Process, System, and Symbol: A New Anthropological Synthesis." *Daedalus* 106(3): 61–80.

———. 1974. *Dramas, Fields, and Metaphors: Symbolic Action in Human Society.* Ithaca, N.Y.: Cornell University Press.

———. 1969. *The Ritual Process: Structure and Anti-Structure.* Ithaca, N.Y.: Cornell University Press.

———. 1967. *The Forest of Symbols.* Ithaca, N.Y.: Cornell University Press.

———. 1957. *Schism and Continuity in an African Society: A Study of Ndembu Village Life.* Manchester: Manchester University Press.

Turner, Victor W., and Edith Turner. 1978. *Image and Pilgrimage in Christian Culture: Anthropological Perspectives.* New York: Columbia University Press.

Vallier, Ivan. 1973. "The Roman Catholic Church: A Transnational Actor." In
    Joseph Nye and Robert Keohane, eds., *Transnational Relations and World
    Politics*, pp. 129–52. Cambridge, Mass.: Harvard University Press.
Vincent, Joan. 1990. *Anthropology and Politics: Visions, Traditions, and Trends.*
    Tucson: University of Arizona Press.
Vogel, Ezra F. 1989. *One Step Ahead in China: Guangdong Under Reform.*
    Cambridge, Mass.: Harvard University Press.
Wakeman, Frederic, Jr. 1988. "Transnational and Comparative Research." *Items*
    42(4): 85–89.
———. 1998. "Boundaries of the Public Sphere in Ming and Qing China."
    Daedalus 127(3): 167–89.
Waley-Cohen, Joanna. 1999. *The Sextants of Beijing: Global Currents in
    Chinese History.* New York: W. W. Norton.
Wallerstein, Immanuel. 1991. "Development: Lodestar or Illusion?" In
    Unthinking Social Science: The Limits of Nineteenth-Century Paradigms,
    pp. 104–24. Cambridge, England: Basil Blackwell.
———. 1974. "The Rise and Future Demise of the World Capitalist System:
    Concepts for Comparative Analysis." *Comparative Studies in Society and
    History* 16: 387–415.
Wang, Gungwu. 1991. *China and the Chinese Overseas.* Singapore: Times Aca-
    demic Press.
Watson, James L., ed., 1997. *Golden Arches East: McDonald's in East Asia.*
    Stanford, Calif.: Stanford University Press.
———. 1996. "Fighting with Operas: Processionals, Politics, and the Spectre of
    Violence in Rural Hong Kong." In David Parkin, Lionel Caplan, and
    Humphrey Fisher, eds., *The Politics of Cultural Performance: Essays in
    Honour of Abner Cohen,* pp. 145–59. London: Berghahn Books.
———. 1993. "Rites or Beliefs? The Construction of a Unified Culture in Late
    Imperial China." In Lowell Dittmer and Samuel S. Kim, eds., *China's Quest
    for National Identity,* pp. 80–103. Ithaca, N.Y.: Cornell University Press.
———. 1991. "Waking the Dragon: Visions of the Chinese Imperial State in
    Local Myth." In Hugh D. R. Baker and Stephan Feuchtwang, eds., *An Old
    State in New Settings: Studies in the Social Anthropology of China in
    Memory of Maurice Freedman,* pp. 162–77. Oxford: Journal of the Anthro-
    pological Society of Oxford Occasional Papers.
———. 1988. "The Structure of Chinese Funerary Rites: Elementary Forms,
    Ritual Sequence, and the Primacy of Performance." In James L. Watson and
    Evelyn S. Rawski, eds., *Death Ritual in Late Imperial and Modern China,*
    pp. 3–19. Berkeley: University of California Press.

———. 1985. "Standardizing the Gods: The Promotion of T'ien Hou (Empress of Heaven) Along the South China Coast, 960–1960." In David Johnson, Andrew Nathan, and Evelyn Rawski, eds., *Popular Culture in Late Imperial China*, pp. 292–324. Berkeley: University of California Press.

———. 1982. "Of Flesh and Bones: The Management of Death Pollution in Cantonese Society." In Maurice Bloch and Jonathan Parry, eds., *Death and the Regeneration of Life*, pp. 155–86. Cambridge: Cambridge University Press.

Watson, Rubie S., 1996. "Chinese Bridal Laments: The Claims of a Dutiful Daughter." In Bell Yung, Evelyn Rawski, and Rubie S. Watson, eds., *Harmony and Counterpoint: Ritual Music in Chinese Context*, pp. 107–29. Stanford, Calif.: Stanford University Press.

———, ed. 1994. *Memory, History, and Opposition Under State Socialism.* Santa Fe, N.M.: School of American Research Press.

———. 1988. "Remembering the Dead: Graves and Politics in Southeastern China." In James L. Watson and Evelyn S. Rawski, eds., *Death Ritual in Late Imperial and Modern China*, pp. 203–27. Berkeley: University of California Press.

———. 1985. *Inequality Among Brothers: Class and Kinship in South China.* Cambridge: Cambridge University Press.

Weber, Max. 1978 [1956]. *Economy and Society.* 2 vols. Eds. Guenther Roth and Claus Wittich. Berkeley: University of California Press.

Weiner, Annette B. 1992. *Inalienable Possessions: The Paradox of Keeping-While-Giving.* Berkeley: University of California Press.

West, Philip. 1976. *Yenching University and Sino-Western Relations, 1916–1952.* Cambridge, Mass.: Harvard University Press.

White, Lynn T. 1989. *Policies of Chaos: The Organizational Causes of Violence in China's Cultural Revolution.* Princeton, N.J.: Princeton University Press.

Whyte, Martin K. 1988. "Death in the People's Republic of China." In James L. Watson and Evelyn S. Rawski, eds., *Death Ritual in Late Imperial and Modern China*, pp. 289–316. Berkeley: University of California Press.

Wiest, Jean-Paul. 1988. *Maryknoll in China.* Armonk, N.Y.: M. E. Sharpe.

———. 1977. "Catholic Activities in Kwangtung Province and Chinese Responses, 1848–1885." Ph.D. dissertation, Department of History, University of Washington.

Wolf, Arthur P. 1974. "Gods, Ghosts, and Ancestors." In Arthur P. Wolf, ed., *Religion and Ritual in Chinese Society*, pp. 132–82. Stanford, Calif.: Stanford University Press.

———. 1970. "Chinese Kinship and Mourning Dress." In Arthur P. Wolf, ed.,

Family and Kinship in Chinese Society, pp. 189–207. Stanford, Calif.: Stanford University Press.

Wolf, Eric. 1982. *Europe and the People Without History*. Berkeley: University of California Press.

———. 1958. "The Virgin of Guadalupe: A Mexican National Symbol." *Journal of American Folklore* 71: 34–39.

Wolf, Margery. 1972. *Women and the Family in Rural Taiwan*. Stanford, Calif.: Stanford University Press.

Wright, Arthur. 1990. *Studies in Chinese Buddhism*. New Haven, Conn.: Yale University Press.

Wu, Cardinal John Baptist Cheng Chung. 1997 [1984]. "The Catholic Church and the Future of Hong Kong." *Tripod* 17(98): 23–24.

Xu Zhichao. 1996. *Shikuhe zhuan* (Stories from the Shiku River). Guangzhou: Guangdong luyou chubanshe.

Xue Fansheng. 1997. *Xingning shi Songsheng zhen Maoxing cun minsu* (Folk customs of Maoxing village, Xingning). In Fang Xuejia, ed., *Meizhou Heyuan diqu de cunluo wenhua* (Village religion and culture in northeastern Guangdong), pp. 106–40. Meizhou: Guoji kejia xuehui, Haiwai huaren yanjiushe, Faguo yuandong xueyuan.

Yan, Yunxiang. 1997. "McDonald's in Beijing: The Localization of Americana." In James L. Watson, ed., *Golden Arches East: McDonald's in East Asia*, pp. 39–76. Stanford, Calif.: Stanford University Press.

———. 1996. *The Flow of Gifts: Reciprocity and Social Networks in a Chinese Village*. Stanford, Calif.: Stanford University Press.

Yang, C. K. 1961. *Religion in Chinese Society*. Prospect Heights, Ill.: Waveland Press.

Yang, Mayfair Mei-hui. 1997. "Mass Media and Transnational Subjectivity in Shanghai: Notes on (Re)Cosmopolitanism in a Chinese Metropolis." In Aihwa Ong and Donald Nonini, eds., *The Cultural Politics of Modern Chinese Transnationalism*, pp. 287–319. London: Routledge.

———. 1994. *Gifts, Favors, and Banquets: The Art of Social Relationships in China*. Ithaca, N.Y.: Cornell University Press.

Yeh Wen-Hsin. 1990. *The Alienated Academy: Culture and Politics in Republican China*. Cambridge, Mass.: Council on East Asian Studies.

Yen, Ching-hwang. 1995. *Studies in Modern Overseas Chinese History*. Singapore: Times Academic Press.

Yuan Ke. 1988. *Zhongguo shenhuashi* (The history of Chinese mythology). Shanghai: Shanghai wenyi chubanshe.

Zen, Bishop Joseph. 1997. "Hong Kong Church Adopts 'Open Door' Policy: Interview with Bishop Zen." *Tripod* 17(98): 6–13.

Zhang Quanqing. 1997. *Wuhua xian Huacheng zhen Hutian cun Zhang shi zongzu yu shenming chongbai* (Gods and lineages in the Hutian Zhang clan of Wuhua). In Fang Xuejia, ed., *Meizhou Heyuan diqu de cunluo wenhua* (Village religion and culture in northeastern Guangdong), pp. 1–76. Meizhou: Guoji kejia xuehui, Haiwai huaren yanjiushe, Faguo yuandong xueyuan.

Zhang, Quanzhang. 1995. "Shilun erci zang de feige" (An analysis of the abandonment of double burial reform). *Kejia yanjiu jikan* (Journal of Hakka research), no. 1: 102–15.

Zhendan Daxue. 1935. *Sili Zhendan daxue yilan* (Guidebook to Aurora University). Shanghai: Zhendan Daxue chubanbu.

Zhongguo tianzhujiao (Catholic Church in China). 1997. "Zhongguo tianzhu jiaotu relie huanqing Xianggang huigui zuguo" (Chinese Catholics warmly welcome Hong Kong's return to the homeland). *Zhongguo tianzhujiao* 1997(2): 4–5.

Zurcher, Erik. 1994. "Jesuit Accommodation and the Chinese Cultural Imperative." In D. E. Mungello, ed. *The Chinese Rites Controversy: Its History and Meaning*, pp. 31–64. Nettetal, Germany: Steyler Verlag.